Population Change in the United Kingdom

Population Change in the United Kingdom

Edited by
Tony Champion and Jane Falkingham

ROWMAN & LITTLEFIELD
INTERNATIONAL

London • New York

Published by Rowman & Littlefield International, Ltd.
Unit A, Whitacre Mews, 26-34 Stannary Street, London SE11 4AB
www.rowmaninternational.com

Rowman & Littlefield International, Ltd. is an affiliate of Rowman & Littlefield
4501 Forbes Boulevard, Suite 200, Lanham, Maryland 20706, USA
With additional offices in Boulder, New York, Toronto (Canada), and Plymouth (UK)
www.rowman.com

British Library Cataloguing in Publication Data
A catalogue record for this book is available from the British Library

ISBN: HB 978-1-78348-591-8
       PB 978-1-78348-592-5

Library of Congress Cataloging-in-Publication Data
Names: Champion, A. G. (Anthony Gerard), editor. | Falkingham, Jane, editor.
Title: Population change in the United Kingdom / edited by Tony Champion and
    Jane Falkingham.
Description: London ; New York : Rowman & Littlefield International, 2016. |
    Includes bibliographical references and index.
Identifiers: LCCN 2016014156 (print) | LCCN 2016022830 (ebook) |
    ISBN 9781783485918 (cloth : alk. paper) | ISBN 9781783485925 (pbk. : alk. paper) |
    ISBN 9781783485932 (electronic)
Subjects: LCSH: Great Britain—Population. | Demographic transition—Great Britain.
Classification: LCC HB3583.A3 P664 2016 (print) | LCC HB3583.A3 (ebook) |
    DDC 304.60941—dc23
LC record available at https://lccn.loc.gov/2016014156

Printed in the United States of America

Contents

List of Figures

List of Tables

Foreword

When, in 1980, I first attended the annual conference of the British Society for Population Studies at the University of York, the workshop on ageing was attended by a tiny number of participants, and I fear I cannot recall major sessions on British migration, either internal or international. This does not reflect the vibrancy of British demography at that time, but rather that different factors, such as the decline in the birthrate, were seen as the most important factors driving population change in Britain.

Population also did not feature heavily in thinking around British social and economic policy in the 1980s, and Heather Joshi should be thanked for putting together the series of seminars at the Centre for Economic Policy Research that led to the wonderful collection of essays that appeared in her book on Britain's population—in many ways a coming of age for the British Society for Population Studies—as it demonstrated the vivid, exciting and multidisciplinary nature of the research challenges that Britain's changing population brings to a huge range of social scientists, and perhaps twenty years ahead of its time, it clearly illustrated the 'impact' that demographic research could have across the social policy spectrum.

If there was any doubt of the importance for social policy of understanding Britain's changing population, then the trends over the past twenty-five years will have dispelled them, probably forever. Childbearing has become ever more common amongst women in their thirties and increasingly in their forties, with implications for generational length, and ageing is a subject rarely out of the national media spotlight, whether it be the implications of increasing longevity for pension provision, the challenges around long-term care or the strategies to maximise healthy life expectancy.

However, it is migration that has perhaps been the most transformational in raising the awareness of the need to understand trends in Britain's population.

Increasing international migration, changing patterns of internal migration and Britain's increasingly multicultural society have become exciting research topics with important social policy implications.

To understand these trends better, demography in Britain has become ever more multidisciplinary. Fuelled by the availability of a rich cadre of data ranging from the census through the UK cohort studies and many surveys, sometimes now including biomarkers, and increasingly administrative data, researchers have risen to the challenge and addressed an increasingly wide, yet vitally important, range of issues. With the passing of its golden anniversary in 2015, the Economic and Social Research Council should be thanked for its continuing support for UK data.

At the heart of this wonderful endeavour has been the British Society for Population Studies. Its wide range of outstanding scholars from many disciplines have led research, nurtured the next generation and provided a forum for debating and understanding these most important of research challenges. And disseminating this knowledge widely is so important, which is why this book—around twenty-five years after Heather Joshi's volume—is so welcome. It is a collection of important chapters that span the challenges faced by Britain's population and do not shirk from the importance of understanding what this means for social policy. We should all thank Tony Champion and Jane Falkingham for their vision, dedication and drive in producing this volume that will, I am sure, stand the test of time.

Professor Sir Ian Diamond

Preface

In the mid-1980s, the British Society for Population Studies (BSPS) and the Centre for Economic Policy Research collaborated on organising a series of lectures highlighting the key challenges facing policymakers and practitioners as a result of the changing demography of Britain; these were then brought together in a book, *The Changing Population of Britain* (1989), edited by Prof. Heather Joshi, then president of BSPS. A quarter of a century on from this landmark publication, understanding the changing population of Britain remains as important today as it was then. Some of the issues covered then remain similar to those today but now take on a somewhat different form, whilst other new issues have surged up the policy agenda.

For this reason, BSPS thought it was timely to revisit Joshi's volume and bring together academics and policymakers to describe and discuss the findings of the latest research on the causes and consequences of demographic change in contemporary Britain and to frame the research agenda for the next twenty-five years. In terms of rationale, this book subscribes to the same sentiments that Joshi expressed in the first sentences of the preface to her 1989 book (Joshi, 1989a: vii): 'The study of population is vital. It is vital in that it is concerned with the vital events of births and deaths and other momentous transitions in people's lives. It is vital for informing forecasting and decision in both public and private sectors. It is also vital . . . in the sense that it is a very lively branch of social science in Britain'.

In conjunction with BSPS Council and through a call for expressions of interest to the BSPS membership, Tony Champion (BSPS president 2013–2015) and Jane Falkingham (BSPS president 2015–2017) selected the topics to be included in the book so as to demonstrate that the 'vitality' evident in the 1989 book continues. This book documents these recent developments, examines their underlying causes and how these are evolving and sets out their implications for both those dealing with the present-day challenges and those who are making decisions about the best way to plan for the future. During the preparation of the book, in conjunction with the British Academy, the BSPS also organised a series of events on several of these topics, notably four policy forums in spring 2015 involving invited representation from key government departments and other stakeholders.

The editors have much cause for gratitude, as a book like this does not come together by itself. First and foremost, they owe a great debt to the contributors to the book, both for initially offering their services and subsequently for all the hard work that has gone into their chapters. Secondly, they are very grateful to the British Academy for hosting the policy forums, which provided useful feedback to the chapter authors as well as a splendid venue for the dissemination of the preliminary findings to the policy community. They are also grateful to the BSPS Council for supporting this initiative and guiding the early stages of its development. In terms of the publication process, thanks go to Rowman & Littlefield International for accepting the book proposal and to their key staff for seeing the book through to fruition, most notably Martina O'Sullivan, her predecessor Alison Howson, Sinéad Murphy and also Editorial Director Sarah Campbell. Last but by no means least, we greatly appreciate Professor Sir Ian Diamond's willingness to contribute the foreword and take this opportunity to echo his key points about the growing salience of population-related issues in contemporary society and the continuing importance of research that helps us to better understand the big changes that are now taking place and anticipate future trends and their implications.

Chapter 1

Population Change in the UK: What Can the Last Twenty-Five Years Tell Us about the Next Twenty-Five Years?

Jane Falkingham and Tony Champion

The population of the UK is undergoing some fundamental transformations that have major implications in key areas of the economy, society, politics and environment. The population is currently increasing in size at a faster rate than for several decades, it is growing progressively older and it is becoming more diverse in ethnic and cultural terms. More school leavers are continuing into higher education, sexual behaviour has altered enormously, cohabitation has been replacing marriage, more children are living in one-parent families or with a step-parent, young adults are finding it harder to get on the housing ladder and to establish their own household, and more women are delaying having children until their late thirties and forties. Many cities have seen population resurgence, but there are still pressures on the countryside, the north-south divide is as great as ever and socio-economic disparities between individuals and communities are widening. This chapter aims to provide an overview of the key changes in the size and composition of the population of the UK and of its four constituent countries over the last quarter of a century since the publication of *The Changing Population of Britain* (Joshi, 1989a), and then looks forward to speculate about what the next twenty-five years might have in store.

POPULATION GROWTH AND THE DRIVERS OF POPULATION CHANGE

Over the past fifty years, the population of the UK has increased by over ten million, from 54 million in 1964 to reach 64.6 million in 2014 (ONS, 2015a). Across this period, however, growth rates have been very uneven, as shown

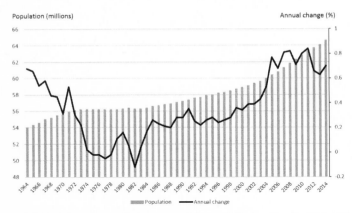

Figure 1.1   Midyear Population Estimates and Annual Change for the UK, 1964–2014.
Source: ONS, NRS, NISRA.

in Figure 1.1. From a high of 0.68 per cent per annum in 1964, reflecting the peak of the 1960s baby boom, over the next decade growth rates fell consistently (with the exception of 1971), and by 1975 annual growth was negative. The UK population actually declined in size between 1975 and 1978, and although positive rates of growth returned, this was short-lived, with 1982 witnessing negative growth of −0.12 per cent per annum, the biggest fall in the postwar period. Population growth rates picked up again in the mid-1980s and then remained fairly stable until the end of the 1990s, at around 0.2 to 0.3 per cent per annum. The dawn of the new millennium marked a change in gear, and growth rates doubled from 0.34 per cent in 2000 to 0.68 per cent in 2006, peaking at 0.82 per cent in 2008 and 0.84 per cent in 2011. Interestingly, although the annual growth rate of the population in the UK in 2014 is very similar to the level witnessed fifty years previously, the drivers behind this current growth are quite different.

The three demographic processes of fertility, mortality and migration determine the size, composition and distribution of a population. Figure 1.2 shows the trend in the annual number of births and deaths in the UK over the past half century. The number of births peaked in 1964 at just over one million and then fell to a low of 657,000 in 1977, when the number of births was almost exactly matched by the number of deaths, resulting in zero rates of natural increase (i.e., births minus deaths) in the population. Although there was then a slight rise in the number of births, reflecting the fact that those women and men born in the 1960s were now starting to form their own families, the annual number of births did not exceed eight hundred thousand throughout the 1980s and 1990s. During the 1960s, 1970s and 1980s, the growth rates in Figure 1.1 almost exactly track the changes in the number

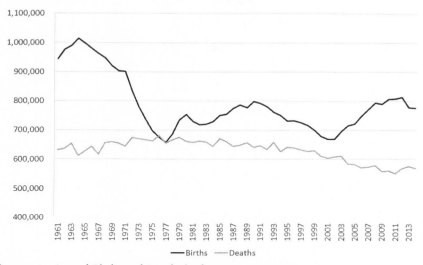

Figure 1.2   Annual Births and Deaths in the UK, 1961–2014.
Source: ONS (2015) Vital Statistics: Population and Health Reference Tables, Summer 2015 update.

of births in Figure 1.2. Thus, at the time of the publication of the *Changing Population of Britain* in 1989, it was principally the rate of natural increase (or the lack thereof) that had determined the rate of population growth for the preceding three decades.

The higher growth rate in recent years has been fuelled by a combination of accelerating natural increase and stronger net immigration from abroad, as shown in Figure 1.3. The annual number of births grew steadily from 679,000 in 2000 to nearly 813,000 in 2012, whilst the number of deaths reduced from 610,500 in 2000 to 570,300 in 2014, giving a much more positive rate of natural increase than for any period since the 1960s (Figure 1.2). Meanwhile, net inward migration added an average of over 240,000 persons per year to the UK population between 2004 and 2014. ONS's estimates of Long Term International Migration (LTIM) show that net migration stood at 336,000 in the year ending June 2015, up from 254,000 in the previous year (ONS, 2015b). EU citizens accounted for 42 per cent of the gross immigration to the UK in 2015, with non-EU citizens comprising 45 per cent and returning British citizens the remaining 13 per cent. The increase in net migration in the mid-2000s was fuelled by the arrival in the UK of migrants from the EU A8 accession countries, most notably Poland, whilst the recent increase in EU immigration in 2014 to 2015 has been partly driven by EU2 (Bulgaria and Romania) citizens. As documented in more detail in Chapter 4 by Jakub Bijak and his colleagues, the majority of these immigrants are in their twenties and

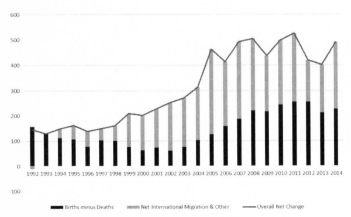

Figure 1.3   Main Drivers of Population Change, mid-1992 Onwards.
Source: Figure 2, ONS (2015a).

thirties and thus of prime reproduction age, so the indirect effect on the size of the population is even greater through their additional contribution to the number of births. Recent data show that around a quarter of all live births in England and Wales in 2014 were to mothers born outside the UK (ONS, 2015c; see also Chapter 5 by Sylvie Dubuc).

The four constituent countries of the UK have not experienced equal population growth. Between 2013 and 2014, whilst the UK as a whole grew by 0.77 per cent, Wales grew by just 0.31 per cent, Scotland by 0.37 per cent and Northern Ireland by 0.59 per cent, with England being the fastest growing at 0.84 per cent. At the regional level within England, the growth rate was highest in London, at 1.45 per cent, followed by the East and South East, at 1.08 per cent and 0.92 per cent, respectively (ONS, 2015a). Although no region of England experienced a population decrease at this time, in some cases this was due to net immigration from overseas offsetting the effect of net migration loss to the rest of the UK. As Chapter 8 shows (see Table 8.2), a net flow into the south and east of England still occurs, but its size fluctuates over time and is much smaller now than in the 1980s, even to the extent that there is a reverse flow in some years.

The most dramatic change in the spatial redistribution compared to a quarter century ago, however, has been at the urban rather than regional scale. As also documented in Chapter 8, the UK has seen an urban resurgence, with the switch from a 'counter-urbanisation' pattern of population change (where growth rates are inversely related to settlement size) to one of 'urbanisation' (where the largest cities are the fastest-growing places). London led the way in the later 1980s, with other large cities following suit a decade or so later. Higher rates of immigration have been the main driver of this urban recovery, along with stronger natural increase, but a contributory factor has been a reduction in the rate of migration from town to country. The latter was particularly marked during the 2008–2009 recession and its immediate aftermath, but its onset predates then, and the subsequent rebound has been slower than after previous recessions, raising questions about whether a different migration regime may be merging—one that may involve a general decline in people's frequency of moving home, as is now being observed in the USA (see Chapter 8 for more detail).

How does the UK compare with other countries in terms of overall growth rate? With a population of 64.4 million, in 2014 the UK had the third largest population in Europe (excluding Russia), just behind France (65.8 million) and Germany (80.7 million) (ONS, 2015d). However, its growth rate of 0.7 per cent was over twice that of Germany (0.3 per cent) and higher than France (0.42 per cent), meaning that other things remaining equal, the UK might look set to move up the EU population league table. However, these data predate the impact of the wave of migrants from Syria, the Middle East and North Africa that arrived in Europe during 2015–2016, many of whom have settled in Germany and France, bolstering their growth rates.

CHANGING COMPOSITION OF THE POPULATION

As well as increasing in size, the composition of the UK population has changed significantly across the last quarter century, most notably becoming older and significantly more ethnically diverse.

Changing Age Structure

Past trends in fertility, mortality and migration all influence the age structure of the population. Births determine the number of people entering the population at its base, and the trends in births presented previously in Figure 1.2 can be clearly seen in Figure 1.4, which shows the UK population by single year of age in 2014. The people born in the peak birth cohort of 1964 are now aged fifty, whilst those born in the baby boom that occurred immediately following the end of World War II, in 1946 and 1947, are aged sixty-six to sixty-seven. Interestingly, however, although the 'baby bust' years of the 1970s are also clearly visible in the dip in the number of people currently aged in their mid-thirties, the numbers in their twenties and mid-thirties are much higher than would be signposted purely by the number of births twenty to thirty years earlier—with their ranks swelled by the in-migration of young people of working age during the past decade.

The UK, in common with all the countries of Europe, is ageing, with the median age of the population having increased from 33.9 years in 1974 to

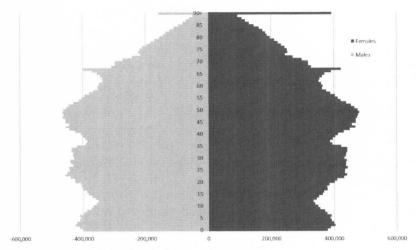

Figure 1.4   UK Population by Single Year of Age, 2014.
Source: Figure 2, ONS (2015a).

40.0 years in 2014, an average rise of 1.5 years each decade. However, the UK has been ageing less rapidly than, for example, Germany, where the median age in 2014 was 45.6, and Italy, where it was 44.7 (Eurostat, 2015), reflecting the arrival of younger migrants in the UK combined with its higher birthrate.

Even so, there are now more older people living longer than ever before. Mortality rates have fallen at all ages over the past fifty years, and these improvements have been most significant amongst infants and for those aged fifty-five and over. Improvements in survivorship mean that the onset of old age is being delayed (see Falkingham, 2016). If one thinks of the onset of 'old age' as being when there is a 1 per cent chance of dying and the onset of 'older old age' as being when there is a 10 per cent chance of dying, it is clear that 'old age' is being increasingly postponed. Levels of mortality that used to prevail for people aged in their early fifties are now prevailing in the early sixties; for men, the age when there is first a 1 per cent of chance of dying has risen from fifty-two in 1955 to sixty-three in 2015, and for women it has shifted from fifty-eight to sixty-eight. Similarly, the onset of 'older old age' has moved from seventy-seven for men in 1955 to eighty-six in 2015, and from eighty to eighty-eight amongst women (ONS, 2015e). The good news is that sixty really is the new fifty.

One of the most noteworthy changes in the UK population over the past twenty-five years has been a rise in the proportion aged ninety and over. This has been the fastest growing age group. In 1989, when the Joshi volume was published, people aged ninety and over accounted for 0.4 per cent of the population (403 per every 100,000 UK residents); in 2014 this figure had more than doubled to 0.8 per cent (853 per every 100,000 UK residents). More-over, in 1989 there were just 4,370 centenarians (people aged one hundred and over) living in the UK; by 2014 the number had risen by 230 per cent to 14,450 (ONS, 2015f). The growth of the oldest-old poses particular chal-lenges for health and social care, as it is these age groups that are most in need of support for everyday living (see Chapter 2 for a fuller discussion).

Changing Ethnic Composition

Perhaps the most significant change to Britain's population over the past quarter of a century has been its increasing ethnic diversity. As discussed in Chapters 4, 5 and 9, the ethnic diversity of the population reflects the various waves of immigration to the UK over the past fifty years. In 2014, 13 per cent of the usual resident population of the UK were born abroad, comprising 8.3 million people (ONS, 2015g). Of these, three million were from the rest of the EU, with an estimated 790,000 born in Poland, 383,000 in the Repub-lic of Ireland, 302,000 in Germany, 170,000 in Romania, 150,000 in Italy and 147,000 in France. Outside the EU, the five most common countries of birth were India (793,000), Pakistan (523,000), Bangladesh (212,000), South Africa (201,000) and China (196,000).

Table 1.1 shows the changing composition of the population of England and Wales by ethnicity. The growing number of UK residents who were born elsewhere in the EU is reflected in the rise in the proportion of the popula-tion who identified as 'White Other' between the 2001 and 2011 Censuses (ONS, 2012a; ONS, 2015h). There has also been an increase in those identi-fying themselves as being of mixed heritage, increasing from 1.4 per cent to 2.2 per cent, reflecting the growing number of children born to inter-ethnic couples. In 2011, nearly one in ten people who were living as part of a couple in England and Wales were in an inter-ethnic relationship, equivalent to 2.3 million people (ONS, 2014a). Moreover, 7 per cent of dependent children lived in a household with an inter-ethnic relationship.

This ethnic mixing is just one line of evidence that suggests that a process of integration is under way. Another is the observation by Sylvie Dubuc in Chapter 5 that the fertility of migrants and minority ethnic groups is converg-ing towards that of White British women. Additionally, in Chapter 9, Nissa Finney and Gemma Catney demonstrate that ethnic mixing is taking place not only between people but also over space, with minority groups moving to new locales away from the places of original settlement. They show that the minority presence is increasing in previously 'White' spaces, and not just due to asylum dispersal strategies but also paralleling the suburbanisation of the White population. Nevertheless, in most cases this dispersal process does little to reduce the size of the ethnic minority concentrations because

Table 1.1   Percentage Distribution of the Population by Ethnic Group, England and Wales, 2001–2011

		2001	2011
White	White British	87.4	80.5
	Irish	1.2	0.9
	Gypsy or Irish Traveller†	n/a	0.1
	Other White	2.6	4.4
Mixed/Multiple ethnic groups	White and Black Caribbean	0.5	0.8
	White and Asian	0.4	0.6
	White and Black African	0.2	0.3
	Other Mixed	0.3	0.5
Asian/Asian British	Indian	2.0	2.5
	Pakistani	1.4	2.0
	Bangladeshi	0.5	0.8
	Chinese*	0.4	0.7
	Other Asian*	0.5	1.5
Black/African/Caribbean/ Black British	African	0.9	1.8
	Caribbean	1.1	1.1
	Other Black	0.2	0.5
Other ethnic group	Arab†	n/a	0.4
	Any other ethnic group	0.4	0.6

*Comparability issues exist between these ethnic groups for the 2001 and 2011 Census.
†No comparable data exists for these ethnic groups in 2001 Census.
Source: Census 2001 and 2011, Office for National Statistics.

the effect of their departure has been offset by new arrivals from overseas, swelling the number of overseas-born there and leading to an expansion of the zones with 'majority minority' populations, with implications for a range of services, most notably education and health, and also potentially for community relations given the steadily increasing diversity within the minority population itself.

Changing Families and Households

Substantial changes are occurring in the patterns of family formation and dissolution in the UK, as very widely across Europe. Declining marriage, increasing cohabitation, the legalisation of same-sex civil partnerships and marriages, delayed fertility and increasing childlessness have resulted in new forms of families and households, with British families becoming considerably more diverse. In Chapter 6, Ursula Henz looks at family change from a child's perspective, examining three aspects of children's families: the size of the sibling group, living with a lone mother and mothers' labour-force participation.

When the Joshi volume was published, one of the most notable changes in families with dependent children over the preceding two decades had been the growth of lone-parent families. In 2015, as shown in Table 1.2, there were

Table 1.2   Families by Family Type in the UK, 1996, 2005 and 2015

Family Type		1996	2005	2015
Married or civil partner couple family*	With dependent children	5.2	4.7	4.7
	Without dependent children	7.4	7.5	7.8
Cohabiting couple family*	With dependent children	0.5	0.9	1.3
	Without dependent children	0.9	1.5	1.9
Lone-parent family	With dependent children	1.6	1.9	2.0
	Without dependent children	0.8	0.8	1.1

Families without dependent children have only non-dependent children or no children in the household.
*Married-couple families include both opposite-sex and same-sex married couples in 2005 and 2015.
Cohabiting couple families include both opposite-sex and same-sex cohabiting couples in 2005 and 2015.
Source: Labour Force Survey, Office for National Statistics.

3.1 million lone-parent families, of which two million contained dependent children (aged under sixteen or aged sixteen to eighteen in full-time education). These lone parents with dependent children comprised around a quarter of all families with dependent children, a figure only slightly higher than the 22 per cent share in 1996. In contrast, the fastest growing family type over the past two decades has been cohabiting couples, more than doubling to 3.2 million in 2015, of which 1.3 million were with dependent children (Table 1.2).

This change reflects the continued shift away from childbearing within marriage highlighted by Kathleen Kiernan's chapter in Joshi (1989a). Even in 1989, 27 per cent of all births were to parents outside a legal union; in 2014, nearly half of all births (47 per cent) were outside a marriage or civil partnership (ONS, 2015j). Births outside marriage or civil partnership can be registered solely by the mother or jointly by both the mother and the father/ second parent. In the latter case, where parents give the same address, it can be inferred that they are cohabiting. The proportion of births registered to cohabiting parents has increased in recent years, with just under a third of all births (32 per cent) being registered to cohabiting parents in 2014, compared with 27 per cent in 2004 and 10 per cent in 1986. In contrast, the percentage of births registered solely by the mother has fallen from 7.2 per cent in 1986 to 5.4 per cent in 2014 (ONS, 2015j). Thus, more births are taking place in the context of both partners being present, this in part being a reflection of the rise in the average age of parenthood, given that the majority of births registered by the mother alone are to younger mothers.

The increases in the likelihood of becoming a lone mother that occurred in the 1970s and 1980s, either through experiencing a birth prior to any residential partnership or through the experience of partnership dissolution, have slowed during the 2000s, explaining why the share of lone-parent families appears to have stabilised (Berrington, 2014). Nevertheless, as Henz discusses in Chapter 6, children growing up with a lone mother remain particularly vulnerable, with 46 per cent of children in lone-parent families in the UK living in relative poverty (Harkness et al., 2012). One of the key reasons for this is the continuing difficulty that lone mothers face in engaging in the labour market. Although the likelihood of lone mothers being in employment has increased over the last decade as a result of policy initiatives such as working family tax credit and nursery vouchers, Henz finds that around half of children of lone mothers lived with a mother who was not in work (see Figure 6.5). Young, single, lone mothers are themselves particularly likely to come from poor socio-economic backgrounds (Rowlingson and McKay, 2005; Kiernan et al., 2011). Breaking the cycle of disadvantage highlighted in Joshi (1989a) continues to remain a key policy challenge.

Interestingly, the most common type of family in the UK is now a married or civil partner couple family *without* dependent children, of which there were 7.8 million in 2015 (ONS, 2015i). As Table 1.2 highlights, there has been strong growth in families with non-dependent children across all three basic family types. This largely reflects the changing living arrangements of young adults in the UK, with more now remaining in the parental home (Stone et al., 2011). Also, more young adults are now living independently outside a family. Shared living is becoming more common for young adults in their early twenties, especially as university students, whilst living as a one-person household becomes more prevalent by their early thirties. As discussed by Berrington and Simpson in Chapter 7, average household size in the UK fell consistently in the twentieth century (though not subsequently), driven first by declining fertility and then by an increased propensity for adults to live alone or as couples only. In 2015, single-person households comprised 29 per cent of all households, corresponding to 7.7 million people and an increase of 1.1 million from the 6.6 million in 1996.

Figure 1.5 shows the proportion living alone by age and gender in 1985 and 2009. Three things stand out. First, the likelihood of living alone is strongly related to age, rising dramatically after sixty-five as the likelihood of widowhood increases. Second, more older women live alone than men, reflecting gender differences in survivorship. Third, looking at changes over time (i.e., the differences between the lines for 1985 and 2009), the propensity to live alone increased in the earlier part of the life course for women, reflecting both the postponement of partnership and the rise of divorce, but remained remarkably unchanged at ages over sixty-five, reflecting improvements in male mortality. However, there has been a significant rise in solo living amongst men across all ages (Demey et al., 2011). Recent analysis of the living arrangements of men in mid-life, using data from the first two waves of the United Kingdom Household Longitudinal Survey (UKHLS), indicates that the dissolution of a marriage with children is the dominant pathway into mid-life solo-living, but it also reveals a substantial group of never-partnered

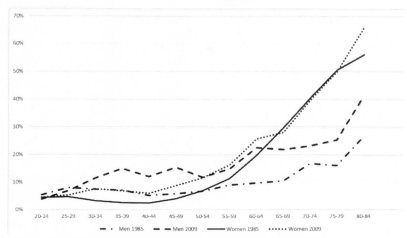

Figure 1.5 Proportion Living Alone by Gender, Great Britain, 1985–2009.
Source: Figure 5 in Falkingham, Evandrou and Vlachantoni (2014).

men living alone (Demey et al., 2013). Those who have not had children, have no educational qualifications, are not economically active and live in rented housing are likely to have only limited social and financial resources as they enter later life and thus be in need of a safety net (as further discussed by Evandrou, Falkingham and Vlachantoni in Chapter 2).

BRITAIN'S FUTURE POPULATION—
THE NEXT TWENTY-FIVE YEARS

According to the principal 2014-based National Population Projections produced by ONS, the UK population is projected to increase by just under ten million over the next twenty-five years, from 65.1 million in 2015 to 74.6 million in 2040, with the population breaking through the 70 million threshold around 2027 (ONS, 2015k). Most of this growth will occur in England, with Wales projected to increase by around 195,000 from 3.1 to 3.3 million, Scotland by some 345,000 from 5.4 to 5.7 million and Northern Ireland by 185,000 from 1.8 to 2 million.

Looking at the drivers of this growth at the UK level, around half (49 per cent) is projected to be due to natural increase (i.e., an excess of births over deaths), and the other half (51 per cent) will be the result of net migration. However, these projections are based on particular assumptions regarding future trends, which might be wrong, and projections become increasingly uncertain the further into the future we go, with migration being especially difficult to predict (Bijak et al., 2015; see also Chapter 4). One area where we can have more confidence than others, however, is the continued ageing of the population and the growth of the oldest old. The number of people aged eighty and above is projected to more than double by mid-2040, the number of people aged ninety and over is projected to more than triple, and the number of centenarians is projected to rise from 14,500 in 2014 to 89,000 in 2040, a more than sixfold increase. This increase in the numbers of older people means that by 2040 one in eleven of the population is projected to be aged eighty and over (ONS, 2015k). With rises in life expectancy, more of the older population may expect to live as couples as opposed to alone, particularly in the earlier stages of later life, with declining widowhood offsetting rising divorce rates. However, a significant minority will be living solo, with implications for the availability of co-residential social care.

Moreover, even if migration flows to the UK reduce or cease altogether, the population in twenty-five years' time will undoubtedly be more ethnically diverse than today, as older cohorts that are more ethnically homogeneous are replaced by younger cohorts that are more heterogeneous. The 2011 Census (Table DC2101EW) shows that, amongst those aged twenty-five to thirty-four, one in five (20 per cent) reported their ethnicity to be other than White, and a further 10 per cent identified as 'White Other', whilst just 69 per cent reported being 'White British'. This contrasts with those aged seventy and over, where 92 per cent are 'White British' and just 5 per cent are from non-White heritage. The ONS does not produce population projections by ethnicity, but Rees et al. (2012) suggest that the ethnic minority share of the population will rise to 20 to 25 per cent by 2051 depending on assumptions made concerning international migration.

As regards family composition, it is likely that the number of cohabiting couple families will rise, continuing the upward trend shown in Table 1.2. Alongside this, the number of dependent children living in cohabiting couple families will also increase. The recognition of children living in such family types, which are themselves quite diverse in terms of other demographic and socio-economic characteristics, will be of growing importance by policy-makers who are tasked with catering for the ever-increasing diversity in the demographic composition of the population.

Over the next twenty-five years, we can say with a fair degree of certainty that the population will get larger, the population will get older and the population will become more diverse in terms of both ethnic composition and family forms. What is less clear is exactly how these changes will impact on particular places and alter their socio-demographic profiles, including whether urban-to-rural migration will pick up further as economic conditions improve, whether the dispersal of ethnic minority groups will accelerate and whether social segregation will intensify, all these being partly related to what long-term solution, if any, is found for the current 'housing crisis'. The need to plan for this changing population remains as critical today as it did twenty-five years ago; so, too, does the need for better intelligence on how the UK's population is altering over time, on what are the principal drivers of these changes and on what policy levers are likely to be more effective in encouraging the more welcome trends and counteracting the less desirable developments.

The remaining chapters of this book aim to move forward our understanding of the UK's changing demography and the opportunities and challenges that arise from this, building on the overview provided in the previous sections. The next two chapters focus on the ageing population, for which the trends appear highly predictable, though this does not diminish the scale of the implications for health and social care (Chapter 2), nor the challenge of ensuring well-being in the later stages of the life course for the many and not just the privileged few (Chapter 3). Attention then turns to the topic of immigration, which is sometimes seen as part of the solution to population ageing but which has much more uncertainty attached to it, in terms of both the numbers and the types of people that can be expected to arrive in any year and as regards their impacts on the economy and social relations (Chapter 4), but it seems that at least in one important respect, that of fertility and family size, there is evidence of convergence towards the national mean by the non-UK born and their descendants (Chapter 5).

Chapters 6 and 7 focus on aspects relating to families and households, with the former taking a children's perspective on the profound changes that have taken place in the structure of British families over recent decades and emphasising the wide diversity of conditions under which children grow up. These are reflected in similarly important changes in household composition and in the increasing difficulty that adults are facing in satisfying their housing needs and aspirations, with the cessation of the century-long decline in average household size, which seems at least partly due to shortages on the supply side (Chapter 7). The historically low levels of housebuilding in recent years can help to explain the reduction in frequency of moving home by almost all types of people apart from those of university age, including the fading of net north-to-south migration since the 1980s and the slowdown in the urban exodus since the early 2000s, with potential implications for the efficiency of housing and labour markets that merit further study (Chapter 8). For ethnic minorities, however, an accelerating dispersal from the original locales of immigrant settlement is a key change, though the main message of Chapter 9 is of increasing diversity both in ethnic composition and in the behaviour of the many ethnic communities.

These many developments, along with alterations in attitudes and values over the past half century, have shaped, and been shaped by, equally fundamental changes in reproductive and sexual behaviour and health, which raise key concerns for the future relating to a range of groups, especially older adults, adolescents, migrants and non-heterosexuals. Chapter 10 examines some of the most salient aspects, including trends in sexual partnerships, contraceptive use, induced abortion, maternal morbidity, sexually transmitted infections, HIV/AIDS and female genital mutilation. Finally, given that deprivation and social exclusion are such important issues, it is vital that we make use of the best tools available for monitoring patterns and trends in these, including comparing like with like over time rather than being overly reliant on cross-sectional studies, as Chapter 11 shows. This final chapter also provides a timely reminder of the need for continuity in the statistical resources needed for monitoring this and all aspects of population change, not least given that the 2021 Census looks like being the last of its kind, with much greater dependence needing to be put thereafter on alternatives like administrative records and sample surveys—this being a major potential opportunity for researchers to gain access to new types of data but also posing significant challenges for data providers in ensuring, at the very least, no diminution of the range and quality of information compared with the existing picture.

Chapter 2

The Ageing Population: Implications for Health and Social Care

Maria Evandrou, Jane Falkingham and Athina Vlachantoni[1]

In the 1980s, when Pat Thane wrote the chapter on 'Old Age: Burden or Benefit?' in the Joshi (1989a) volume, the share of Britain's population aged sixty-five and over was just over 15 per cent. At the time of the 2011 census, nearly twenty-five years later, individuals aged sixty-five and over constituted 16 per cent of the population (ONS, 2012b), suggestive of a remarkable period of stability in the relative size of the older population. However, all is not quite as conveyed by the headline figure. As was discussed in Chapter 1, there have been significant changes in the age composition of the population of working-age and older population itself, with the age structure of the working-age population increasingly weighted towards higher age cohorts and with a growing number of 'very old' amongst the retired population. Nevertheless, as Thane suggested, the period of stability has given us the 'breathing space in which to research and to plan for future policy' (Thane, 1989: 62).

In contrast to the 1960s and 1970s, when Thane noted that 'the work of gerontologists seems often not to have reached the policymakers, the economists and the public' (Thane, 1989: 60), the last two decades have witnessed a plethora of policy reports and enquiries, notably including the Pensions Commission chaired by Lord Adair Turner, which laid the foundation for a radical overhaul of the UK pension system (Pensions Commission, 2004; 2006), and the Commission on Funding of Care and Support, chaired by Andrew Dilnot, tasked with reviewing the funding system for care and support in England (Department of Health, 2011). The academic community has also been extremely active, in part reflecting the availability of dedicated research funding under the 'Growing Older' initiative and the 'New Dynamics of Ageing Programme' (Harding, 2014). However, despite this, in its report published in 2013, the House of Lords Select Committee on Public Service (chaired by Lord Filkin) concluded, 'The UK population is ageing rapidly, but we have concluded that the Government and our society is woefully underprepared' (House of Lords, 2013: 1, para. 1), highlighting that more remains to be done.

This chapter takes a demographic perspective on ageing, updating the evidence base presented in Thane (1989). It first outlines the changing age structure of the population over the last century before discussing trends in life expectancy and how improvements in survival are reframing the meaning of old age. The chapter then briefly examines the health of older people and how this has changed over time and across sections of society. In particular, it addresses the question of whether the improvements in life expectancy over the last twenty-five years have been matched by improvements in health. Maintaining its demographic focus, the final section of the chapter discusses how changes in patterns of family formation and dissolution are reflected in changes in the life course across cohorts. In particular, we highlight the need to take a holistic view of demographic change and ageing, including the impact of shifts in patterns of family formation and dissolution on the future 'availability' of kin (both spouse and adult children) to provide care.

THE CHANGING AGE STRUCTURE

Figure 2.1 shows the percentage of Britain's population aged sixty-five and over, along with the percentage aged eighty-five and over. Over the course of the twentieth century, the proportion of those aged sixty-five and over increased dramatically. In 1901, the proportion of the population aged sixty-five and over was just under 5 per cent; by 1941 it had doubled to 10 per cent, and by 1981 it had tripled to reach 15 per cent. Since then, there has been a period of stability. However, the proportion of older people in the population is now rising again as the cohort of people born just after World War II reach their mid-sixties. In 2014, 17.7 per cent of the population were aged sixty-five and over, and this figure will increase significantly over the next twenty years as the baby boom cohort (those born in the late 1950s to mid-1960s) enters retirement. In 2021, older people will make up one in five of the total population (19.1 per cent), and by 2041 this will have risen to almost one in four (24.4 per cent). The graph also highlights the ageing of the older population itself, reflecting an increase in the proportion of the 'oldest old'. The proportion of Britain's population aged eighty-five and over in 1901 was just 0.2 per cent. In 2014, these 'oldest old' accounted for about 2.3 per cent of the total population, and by 2041 they will constitute 5 per cent, the same share of those aged sixty-five-plus in 1901.

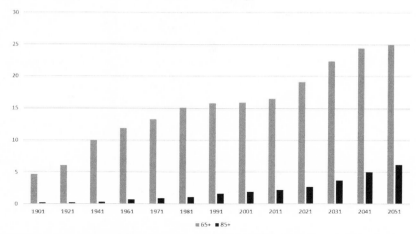

Figure 2.1   Percentage of the Population Aged 65+ and 85+, Great Britain, 1901–2051.
Source: 1901–2011 from ONS Population Trends (selected volumes); 2021–2051 from ONS 2014–based Population Projections.

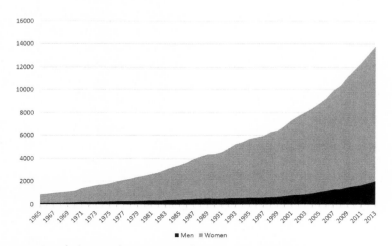

Figure 2.2   Population Aged 100 Years and Over, UK, 1965–2013.
Source: ONS (2015a) Estimates of the Very Old (including Centenarians) for England and Wales, United Kingdom, 2002–2013.

Centenarians are the fastest-growing age group in the population. As illustrated in Figure 2.2, the number of centenarians living in the UK has risen dramatically over the past fifty years, from just 860 in 1965 to 14,450 in 2014. Moreover, 780 of the 14,450 centenarians in 2014 were estimated to be aged 105 or more, compared with just 120 in 1984 (ONS, 2015f).

The vast majority of centenarians are women, but the ratio of women to men is decreasing as more men reach their one-hundredth birthday. In 1996, there were nine women aged one hundred and over for every man, but by 2014 this had fallen to less than six, reflecting the narrowing of the gap in overall life expectancy between the genders.

INCREASING LIFE EXPECTANCY

The improvement in average life expectancy over the past one hundred years is one of the great success stories of the twentieth century. Given the mortality rates prevailing at the start of the last century, a baby boy born in 1901 could, on average, expect to live to age forty-five and a baby girl to forty-nine years. By the beginning of this century, average male life expectancy had risen to 75.7 years, whilst average female life expectancy in 2001 was 80.4 years. These improvements in life expectancy reflect advances in medicine and public health across the last century, as well as rising standards of living, better education, improved nutrition and changes in lifestyles.

Figures 2.3a and 2.3b show the annual mortality schedule—that is, the probability of dying per 100,000 population of that age, for men and women over the period 1955–2015 using the 2014-based life tables (ONS, 2015k, Table D1.1, 1951–2064, UK principal projection). The probability of dying is plotted on a logarithmic scale. The underlying shape of the curves has not changed significantly over time, with both boys and girls experiencing a relatively high chance of dying at birth; then the mortality risk decreases and remains low until age sixteen, after which it begins to rise. Over time, death rates have fallen at virtually every age, with each curve lying below that of the previous one. These improvements in survivorship have given rise to discussions around the meaning of age itself. As was briefly discussed in Chapter 1, the levels of mortality that used to prevail for people aged in their early fifties are now prevailing in the early sixties; for men, the age when there is first a 1 per cent annual chance of dying has risen from fifty-two in 1955 to sixty-three in 2015, and for women it has shifted from fifty-eight to sixty-eight. The data in Figures 2.3a and 2.3b use period-based age-specific mortality rates; the improvement in survivorship across cohorts has been even more remarkable. Amongst girls born in 2015, the age at which they first experience a 10 per cent chance of dying, signifying the onset of 'older old age', may well be at age one hundred (Falkingham, 2016).

As discussed in greater detail in Chapter 3 of this volume, there are significant variations in life expectancy both across social groups and spatially. In 2012–2014, life expectancy for a newborn baby boy in Kensington and Chelsea was 83.3 years, whereas life expectancy for a baby boy born in Blackpool was 8.6 years less (74.7 years). The inequalities between local

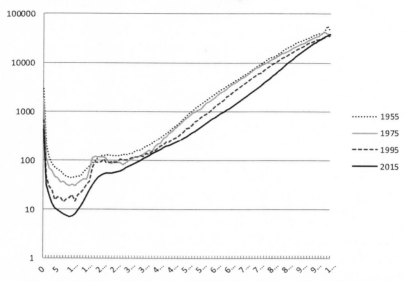

Figure 2.3a   Probability of Dying Per 100,000 Population, UK, 1955–2015, Males.
Source: ONS 2014-based National Population Projections Lifetable template.

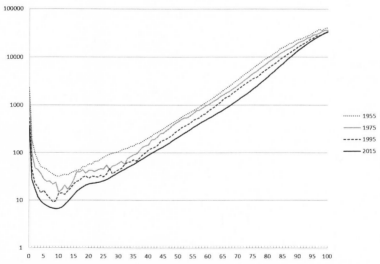

Figure 2.3b   Probability of Dying Per 100,000 Population, UK, 1955–2015, Females.
Source: ONS 2014-based National Population Projections Lifetable template.

areas with the highest and lowest life expectancy at birth have widened over the last two decades (ONS, 2015l). So, too, has the gap in life expectancies according to social class. Figure 3.1 (Marshall and Nazroo, this volume) presents data on the changes in life expectancy at age sixty-five for England

and Wales across the period 1982–2006. The gap in life expectancy between the lowest social classes (routine occupations) and the highest social classes (managers and professionals) for men has widened from 3.6 years in the early 1980s to 5.5 in 2012, and for women the gap in life expectancy has increased from 3 years to 4.2 years. The largest gains at age sixty-five over the thirty-year period were to men from the higher managerial and profes-sional class and for women from the intermediate class (ONS, 2015m). This has implications for current debates around linking future increases in the age at which people are entitled to the UK state pension to changes in average life expectancy (Sinclair et al., 2014). Such a link has been proposed in the 2013 Pension Act, with the aim of maintaining the proportion of adult life spent in receipt of a state pension. If enacted, such a change would disadvantage those groups whose life expectancy is lower than the average. This is already the case where eligibility is a fixed chronological age (currently sixty-five and set to rise to sixty-six by 2020 and sixty-seven by 2028), as some people enjoy a longer period in retirement than others; linking future rises to aver-age improvements in life expectancy would then preserve these inequalities in perpetuity.

HEALTH, DISABILITY AND HEALTHY LIFE EXPECTANCY

Pensions can be viewed as one side of the 'public expenditure coin' for older people, the other side being the cost of health and social care provision. Indi-viduals aged seventy-five and over account for a significant share of spending on health and social care services. Data published by the Health and Social Care Information Centre indicates that 51 per cent (£8.8 billion) of total expenditure on personal social services in England in 2013–2014 was on indi-viduals aged sixty-five and over (HSCIC, 2014). McKinsey (2013) estimated that health and social care expenditure on individuals over seventy-five was thirteen times greater than that on the rest of the adult population. A key ques-tion for policymakers, and indeed for older people themselves, is whether the years of life added by the improvements in mortality over the past twenty-five years have been years in good health. The Office for National Statistics (ONS) routinely publishes two types of health expectancies. The first is Healthy Life Expectancy (HLE), which estimates the length of life spent in 'very good' or 'good' health based upon how individuals perceive their general health (ONS, 2015n). The second is Disability-Free Life Expectancy (DFLE), which estimates the numbers of years expected to live free from a limiting persis-tent illness or disability. DFLE is based upon a self-rated assessment of how health limits an individual's ability to carry out day-to-day activities (ONS, 2014b). Both are summary measures of population health and key indicators of the well-being of society. From these it is possible to calculate the proportion of life spent on average in a health state. Moreover, these measures can also be calculated for different sub-groups of the population.

Table 2.1 shows life expectancy and healthy life expectancy for women and men at ages sixty-five, seventy-five and eighty-five in England in 2011–2013. The proportion of later life spent in 'good' health is higher for men than women and, not surprisingly, drops with age. Amongst those who have survived to age eighty-five, women can expect around 40 per cent of their remaining years to be in good health and men 44 per cent. There are difficulties in examining trends across time due to changes in question wording. However, Jagger (2015), in her paper for the recent UK Government Foresight 'Future of an Ageing Population' project, concluded that the increases in health expectancies in the UK have not kept pace with gains in life expectancy, particularly at older ages, meaning that a greater proportion of later life is now spent in not good health than in the past. Moreover, some groups are less likely to reach state pension age in good health, reflecting the significant variations in healthy and disability-free life expectancy by region, social class and ethnicity (ONS, 2014b, 2015n; Wohland et al., 2015; see also Marshall and Nazroo, this volume). In 2011–2013, HLE was lower than the state pension age in three-quarters of areas for males and two-thirds of areas for females, presenting a challenge to policies aimed at extending working life. It may be that the planned increases of the state pension age will, in some instances, simply transfer spending from the state pension to disability and unemployment benefits (Sinclair et al., 2014). Furthermore, the additional benefits tied to the state pension age, such as the free bus pass and winter fuel allowance, will, on average, not be available to some disadvantaged groups until well beyond their disability life expectancy. Yet it is these groups of individuals who are likely to benefit most from it.

Table 2.1   Life Expectancy and Healthy Life Expectancy for Females and Males at Age 65, 75 and 85 and Over in England, 2011–2013

	Life Expectancy	Healthy Life Expectancy	Proportion of Life Spent in 'Good' Health (%)
Women			
At age 65	21.1	11.3	53.4%
At age 75	13.3	6.1	45.7%
At age 85	7.1	2.9	40.3%
Men			
At age 65	18.7	10.5	56.2%
At age 75	11.5	5.8	50.6%
At age 85	6.3	2.8	43.9%

Source: ONS (2015e).

These trends in HLE and DFLE will also have an impact on the need for social care during later life. The ageing of the population over the last twenty years has been accompanied by important shifts in the policy context of social care provision, with a greater emphasis on the provision of care in the community and the 'intensification', or targeting, of council services to fewer people (Humphries et al., 2010; Vlachantoni et al., 2011). Interestingly, the £8.8 billion spent on older people's social care by local authorities in England in 2013–2014, cited previously, compares to a real-terms figure of £10.1 billion (56 per cent of the total) in 2008–2009, a decrease of 12 per cent in real terms spending in the last five years (HSCIC, 2014), reflecting the squeeze on the public sector during the recent period of 'austerity'. Previous analysis of survey data by the authors and other colleagues within the Centre for Population Change highlight that there is significant unmet need for social care amongst older people and, where they do receive support, that older people are more likely to receive support from formal sources for assistance with instrumental activities of daily living (IADLs), such as shopping, than for the more intensive activities of daily living, such as bathing and dressing, where the main source of support was from the informal sector (Vlachantoni et al., 2011).

CARE AND CARERS

Over the past two decades there has been a growing recognition of the key contribution made to social care by the unpaid care provided by family, neighbours and friends (Evandrou et al., 2015). The increasing importance of informal care for the policy agenda is reflected in the inclusion of a question in the 2001 UK Census on the provision of unpaid care. This provided the first data on the prevalence of informal care at the national level, highlighting that an estimated 5.9 million individuals were providing such care (Doran et al., 2003). Of these, over one million were aged sixty-five and over, and more than a fifth were cared for at least fifty hours per week (Evandrou, 2005). Inclusion of a repeat question in 2011 highlighted that in England and Wales the prevalence of informal care had increased across the decade, especially amongst those providing twenty to forty-nine hours and fifty hours plus per week (ONS, 2013a). The prevalence of caring in 2011 was higher amongst women than men and peaked in mid-life (forty-five to sixty-four), reflecting the provision of care by adult children to their parents. However, the numbers of hours of care provided rises with age, and the increase in the prevalence of very intensive care (fifty or more hours) across the decade has been most marked amongst men aged seventy-five and over, reflecting improvements in male life expectancy and thus increases in intensive spousal care at later old ages (Evandrou et al., 2015).

The role played by informal care provision is substantial. In 2011, Carers UK estimated the economic contribution made by carers in the UK to be around £119 billion per year, exceeding all spending on the NHS (Carers UK, 2011). Caring is not without costs to the individual, in terms of both their ability to continue to participate in paid work and their health. Economically active individuals are less likely to provide care compared to inactive individuals (Vlachantoni, 2010), and when informal carers are in paid work, they earn significantly less (Carmichael and Charles, 2003). There is a growing body of work examining the relationship between care provision and health. Cross-sectional analysis frequently points to a positive association between caring and health, with carers being less likely to report a limiting long-term illness than non-carers. However, the picture may be complicated by a healthy carer selection effect, with only those in better health being in a position to provide care. Recent research, using the ONS Longitudinal Study's linked census records, found the provision of intensive (i.e., over twenty hours a week) informal care repeatedly or over an extended period of time to be associated with poor health outcomes (Evandrou et al., 2016). Amongst all informal carers in 2001, over one-third were also providing care ten years later, suggesting that for a significant sub-group of people the duration of caring may be extensive (Robards et al., 2015). It is those carers providing high-intensity care for long durations who are in most need of additional support, including respite care. Such support is cost-effective compared to the alternative of hospital or long-term residential care; yet in many local authorities such services are under pressure.

THE CHANGING LIFE COURSE AND THE FUTURE DEMAND AND SUPPLY OF HEALTH AND SOCIAL CARE

To what extent will we be able to continue to rely on adult children and partners as the main sources of social care and other forms of support in later life? Timaeus, writing in the mid-1980s, suggested that kin support was likely to increase rather than decline over the next two decades, as those cohorts reaching the age of sixty during the 1990s and 2000s were more likely to have married and have had children than previous generations (Timaeus, 1986). Since then, however, there have been significant changes in the patterns of family formation and dissolution that commentators in the 1980s could not have envisaged. Declining marriage, increasing cohabitation, the legalisation of same-sex civil partnerships (in 2004) and marriages (in 2014), delayed fertility and increasing childlessness have resulted in new forms of families and households, with British families becoming considerably more diverse. Examining the trends in partnership formation and dissolution across the cohorts allows us to speculate what the living arrangements of the 1960s baby boomers might look like when they begin to retire and to comment on their potential situation with regard to the future availability of informal care from adult children or partners.

Figure 2.4 shows the proportion of women ever married by a certain age by birth cohort for England and Wales. Successive cohorts of women (and men) have married later, and marriage has become less popular overall. The majority of women born in 1945 had married by their early thirties; however, amongst those born in 1965, a significant minority (over 20 per cent) had not entered into a first marriage by age forty, and amongst men born in 1965 the level was even higher, at around 30 per cent. This in part reflects the trend towards increasing cohabitation, but recent research has also shown that there is a substantial group of men who have never partnered by mid-life (Demey et al., 2013).

Amongst those who have married, divorce has also become more common (Figure 2.5), with dissolution of a marriage with children being the dominant pathway into mid-life solo living. Of those women born in 1945, 25 per cent had divorced at least once by age fifty; this had risen to 30 per cent amongst women born in 1955, with similar proportions divorcing amongst men. Moreover, amongst those born in 1955, the proportion ever divorced continued to increase through their fifties, highlighting that divorce is becoming more common later in the life course than previously. Solo living has become more common in mid-life amongst successive cohorts; in 1985 10 per cent of men aged sixty to sixty-four were living alone; by 2009 this had risen to 22 per cent amongst the same age group, whilst the proportions for women were 20 per cent and 26 per cent, respectively (Demey et al., 2011; see also Figure 1.5 in this volume). The trends in patterns of family formation and dissolution experienced by different birth cohorts suggest that more of the 1960s baby boomers may be living alone in later life than previous cohorts, despite the improvements in longevity that will mean fewer will experience prolonged periods of widowhood.

Adult children are the other main source of support in later life. As Table 2.2 shows, the average completed family size has fallen from 2.19 children amongst women born in 1945 to 1.91 amongst those born in 1965. Interestingly, there has been little change in the percentage of women with large families across cohorts. Rather, it is the decision to have any children at all that has changed, with one in five of women born in 1965 being childless at age forty-five compared to one in ten of those born two decades earlier in 1945.

The fact that a higher proportion of the 1940s cohort ever married and had children means that a higher proportion than in previous generations are likely to be living as couples in later life, especially given improvements in

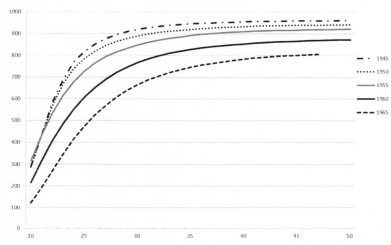

Figure 2.4   Proportion of Women Ever Married by Age, by Birth Cohort, England and Wales.
Source: ONS (2014h) Marriages in England and Wales 2012.

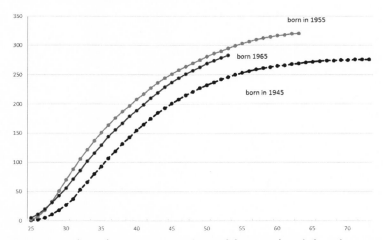

Figure 2.5   Proportion of Women Ever Divorced by Age, by Birth Cohort, England and Wales.
Source: ONS (2015f) Divorces in England and Wales 2013.

mortality, and more will have adult children, thus potentially the availability of informal care is likely to rise for this cohort. However, the future is much less clear-cut for those baby boomers born in the 1960s. Changes in partnership behaviour may mean that more people from the 1960s cohort enter later life without a partner than in previous cohorts. Modelling work carried out by Pickard and colleagues suggests that, given increases in female employment

Table 2.2   Completed Family Size at Age 45 Amongst Women in England and Wales, by Birth Cohort

Year of Birth of Woman	Average Family Size	Number of Live-Born Children (Percentages)					
		Childless	1	2	3	4+	Total
1945	2.19	10	14	43	21	12	100%
1950	2.07	14	13	44	20	10	100%
1955	2.02	16	13	41	19	11	100%
1960	1.98	19	12	38	20	11	100%
1965	1.91	20	13	38	19	10	100%

Note: Individual numbers are rounded to nearest integer, so the total may be more or less than 100.
Source: ONS Birth Statistics.

and other social changes affecting the willingness to care, even over the next two decades the supply of unpaid care to older people with disabilities by their adult children in England is unlikely to keep pace with demand and that by 2032 there is projected to be a shortfall of 160,000 caregivers in England (Pickard, 2015). Bearing in mind that the 1960s baby boomers will only be entering their seventies at this date, it is highly likely that this care gap will continue to widen further. Of great concern are men who are living alone and who have never had children, have no educational qualifications, are not economically active and who live in rented housing; they represent an especially vulnerable group, having both low social capital and poor economic resources (Demey et al., 2013).

CONCLUSION

This chapter has highlighted the progress made over the past century in terms of improving life expectancy, as well as the challenges presented by an ageing society. The fact that more people are living longer is something to be celebrated. However, we also need to plan for our longer lives, as the Filkin Report notes: 'Without urgent action this great boon could turn into a series of miserable crises' (House of Lords, 2013: 1, para. 1) for individuals, families and society.

Progress has been made over the past twenty-five years, and Pat Thane would be amongst the first to recognise that it is no longer the case that the work of gerontologists and demographers is invisible to policymakers and economists. There remains, however, work to do in reaching the public. Many people remain unaware of the improvements in mortality and the consequent increase in the number of years that they may expect to live in retirement. As a consequence, many remain under-provisioned in terms of their pension savings.

Moreover, it remains important to alert policymakers to the drivers and consequences of demographic change. There remain considerable differences in both life expectancy and disability-free life expectancy across society. Thus, care is needed to ensure that policy changes act to reduce rather than perpetuate disadvantage. The equity implications of linking of the qualifying age for entitlement of state pension to rises in average life expectancy need careful consideration.

Furthermore, in terms of recent demographic changes, it is not just living longer that is significant within the context of an ageing population. Policymakers need to be aware of the potential impact of changes in other spheres, including changes in patterns of family formation and dissolution. The number of older people requiring some form of social care and support is expected to double over the next thirty years, and meeting this need will present a major challenge for society. The majority of older people will continue to rely on support from partners and adult children, but the rise in the proportion of older people living alone and the increase in childlessness mean that not all older people will be able to do so. Neighbours and friendship networks may go part way to fill the gap, but formal care services will also need to be configured to be able to respond.

Employers will also need to adapt to an ageing society. On the one hand, many governments are now introducing policies to extend working lives, including in the UK raising the state pension age. However, in order to meet the growing care needs of the ageing population, an increasing number of mid-life adult children will need to provide care. Currently, the prevalence of informal care peaks at ages forty-five to sixty-four, coinciding with a time when many people are at the height of their career in terms of seniority, skills and experience. Carers UK suggest that amongst current carers, one in four have given up paid work to care. This incurs costs both for the individual carer in terms of current wages and future pension benefits foregone and for the employer in terms of lost skills. Since June 2014, within the UK, all employees with twenty-six weeks of service have the right to request flexible working hours, and most employers now recognise the need to support families in their childcare. Going forward, employers will also need to be more flexible in supporting adult children to successfully reconcile employment and *parental* caregiving, retaining vital skills in the workplace.

Celebrating and harnessing the benefits of an ageing society, as well as meeting the challenges of an ageing society, requires a holistic response. Academics can inform the debate, but ultimately it will be national and local policymakers, third-sector organizations and employers, along with families and older people themselves, who will determine whether we are 'ready for ageing'.

NOTE

1. The authors gratefully acknowledge the Economic and Social Research Council (ESRC) Centre for Population Change grants (RES-625-28-0001 and ES/K007394/1). The authors also thank the participants of the policy forum on ageing held at the British Academy in July 2015 for their valuable comments.

Chapter 3

Inequalities in the Experience of Later Life: Differentials in Health, Wealth and Well-Being

Alan Marshall and James Nazroo

This chapter is concerned with the unequal *experience* of growing old in Britain. We deliberately turn our attention away from a focus on the future numbers of older people and the abilities of societies to cope, as this is addressed in Chapter 2, except to briefly echo the often-made observation that the UK has the resources to deal with the demands of population ageing over the coming century, as it has in the past (Mullan, 2002; Wilson and Rees, 2005). Instead, drawing on research from a variety of disciplines, we consider the extent, trends and causes of social and spatial inequalities in mortality, morbidity, well-being and wealth. We reflect on the inequalities in the experience of old age, focussing on retirement and the degree of participation in social, civic and cultural activities at the older ages. Throughout, we reflect on how these inequalities in various outcomes interrelate with, and at the same time are influenced by, wider contextual factors such as the characteristics of residential neighbourhoods. Whilst our focus is on inequalities according to social class and place, we acknowledge that important inequalities also exist according to other characteristics such as gender and ethnicity.

The key message of this chapter is that there remain two very different experiences of old age in Britain. For the most affluent, life after retirement is likely to be one of health and opportunity in line with Laslett's (1996) vision of the 'third age'. However, for the rest of the elderly, this part of the life course comprises fewer years, poorer health, fewer resources and greater constraint to social, cultural and civic participation. A preoccupation with negative and narrow views of the challenges of population ageing could lead to policy choices that further differentiate the experience of old age in Britain in years to come. Instead, it is vital that there is a focus on the inequalities in later life.

HEALTH AND MORTALITY

For many people entering the postretirement phase of life, a key question concerns how many years they might expect to live in retirement and what proportion of them will be spent in good health. In Britain, there have been strong improvements in life expectancy and healthy life expectancy over the past thirty years, yet health and mortality remain strongly graduated by social class and place. The previous chapter has considered the increase in life expectancy over the past three decades, as well as increases in healthy and disability-free life expectancy that are thought to have occurred at a slower rate of change compared to life expectancy (Jagger, 2015). Here, our focus is on how social and spatial inequalities in life expectancies at the older ages have changed in the context of improvements in mortality and health in later life.

Analysis is complicated by changes in the definitions of social class and understandings of 'health', particularly in relation to self-reported measures. There are also methodological challenges relating to the changing geographical boundaries of data release that hamper evaluation of area-level trends in mortality and morbidity, not to mention the ongoing changes to the format and wording of questions of health. As an example of the latter, Bajekal et al. (2004) show how the 1991 and 2001 censuses yield very different estimates of limiting long-term illness because the relevant question used the word *handicap* in 1991 but then *disability* in 2001. However, the latest evidence suggests that inequalities have, at best, remained constant, but most likely have widened over the past twenty-five years.

Figure 3.1 illustrates life expectancies according to social class at age sixty for England and Wales. For men we see an increase in the gap in life expectancy between the lowest social classes (routine occupations) and the highest social classes (managers and professionals) from 3.6 years in the early 1980s to 5.5 years in 2012. For women, the social gap in life expectancy has grown from 3.0 years to 4.2 years over this period. Evidence for widening inequalities in other health outcomes is also observed elsewhere in the literature. For example, Jivraj et al. (2015) use data from the Health Survey for England to demonstrate growing inequalities in more recent years compared to earlier cohorts in limiting long-term illness, self-reported health and high blood pressure.

Spatial inequalities in mortality across Britain are particularly stark; the World Health Organisation report on the Social Determinants of Health (CSDH, 2008) noted the twenty-eight-year difference in life expectancy between the Carlton and Lenzie neighbourhoods of Glasgow, a mere 12 kilometres apart. Mortality is highest in Scotland and the North of England, within deprived areas of the larger cities and, in particular, in the former mining and industrial areas, the latter perhaps reflecting the

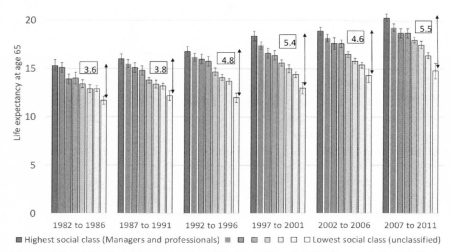

Figure 3.1a Life Expectancy at Age 65 According to Gender and Social Class, 1982/1986–2006/2011, Male.
Source: Office for National Statistics Longitudinal Study estimates of life expectancy by the National Statistics Socio-Economic Classification.

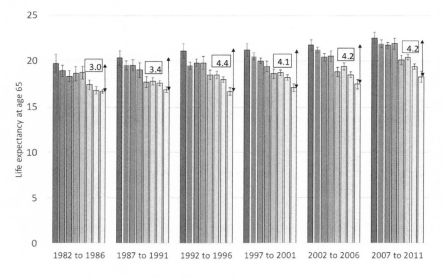

Figure 3.1b Life Expectancy at Age 65 According to Gender and Social Class, 1982/1986–2006/2011, Female.
Source: Office for National Statistics Longitudinal Study estimates of life expectancy by the National Statistics Socio-Economic Classification.

health-harming effects of particular industries as well as the persistent high
levels of deprivation and unemployment that have afflicted such areas since
the loss of these industries.

A body of evidence suggests widening inequality in spatial inequalities in
all-age mortality across Britain over the past three decades (Shaw et al., 2005;
Bennet et al., 2015). At the oldest ages, the picture is one of a slight expansion
in the extent of inequality in measures of life expectancy (Jagger, 2015) and
disability-free life expectancy across areas (see Figure 3.2) (ONS, 2012b).
A widening of spatial inequalities in mortality and morbidity may reflect,
in part, the trends observed in these outcomes according to social class (see
Figure 3.1, for example) but also other area-based processes, such as the selective migration of healthy migrants away from deprived areas (Norman et al.,
2005) and the polarisation of the UK according to other social and economic
correlates of mortality over the past decades (Dorling and Thomas, 2004).

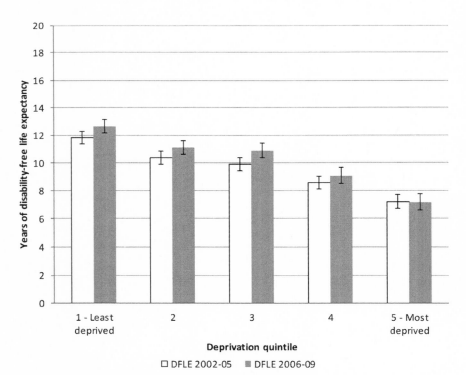

**Figure 3.2a   Disability-Free Life Expectancy (at Age 65) by Gender and Area Deprivation
Quintile between 2002/2005 and 2006/2009, Male.**
Source: Adapted from Office for National Statistics (2012b) Inequality in disability-free
life expectancy by area deprivation: England 2002–2005 and 2006–2009. ONS Statistical
Bulletin. 2012; http://www.ons.gov.uk/ons/dcp171778_265133.pdf.

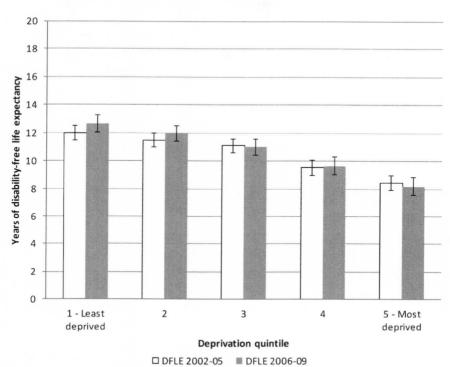

Figure 3.2b Disability-Free Life Expectancy (at Age 65) by Gender and Area Deprivation Quintile between 2002/2005 and 2006/2009, Female.
Source: Adapted from Office for National Statistics (2012b) Inequality in disability-free life expectancy by area deprivation: England 2002–2005 and 2006–2009. ONS Statistical Bulletin. 2012; http://www.ons.gov.uk/ons/dcp171778_265133.pdf.

These analyses of trends in mortality and health rely on cross-sectional data that has obvious limitations in terms of comparing change in health outcomes across cohorts. We now turn to the evidence from longitudinal analysis on how social inequalities in mortality and frailty are changing across cohorts. We focus on wealth as a proxy for social class, as it is thought to provide a more reliable indicator of social position compared to other sources (e.g., education and occupation). For mortality, Nazroo et al. (2008) have shown that those in lowest wealth quintiles have over 50 per cent higher odds of mortality compared to the most affluent *after* controlling for other social, demographic and behavioural correlates of mortality.

The progression of frailty with stratification by cohort (based on five-year intervals), wealth (tertiles) and gender over an eight-year period (2002–2010) is shown in Figure 3.3. This uses a frailty score that is expressed as the proportion of sixty problems, including falls, activity restrictions, measures

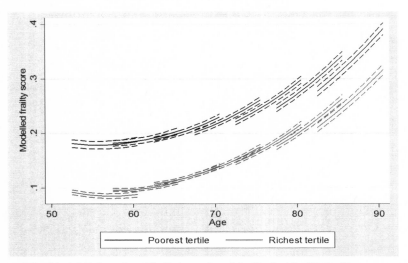

Figure 3.3   Model Cohort-Specific Trajectories of Frailty by Wealth Tertiles.
Source: Adapted from Marshall et al. (2015) using data from the English Longitudinal Study of Ageing.

of cognition and cardiovascular disease and chronic diseases that are held by an individual. The average trajectory of frailty for an affluent individual aged between seventy and seventy-four is comparable to that observed for an eighty-to-eighty-four-year-old in the poorest quintile; thus, we see a ten-year difference in experiences of frailty between the richest and poorest thirds of the population. Figure 3.3 also suggests that inequalities in levels of frailty widened between 2002 and 2010; at particular overlapping ages, the younger cohorts amongst the poorest tertile appear to have higher levels of frailty than its older cohorts, such as between the ages of seventy-five and eighty for the cohorts aged seventy to seventy-four and seventy-five to seventy-nine in 2002. By contrast, for the richest tertile there is little difference in frailty across cohorts.

WELL-BEING

There has been an increasing interest in the measurement of well-being over the past twenty-five years amongst social scientists and policymakers as an outcome alongside traditional indicators of mortality and morbidity. Van-houtte (2014) provides a review of the measures used to capture well-being in the older population, including their theoretical and statistical properties. Whilst most measures of ill health display a characteristic age pattern of increasing prevalence with age, a U-shaped age pattern is observed for well-being, with the highest levels of well-being in later life and amongst younger adults, and the lowest well-being for the middle ages. Nevertheless, the consequences of poor well-being in later life are thought to be particularly serious. For example, depression is a strong predictor of suicide in older people and has important implications for the onset and progression of other health problems such as disability, morbidity and mortality (Beekman et al., 1995; Blazer, 2003). Thus, maintaining well-being in later life is an important aspect of 'healthy ageing' (Simons et al., 2000) that is recognised as essential to mitigate the challenges associated with global projected trends towards more elderly populations.

Just as for health and morbidity, so, too, for well-being are social and spatial inequalities strong across the older ages; for example, lower levels of well-being are found with decreasing wealth or education and as area deprivation increases (Marshall et al., 2014; Jivraj et al., 2014). Analysis of the cross-sectional relationship between well-being and age in later life reveals striking declines in well-being from age seventy after initial improvements in well-being from age fifty, as shown by the 'age' line in Figure 3.4, adapted from Jivraj et al. (2014) using data from the English Longitudinal Study of Ageing (ELSA). However, once socio-economic and demographic factors are controlled for, the age pattern of declining well-being across the older ages is much less clear. The other lines in Figure 3.4 show that, where older people remain in partnerships, retain high socio-economic status, maintain good self-reported health and have strong social contacts, there is no clear decline in cross-sectional age pattern of well-being in the final period of life.

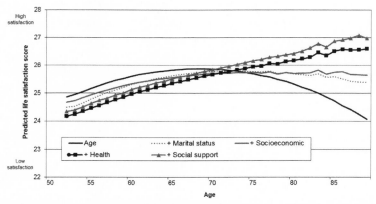

Figure 3.4 Age Pattern of Well-Being (Life Satisfaction) in an Uncontrolled Age-Based Model and After Progressively Adding Controls for Marital Status, Socio-Economic Factors, Health and Social Support.
Source: Adapted from Jivraj et al. (2014).

In effect, it is events and characteristics correlated with age and occurring predominantly as individuals progress through the older ages that drive the cross-sectional age pattern of declining well-being in the final years of life. However, it is important to note that, within cohorts, *longitudinal* analysis reveals that the rate of decline in well-being is greatest for those at the oldest ages independent of their social, economic, partnership and health status, suggesting that other events and feelings are important in terms of the progression in well-being amongst individuals in the final stages of life (Jivraj et al., 2014).

WEALTH AND INCOME

Wealth and income provide the means for older people to live a comfortable and fulfilling life but are also indicators of social position in later life. Information on the financial resources of older people is collected in the surveys of ageing populations in Britain (e.g., ELSA) and overseas (e.g., Health and Retirement Survey of Americans aged over fifty).

Inequalities in wealth are much greater than those observed in income. According to ELSA, the mean level of net financial assets (excluding pensions, housing and other physical wealth) amongst the community dwelling population aged over fifty was £43,400 in 2002. However, the skewed nature of the wealth distribution is such that half the population aged over fifty have a total wealth less than £12,000, with a quarter holding less than £1,500. A quarter of single (never married) men and women aged over fifty have almost no wealth whatsoever (Banks et al., 2004).

Incomes amongst couples tend to decrease from age fifty, reflecting withdrawal from the labour market and a shift in composition from employment to pensions, state benefits and income derived from other assets (Banks et al., 2004). Couples tend to have higher incomes than those who are single, and for those who are single, women are worse off than single men (Emerson and Muriel, 2008). Analysis of changes in the level and distribution of income at the older ages suggests that although incomes have increased, inequality across the income distribution has grown (Muriel and Oldfield, 2010). Financial poverty amongst older people has also increased over the first decade of the twenty-first century; those in the poorest income quintile were seventeen percentage points more likely to have seen a 10 per cent increase in the proportion of their income spent on basics (food, fuel, clothing) over the period 2002/2003–2008/2009 (Muriel and Oldfield, 2010). More generally, the literature suggests that income inequality in Britain increased steeply during the 1980s and has been sustained throughout the 1990s and 2000s at historically high levels (Shaw et al., 2005).

EXPERIENCES OF LATER LIFE

In this section, we consider social patterns in the experiences of later life, focussing on the key life course event of retirement and on the subsequent social, civic and cultural participation and lifestyle choices amongst retirees.

Retirement

Retirement has come to represent an important event marking a move to a new phase of life with the potential for individuals, freed from the constraints of work, to pursue new interests, responsibilities and aspirations (Laslett, 1996). Retirement has become an important political issue within policy debates on population ageing. It is argued that a population that is living longer has greater capacity to work to older ages and that, at the same time, increased numbers of workers are needed to cope with the demands and costs of a relatively larger share of the population at the older ages (Harper et al., 2011). Within the UK, the Pension Act of 2011 laid out a timetable for increasing the women state pension age from sixty to sixty-five by 2018 and increasing the state pension age of both men and women to sixty-eight by 2046.

The policy changes to increase the statutory retirement age come at an interesting time following a period, from 1970 to the late 1990s, in which the proportion of people working immediately prior to the statutory retirement ages steadily declined. For example, the proportion of men aged sixty to sixty-four in work fell from 80 per cent in 1970 to just under 50 per cent in 2000 (Chandler and Tetlow, 2014). The first decade of the twenty-first century has witnessed modest increases in economic activity at the oldest working ages, perhaps reflecting the changing policy climate and the proposals to increase the statutory retirement age; the proportion of sixty-to-sixty-five-year-old men in work rose to around 55 per cent in 2014 (Chandler and Tetlow, 2014). However, it remains the case that a substantial proportion of people in the UK retire *before* the statutory retirement age even as plans are implemented to increase this retirement age.

Banks and Smith (2006) distinguish two pathways into retirement over past decades that are strongly patterned according to wealth and social position. The poorest individuals have tended to transition out of the labour market into retirement through sickness benefits, a retirement route that is thought to have been driven in part by the collapse in the demand for unskilled labour in many developed countries from the 1980s (Burstrom et al., 2000). For the richest individuals, early retirement is commonly financed through occupation pension schemes or through accumulated wealth and investments.

How does retirement affect subsequent outcomes such as health? Clearly this is a complicated question that depends on the particular measure of

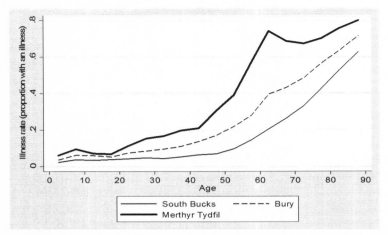

Figure 3.5a   Age Patterns of Self-Reported Limiting Long-Term Illness at Retirement in Bury, Merthyr Tydfil and South Bucks.
Note: Merthyr Tydfil: group of districts with a large post-retirement improvement in illness rates; Bury: group of districts with a modest post-retirement improvement in illness rates; South Bucks: group of districts with no post-retirement improvement in illness rates.
Source: Calculated from 2001 census, adapted from Marshall and Norman (2013).

health used, the nature of the reason for retirement and the potential for reverse causation whereby poor health itself leads to retirement. A set of research papers has focussed on longitudinal analysis of trajectories (or change) in self-reported measures of health throughout retirement. Such health measures are thought to be useful for a number of reasons. First, their general use is supported by a large body of research (e.g., Charlton et al., 1994; Bentham et al., 1995; Idler & Benyamini, 1997; Mitchell, 2005), and they are especially valid for more serious health conditions (Manor et al., 2001) and for physical limitations rather than with psychological health (Cohen et al., 1995). Secondly, they provide a useful global measure in summarising a diverse set of health components (Rijs et al., 2012). Thirdly, they provide an individual's evaluation of their health given the conditions in which they are placed and particularly during the final years of work and into retirement. This context-specific evaluation of health is important given the policy of extending working lives and the parallel need to ensure that those approaching retirement are satisfied with their work and that the working conditions they experience are not damaging to health or well-being.

Several recent studies that use longitudinal data to track self-reported health throughout retirement have shown an improvement in general health after retirement that is observed for particular groups and not others. What

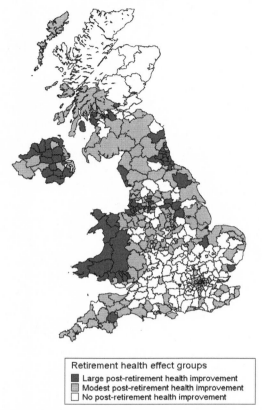

Figure 3.5b Spatial Distribution of Districts according to Three Patterns of Self-Reported Limiting Long-Term Illness at Retirement.
Source: Calculated from 2001 census, adapted from Marshall and Norman (2013).

this body of research suggests is that retirement appears to have a beneficial effect on health for vulnerable groups who are in, for example, the least favourable working conditions (high demands, low job satisfaction) (Westerlund et al., 2009), who are least able to exercise choice over the retirement decision (van Solinge 2007) or who are in lower social classes (Marshall and Nazroo, 2015). One argument is that vulnerable individuals at the older working ages are less able to cope with the demands of work as a result of a range of factors experienced more frequently by those in lower social classes, including poverty and ill health, the extent of job stability and the nature of work in terms of its demands and rewards. This vulnerability—a result of an accumulation of disadvantage across the life course—means that people in the lower social classes have fewer resources to draw upon to continue in work and to maintain good health in the final years of work, and so they experience benefits in terms of self-reported health after they retire (Marshall and Nazroo, 2015).

Marshall and Norman (2013), classifying UK districts according to the aggregate area age patterns of self-reported illness at retirement, found spatial patterns in line with the longitudinal analysis of self-reported health measures throughout retirement. As shown in Figure 3.5a, districts in the affluent South East of England (e.g., South Buckinghamshire) have illness rates that rise smoothly with age through retirement. However, districts in the former industrial and mining areas of the UK (e.g., Merthyr Tydfil) exhibit a levelling off or decline in illness rates after the statutory retirement age, whilst the case of Bury shows just a modest post-retirement improvement. The geographical distribution of these three patterns across the UK (shown in Figure 3.5b) may reflect the spatial clustering of vulnerable groups experiencing such benefits in health in retirement. However, it may also reflect spatial processes, such as health-selective migration of healthy working-age migrants away from deprived areas, or the effects of hidden unemployment in particular areas where working age self-reported illness rates are thought to be particularly high, partly as a result of a political decision to move individuals on to sickness rather than unemployment benefits during the de-industrialisation of the 1980s (Beatty and Fothergill, 2005). Two further potential explanations for these spatial patterns do not stand up to empirical testing. The extent of premature mortality prior to retirement in deprived areas is not sufficient to account for the slower increases in self-reported illness rates after retirement that might be observed in a healthy group of survivors. Secondly, a cohort effect, whereby those at retirement in 2001 suffered particularly high illness rates, does not seem convincing because the retirement patterns in self-reported illness rates are also observed in other census years (see Marshall and Norman, 2013, for further details).

Social, Civic and Cultural Participation

A body of literature suggests that social and civic participation in later life has a beneficial influence on health outcomes. For example, Steptoe et al. (2013) reported a significant association between social isolation and mortality that is independent of other social and demographic predictors of mortality. Similarly, in a systematic review of interventions intended to provide meaningful social roles through retirement, Heaven et al. (2013) found that involvement in activities such as grand-parenting, volunteering, paid work, education and training led to increased levels of physical activity, decreased sedentary activities (such as watching TV) and improved life satisfaction, cognitive function, self-assessed health and, in some cases, physical health.

A key correlate of social and civic participation is wealth. Analysis of ELSA (wave 6) reveals that older adults with higher levels of wealth are more likely to be involved in medium-to-high levels of social, civic and cultural activities (Matthews et al., 2014). Jivraj, Nazroo and Barnes's (2015) investigation of the effect of short-term changes in employment, marital status and health status on social detachment found recent deterioration in health to be associated with movement into social detachment, with little effect on social detachment stemming from changes in marital or employment status. This suggests the potential for a reciprocal relationship between health and social detachment; poor health leads to, but is also exacerbated by, social detachment. Matthews et al. (2014) demonstrated lower levels of social, civic and cultural engagement for those without a car as well as decline in such engagement should access to a car be lost.

An important question is how and to what extent lifestyles in later life, including social, civic and cultural participation as well as health-related behaviours, influence health outcomes in the context of class-based inequalities in wealth. McGovern and Nazroo (2015) investigated the relationship between social class and health, using the path analysis depicted in Figure 3.6, where the connecting lines indicate the strengths of the mechanisms through which class and education influence health and well-being. It can be seen that class and education have a strong influence on the work and work quality, wealth and subjective social status as well as lifestyle choices.

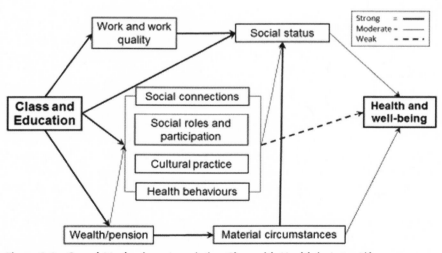

Figure 3.6   Causal Mechanisms Associating Class with Health in Later Life.
Source: Adapted from McGovern and Nazroo (2015); data from the English Longitudinal Study of Ageing.

Interestingly, this analysis not only shows the importance of material circumstances, employment quality and lifestyle factors, and their interrelationships for health but also reveals that in some circumstances these effects appear to operate through *subjective* social status.

Health-Related Behaviour in Later Life

Differences in the prevalence of health-related behaviours have long been thought to be one of the influences on inequalities in health outcomes. Indeed, it is proposed by some that increases in the prevalence of unhealthy lifestyle choices have the potential to halt the improvement in life expectancy observed in the past (Olshanky, 2005). If unhealthy lifestyle choices, such as smoking, alcohol consumption, poor diet and sedentary lifestyles, have a cumulative effect over the life course and are socially patterned, then they could explain the apparent widening in health inequalities at the older age like those shown above in Figures 3.1–3.3. Analysis of ELSA data between 2004 and 2008 (de Oliveira et al., 2010) reveals mixed evidence for this theory. First, whilst some unhealthy lifestyle choices (e.g., inactivity, lack of fruit and vegetable consumption and smoking) are most prevalent for the poorest individuals, the social patterning is less clear for others (e.g., alcohol consumption and obesity). Secondly, not all unhealthy lifestyle choices are increasing in the more recent cohorts. Comparison of the cohort-specific extent of smoking and daily alcohol consumption within ELSA reveals *declines* in prevalence between 2004 and 2008, although there was an increase in the prevalence of sedentary lifestyles and waist circumference over this period. The review above points to the need for further analysis on cohort-specific trends in specific unhealthy lifestyle choices (including prior to the period of this study) in order to fully understand their impact on the cohort differences in later-life frailty. We also need to consider the drivers of such changes in lifestyle.

NEIGHBOURHOOD CONTEXT

Older people are thought to be particularly susceptible to the influence of place on health and other outcomes as a result of greater attachments to their neighbourhood that stem from living in an area longer, spending more time day to day within their neighbourhood (especially if retired or less mobile) and making more use of local services compared to younger people (Bowling & Stafford, 2007; Beard et al., 2009; Stafford et al., 2011). Area effects are usually small, meaning that determining such an effect, after accounting for the relevant individual characteristics, is often difficult. However, a small area effect can have a significant impact on population health as it applies to each member living within an area (Craig, 2005).

A number of researchers have found an association between the physical and social aspects of a neighbourhood in which an individual lives and the physical and mental health of that individual (Duncan et al., 1995; Pickett and Pearl, 2001; Cummins et al., 2005; Diez Roux and Mair, 2010). In the England context, Marshall et al. (2015) demonstrated significantly higher levels of depression in more deprived and more economically mixed neighbourhoods (middle super output areas, average population 7,200) that hold after controlling for individual correlates of depression including wealth and education. Their multilevel modelling techniques enable the variability in depression to be apportioned into individual and neighbourhood components, suggesting around 10 per cent of the variability observed in depression is attributable to neighbourhood factors. After controlling for individual correlates of depression, this analysis finds a 10 per cent increase in the odds of depression for a 1 standard deviation increase in the neighbourhood deprivation score. The odds of depression are around 20 per cent lower in the most mixed (or unequal) areas compared to the least mixed, suggesting that heterogeneous, or more unequal, neighbourhoods can be protective in terms of depression risk, possibly as a result of the general benefits associated with the presence of more affluent individuals in the area.

DISCUSSION AND CONCLUSIONS

The research reviewed in this chapter demonstrates the latest understandings of differences in the experience of later life across social classes and place in Britain. The overall trend is one of improvement; older people are living longer lives, experiencing more time in good health and have increasing wealth—a combination of factors that contribute towards more fulfilling and productive experiences in later life. However, these overall trends mask the persistence or expansion of two different experiences of old age over the past three decades. We have seen, for example, a ten-year gap in the health of older people across the distribution of wealth (Figure 3.2b), with social and spatial inequalities in life expectancy and healthy/disability-free life expectancy appearing at best stable but that may well have widened. Pathways into retirement are strongly patterned by social class and place, as are the capabilities of different groups to continue to work and maintain good health in the final years of employment. Also, whilst retirement offers opportunities for increased social, civic and cultural participation, such opportunities are enjoyed predominantly by the richest. For those individuals growing older in the most deprived areas, the characteristics of their neighbourhoods appear to put them at a disadvantage in terms of health and other outcomes.

Why do we observe such stark and growing inequalities in experiences of later life? One explanation is rooted in the psychosocial model of health inequality that proposes that health is influenced by the psychological effects of stressful conditions encountered at work or at home or that result from low social status (Bartley, 2004). Figure 3.4 demonstrates the importance of subjective social status in later life as a pathway through which health inequalities are produced. The accumulation of stress and disadvantage relating to social position across the life course (Dannefer, 2003), combined with the growth in economic inequality in England from the 1930s, offers one explanation for the relatively worse health outcomes for the poorest older people now compared to thirty years ago. In other words, the current cohort of older people has lived through a time of greater inequality with correspondingly greater psychological penalties that are associated with low social position compared to earlier cohorts. Alternatively, if improvements in medical and care services across the life course have served to increase the survival of individuals in poor health and such effects are more concentrated amongst poorer individuals who tend to have the worst health, then a widening in socio-economic inequalities in morbidity might be expected. Another potential driver of growing inequality in health outcomes is the increasing prevalence of unhealthy lifestyle choices that are strongly socially patterned (such as the prevalence of sedentary lifestyles) and concentrated in more recent cohorts compared to earlier ones. Clearly these explanations are not mutually exclusive, and a combination of each is plausible.

The extent and growth of inequality in the experience of later life is concerning for a number of reasons linked to fairness, the related adverse impacts on wider society, the avoidable nature of health inequality and its impact on the cost-effectiveness of welfare spending (Woodward and Kawachi, 2000). Improving the circumstances of the poorest older people is crucial, not just from a moral perspective but also in order to reduce the care costs in the context of population ageing. Unfortunately, many of the current responses to population ageing are serving to reduce welfare benefits to older people, which disproportionately affect the poorest, worsening their relative position with the likely effect of exacerbating the health inequalities currently observed. One clear example is the proposal to increase the statutory retirement age, which does not take into account inequalities in health and mortality at the older ages. As shown in Figure 3.3, less affluent older individuals are considerably frailer than richer people and appear less able to continue work beyond the current retirement age without incurring further health problems, particularly as their work is often more physically demanding and less rewarding, and it offers less scope for autonomy than the work experienced by those in professional jobs. Thus, a policy intended to reduce the costs of population ageing might actually have the opposite effect if the health of poorer older people deteriorates as a consequence.

This chapter has documented the progress in research and understandings of the unequal experience of ageing that has been made since the 1980s. Looking to the future, particularly important themes are the trend towards interdisciplinary research and the maturation of internationally harmonised longitudinal data sources on the social circumstances and the biological characteristics of older people. These developments open new questions such as: How do social, biological and contextual factors interact to produce the inequalities in health and other outcomes observed in later life? In what ways do different social and institutional contexts (national and local) influence experiences of ageing? These questions are challenging but vitally important. The answers to these have the potential to further increase knowledge and understandings of the unequal experiences of later life in Britain.

Chapter 4

International Migration and Asylum Seekers

Jakub Bijak, George Disney, Sarah Lubman
and Arkadiusz Wiśniowski[1]

A quarter of a century ago, international migration was not even considered a key element of the demographic puzzle of the UK. For example, there was no dedicated chapter in Joshi's (1989a) book, though the chapter there on ethnicity (Diamond and Clarke, 1989) discussed some of the impacts of immigration, as does Finney and Catney's chapter in this book. However, over the past two decades the situation has changed considerably, such that immigration is now one of the most salient of political issues. This chapter looks at the history of migration into and out of the UK since World War II and at the role that migration has played in influencing public policy and discourse. We focus on the successive waves of migrants from the 'Windrush' generation of 1948 onwards through to the citizens of the countries that joined the European Union (EU) in 2004 and subsequently.

In this chapter, we summarise current knowledge about the trends in the numbers of migrants and their socio-economic composition. We also look at some specific areas of interest, including refugees and asylum seekers. We then challenge some of the migration-related myths, especially concerning the uniqueness of the recent UK migration experience and about the social impacts of migration. The substantive analysis of the UK's international migration faces several methodological difficulties, most notably that despite the importance of migratory processes for population change and their prominence in public perception, quantitative evidence on population flows remains deficient, inconsistent and sometimes even contradictory. However, many of the apparent shortcomings of the existing estimates can be resolved, as we show in the final section where we make suggestions for the research agenda for the next twenty-five years. We present a framework for facilitating policy and planning decisions under uncertainty about the true magnitude and the likely future developments of UK migration.

INTERNATIONAL MIGRATION: DRIVERS AND PATTERNS

The main drivers and patterns of international migration are complex. However, there are clear triggers and patterns in the development of migration flows to and from the UK. Key changes in immigration policy, such as the British Nationality Act of 1948 and the expansion of the EU and associated freedom of labour movement in 2004, have been two such triggers. Furthermore, the establishment of large migrant communities and networks sustains the flows that began many years ago and will sustain newer flows into the future. What follows is a detailed account of the main international migration flows of the last fifty years, including reference to the key events and policies, which have significantly shaped them. The general trends in migration are well documented in the literature. We draw on that literature and the best publicly available evidence from the International Passenger Survey (IPS) on the migration flows and from the Population Census on stocks of foreign nationals and the overseas-born.

Overview

The UK was mainly a country of emigration up until the 1980s, with 1979 being the first year of net immigration, according to the available evidence. Patterns of emigration from the 1950s tend to mirror the traditional routes to the USA and the English-speaking countries of the British Commonwealth. Immigration from the late 1950s was characterised by waves of migration from India, Pakistan and Bangladesh, successively, flows that have since been less pronounced but still continue. From the 1980s onwards, however, international migration has become more diverse, particularly with migration from the European Economic Community (EEC), and subsequently the European Union, becoming more important. The flows from the Commonwealth, South Asia and the EEC/EU remained quite stable during most of the 1990s, but there was a large increase in immigration in the late 1990s. A further increase occurred after the enlargement of the EU in 2004 and the removal of labour market controls on Romanian and Bulgarian citizens in 2014, following their accession in 2007. Over the last decade, therefore, the main fluctuations in immigration have been driven by changes in policy, at both the national and the EU scale, which run alongside the more long-established flows from Commonwealth and South Asian countries (for an overview and an interesting analysis of postwar migration and integration, see Goodhart, 2013).

Postwar UK Migration in Context

Since the 'age of mass migration' in the nineteenth century, with approximately fifty-five million Europeans migrating to North America and Australasia between 1850 and 1914 (Hatton and Williamson, 1998), scholars have striven to explain the phenomenon of human migration (Arango, 2000). The UK has traditionally been a country of emigration; in the late nineteenth century—from 1870 to 1913—the total net loss of the population due to emigration was 5.6 million people, with the overwhelming majority of emigrants going to other English-speaking countries (Hatton and Price, 1999). However, it should be noted that these figures include emigration from Ireland, which was part of the then–United Kingdom of Great Britain and Ireland at that time. With the American Immigration Acts of 1921 and 1924 restricting immigration to the USA, the numbers leaving the UK fell significantly.

Over the last half a century, the general pattern of international migration has changed markedly, which is reflected in the nature of overall UK flows. After the Second World War, with declining costs of travel, international migration revived (Hatton and Price, 1999). Traditional immigrant receiving countries such as Australia, Canada and the USA began to receive migrants from Asia, Africa and Latin America rather than Europe (Massey et al., 1993). This change is also evident in western and northern Europe after 1945. Countries that were traditionally migrant sending became net receivers of migrants, initially from southern Europe, but later in the twentieth century from Africa, Asia and the Middle East (Massey et al., 1993).

As regards the UK, the IPS data collected from 1964 onwards show that the switch to net immigration first became evident in 1979, as shown in Figure 4.1, with net immigration to the UK averaging 44,600 people a year during the 1980s (Hatton, 2003; Hatton and Tani, 2005). This switch occurred mainly because of emigration falling; especially to Canada, where net emigration dropped from 148,000 people in the 1970s to 47,000 in the 1980s, according to IPS estimates (Hatton 2005). The net inflow of migrants has continued right through the 1990s and 2000s (see Figure 4.1).

The Early Postwar Decades

During this period of net emigration, up till the late 1970s, the general destination of UK emigrants remained similar to earlier patterns, focussed primarily on the USA, Australia, Canada, New Zealand and South Africa. However, care needs to be taken when assessing trends of net migration flows: *net migration* is simply a measure of the difference between immigration and emigration. With immigration and emigration flows not being analysed separately in the earlier years, there is no way of knowing whether

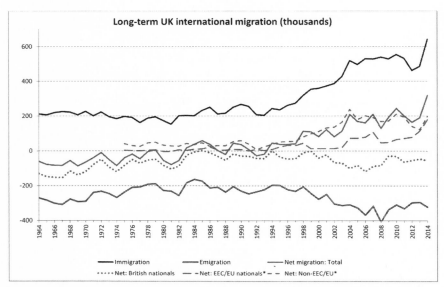

Figure 4.1   IPS-Based Estimates of UK Immigration, Emigration and Net Migration, 1964–2014.
*Data for European Economic Community [1975–1992]/European Union [since 1993].
Note: The UK joined the EEC in 1973; separate data for the EEC are available since 1975.
Source: Office for National Statistics, International Migration collection, various years.

changes in net migration result from a change in immigration or in emigration (Rogers, 1990).

A key driver of immigration to the UK, as has become evident throughout the second half of the twentieth century, is the impact of immigration-related policy on the nature and magnitude of flows to the UK. For example, the passing of the British Nationality Act in 1948, by the Attlee Government, meant that all 'British subjects' had the right to enter the UK and enjoy all the social, economic and cultural rights of full British citizenship (Hansen, 1999). Following this, there were increasing levels of immigration to the UK from the Caribbean, accompanied by increasing numbers from South Asia. Between 1948 and 1962, approximately five hundred thousand new Commonwealth immigrants had entered the UK, with the majority originating from India and Pakistan (Hansen, 1999: 95). Then the Commonwealth Immigrants Act of 1962 restricted immigration from the New Commonwealth nations.[2]

The immigrant flows from the Caribbean started, symbolically, with the docking of the 'Empire Windrush' at Tilbury in 1948. Caribbean immigration was driven by both a recruitment push by employers, including the National Health Service, British Rail and London Transport, and by family and island-specific social networks that helped people establish their new lives in the

UK (Byron, 1994). This particular migration flow peaked in the 1960s and was effectively over by 1973, possibly due to the reduced size of the pool of potential migrants there but also coinciding with the introduction of new legal restrictions on immigration.[3]

By contrast, flows of South Asian migrants, mainly from Pakistan and India, are still significant today, along with those from Bangladesh (formerly East Pakistan). These flows date all the way back to the seventeenth century (Peach, 2006) but increased dramatically following the British National-ity Act of 1948. The composition of these flows also changed from mainly skilled Indian people to people of rural background (Peach, 2006). Like the flows from the Caribbean, they were driven by UK employers' demand for labour—initially during the economic boom of the later 1950s when the already UK-based labour supply was restricted by the small numbers of school leavers (due to the low birthrates of the 1930s and in wartime) and, subsequently, due to the attempt to use cheap imported labour to keep the textile industry internationally competitive.

The pioneer migrants of the 1950s went out of their way to assist fellow would-be migrants from villages back at origin (Ballard, 1990). This resulted in surges of immigration from India in the late 1950s, peaking in the 1960s. The 1960s, in turn, saw increasing levels of immigration from Pakistan, peak-ing in the 1970s, and then increasing levels from Bangladesh that peaked in the 1980s (Hatton and Price, 1999). These respective specific waves of immi-gration to the UK, it is argued by Peach (2006), were a result of the partition of parts of South Asia from 1947 onwards, with Indian and Pakistani Punjab-and Pakistan-administered Kashmir being the major contributors.

The migrants from South Asia at this time were mainly single male labour migrants who sent remittances back to their extended families (Peach, 2006). However, following the 1962 Commonwealth Immigration Act, which attempted to restrict immigration to the UK, many were faced with the issue of whether to bring their wives and families with them. According to Peach (2006), Sikh and Hindu men, mainly from India, were the first to bring their families. This trend was followed by a large number of Pakistani family reunifications in the 1970s, with Bangladesh family migration fol-lowing in the 1980s (Peach, 2006). This pattern of pioneer labour migration, followed by family reunions for migrants from South Asia, may go some way towards explaining the aforementioned surges and sustained flows of these immigration flows. Even now, for the citizens of countries outside the Euro-pean Union, their close family members, such as spouses, parents and chil-dren, are entitled to apply for leave to remain in the UK. The family ties that these migration flows have brought, coupled with the large populations in countries of origin such as Pakistan and India, help to explain why migration from South Asia is still significant today.

The 1980s Onwards

If one of the main stories of UK immigration in the 1950s, 1960s and 1970s is the establishment of South Asian migration, the emerging story of the 1980s onwards is of an increasing diversity of origins. Whilst immigration continued in the 1980s from South Asian countries, with net immigration from Bangladesh, India and Sri Lanka combined totalling 109,000 people during this decade, European flows started to become more important then.

This diversification came about alongside changes in the wider European context of migratory flows. Since the 1960s, major political and social transformations in Europe have influenced the patterns of international migration affecting the UK. The 1960s were dominated by labour migration (Jennissen, 2004), with a general south-to-north movement within Europe, with the exception of the Eastern bloc, from where emigration was highly restricted for political reasons. In a similar vein to the South Asian migration outlined above, following this initial flow, there was a shift towards family and return migration in the 1970s (Hatton and Price, 1999). In terms of origin and destination flows, international migration in Europe became even more diverse from the 1980s onwards (Hatton and Price, 1999). This increasing diversity can largely be attributed to immigration policy changes at the European level, as detailed below.

The UK joined the EEC on January 1, 1973. Its overall net emigration balance with other European countries switched to net immigration in the 1980s. Political events and changes to migration-related policy can be identified as playing a significant role in shaping UK international migration flows. In 1981, Greece joined the European Economic Community, followed by Spain and Portugal in 1983, leading to the increase in net immigration from the EEC in the late 1980s. This continued in the 1990s, when—following the Maastricht Treaty, which transformed the EEC into the EU—most countries became both significant senders and receivers of international migration (Castles and Miller, 2009). Total net immigration to the UK continued to rise, up from 13,800 in 1993–1995 to 37,700 in 1996–1998 (Hatton, 2005; see also Figure 4.1), now driven mainly by a rise in gross inflow rather than any further reduction in emigration. By 1999, the estimated inflow had reached 450,000 (Salt et al., 2001).

Foreign citizens drove this increased inflow in the 1990s. According to IPS data, inflows of non-British nationals were consistently higher than inflows of British emigrants returning to the UK, with the latter remaining relatively stable at around 100,000 per year. Non-British inflows, by contrast, rose steadily (apart from a slight dip in 1992 and 1993) from 234,000 in 1990 to 331,000 in 1999 (Salt et al., 2001; see also Figure 4.1). Also, its composition by origin region was changing. As documented by Salt et al. (2001), the main change occurred in the late 1990s, first with a big increase in the inflow from 'Other Foreign' countries (i.e., all but the EU and the Commonwealth) from 76,500 in 1997 to 142,000 in 1999, and, secondly, with a fall in arrivals of EU nationals from 77,600 to 65,700 in the same period.

However, the 2000s saw a further reversal in inflows from Europe, with the enlargement of the EU. Following the signing of the Treaty of Accession in 2003 there have been three subsequent expansions of the European Union. The first and most significant enlargement with regard to the UK migration occurred in 2004, with the accession of ten countries: Czech Republic, Estonia, Hungary, Latvia, Lithuania, Poland, Slovenia and Slovakia (collectively known as the 'A8'), plus Cyprus and Malta. This was followed in 2007 by a further two countries, Romania and Bulgaria (commonly referred to as the 'A2'), though restrictions were placed on their freedom of labour movement until 2014, and then in 2013 by Croatia.

These progressive enlargements led to a rapid and significant increase in the levels of immigration from A8 countries post 2004, not least because the UK—unlike all the other 'old' EU member states except Ireland and Sweden—did not impose temporary labour-market restrictions on these nationals. As a result, the number of migrants to the UK exceeded the pre-enlargement forecasts (Dustmann et al., 2003) by nearly an order of magnitude. Estimates based on the Labour Force Survey (LFS) indicate that in 2008 there were 665,000 A8 and A2 residents in the UK, an increase of 550,000 from pre-enlargement estimates (Pollard et al., 2008).

The vast majority of the post-enlargement EU migration increase came from Poland. According to Pollard et al. (2008), in 2008 Poles became the largest foreign national group in the UK. This was facilitated by the opening up of many transport links between the UK and Poland. Whilst in December 2003, around forty thousand passengers flew between only three British airports and Warsaw and Kraków in Poland, by December 2007 one could fly from twenty-two British airports to ten Polish cities (Pollard et al., 2008). By the 2011 Census, the number of Polish-born amongst the usual residents of England and Wales had increased to 579,000, a ninefold increase on its 2001 level (ONS, 2012e). Moreover, this migration from Central and Eastern Europe during the 2000s was very different in character from the established labour and family reunification flows from South Asia outlined previously, in particular including more temporary and circular migration.

Another key development of the early twenty-first century, which has further fuelled the more transient nature of recent migration, has been the increasing volume of international students coming to British universities and Further Education colleges. Globally, student migration flows are growing at a faster rate than overall international migration flows (King et al., 2010). IPS estimates show that the total number of international students has been

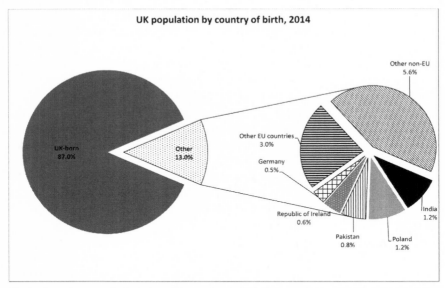

Figure 4.2   UK Population Shares by Country of Birth, 2014 Estimates (Components Are Rounded to the Nearest One DP).
Source: Office for National Statistics, Population by Country of Birth and Nationality, 2014.

increasing since the early 1990s (Blinder 2014). In the first decade of the twenty-first century, India and China were the main countries of origin of international students (HESA, 2010).

In sum, the history of UK international migration since World War II is punctuated by key events and policy changes that have triggered new migration flows. Having been established, these flows have then been driven, and their nature changed, by economic pressures: whether it is Pakistani migrants settling in Manchester to work initially in the textile industry in the 1960s or Eastern European seasonal workers in Lincolnshire after the 2004 EU enlargement. Through gaining an understanding of the recent history of UK international migration, one can begin to understand the present-day diversity of the UK's residents, as reflected in the most recent estimates of population by country of birth shown in Figure 4.2 (see also the comprehensive overview of contemporary migration statistics in Salt, 2009–2014).

ASYLUM SEEKERS AND REFUGEES: POLICY AND TRENDS

Forced migration is a special category of population flows, driven by armed conflict or persecution and far less predictable than other types of migration

(Disney et al., 2015). This category includes asylum seekers and refugees admitted to the UK based on the very specific provisions of international humanitarian law. As such, they are not covered by the IPS-based data used for Figure 4.1, but are added separately to the long-term migration estimates (ONS, 2012d). This section summarises asylum policy in the UK and identifies currently available data sources on asylum, briefly describing the trends.

The 1951 United Nations Refugee Convention was the first formal framework setting out the rights of individuals fleeing their own country as a result of a 'well-founded fear of persecution' on the specific grounds of race, religion, nationality, membership of a particular social group or political opinion (UNHCR, 2010). Migration for international protection differs from other migrations in that application for permission to stay is usually made on or after arrival rather than in advance through visa applications. Whilst waiting for a decision, applicants are defined as 'asylum seekers', and those who are granted leave to remain then become 'refugees'. In the UK, another category of 'permission to stay' may be granted for humanitarian or other reasons if an applicant does not qualify for refugee status.

Since the mid-1990s, the UK has introduced a new piece of legislation on immigration and asylum issues every few years, mostly focussing on restriction and deterrence but also amending the application process and re-organising enforcement agencies. The 1999 Immigration and Asylum Act introduced a system of dispersal, changing the focus of settlement away from London and removing the element of choice, whilst the right to work was removed from asylum seekers through the Nationality, Immigration and Asylum Act of 2002. These rules were later amended so that an applicant who has not received an initial decision within twelve months may apply to work in the UK. In 2004, the Asylum and Immigration Act was introduced to streamline the appeals process for those refused asylum.[4]

The UK asylum system should also be seen in the context of EU law. The main aim of the so-called Dublin system—introduced initially with the Dublin Convention and replaced by later Dublin Regulations I, II and III[5]— was to prevent multiple claims from being made in different countries, as well as allowing for the transfer of asylum seekers between member states. Applicants would be transferred when they were judged to have passed through a 'safe country'. Alongside Dublin, a process of 'harmonisation' was being implemented through the creation of a Common European Asylum System (CEAS), aiming to provide a common minimum standard in legal frameworks to ensure 'fairness, efficiency, and transparency' (Commission of the European Communities, 2007: 2) and to give equal treatment for asylum seekers wherever they lodged their claim.

The recent civil war in Syria and the scale of the resulting displacement has increasingly meant that border countries most often used as the point of entry to the EU, especially in the Mediterranean basin, have been receiving a greatly disproportionate share of asylum seekers compared to the rest of Europe. These developments have cast doubts on the fitness for the purpose of the Dublin asylum system, which, at the time of writing this chapter, is coming under intense scrutiny and revision.

In terms of data, the recording of absolute numbers of asylum seekers is inherent in the system, as an application must have been submitted to the authorities in order for an individual to be defined as seeking asylum. These data are published in the regular quarterly Home Office Asylum Statistics, along with other characteristics (such as age, sex, nationality), but data on timing and transitions between statuses are lacking. The absence of information on length of time between stages of the asylum process limits analytical potential considerably. Other data on the UK refugee population are notably scarce. Since 2010 the LFS has included a question on 'main reason for migration' (Home Office, 2014), but it does not constitute a part of the standard LFS dataset and also suffers from sample size issues in relation to small populations. Below, we draw principally on Home Office statistics but also on a study based on the Survey of New Refugees (SNR) commissioned in 2010.

The Home Office statistics show considerable fluctuations in the patterns of asylum applications and outcomes over the last three decades, as shown in Figure 4.3. This variation reflects a changing global context, including different regions experiencing conflict and instability at different times, the increasing availability of transport links and changes to UK asylum policy and legislation. The number of applicants rose in the early 1990s with the breakup of the Soviet Union and the conflict in former Yugoslavia. The peak in grants and refusals in 2001 results from 'clearing the backlog' of asylum cases, which reached the top of the government agenda then. The subsequent reduction in applications, decisions and grants is largely a result of three changes: the introduction of progressively more stringent controls, the placing of limits on asylum support and greater focus on removals (Somerville, 2007). Alongside restriction and the aim to differentiate those 'genuinely in need of protection' from 'economic migrants' was a desire to better understand and encourage refugee resettlement and community cohesion (Home Office, 2002).

The SNR was introduced in an attempt to address the data limitations recognised in assessing asylum and refugee policy, primarily to provide information on the integration of refugees in Britain (Home Office, 2010). A baseline survey was sent to all those over the age of eighteen in Britain who were granted asylum, humanitarian protection or discretionary leave to remain between December 2005 and March 2007. This recorded background characteristics (such as education) as well as data on their current situation

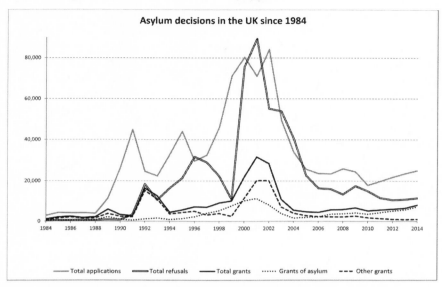

Figure 4.3   Annual Asylum Applications, Grants and Refusals, UK, 1984–2014.
Source: Home Office (2015).

(such as housing and health) and was followed by three subsequent question-naires eight, fifteen and twenty-one months later, recording socio-economic outcomes such as employment status. As a panel survey following the same individuals in multiple waves over time, it enables the relationships between background characteristics, experience and outcomes to be analysed.

Cheung and Phillimore (2013) used SNR data to explore social capital in relation to other indicators and, based on their findings, recommend that inte-gration can be promoted through improving access to good-quality language training, encouraging the development of social networks (for example, fam-ily reunification) and ensuring that refugees have access to employment and financial support. They also suggest that allowing asylum seekers to choose dispersal locations with friends and family as well as actively providing pro-tection from harassment could support integration. Although this research can contribute to the body of knowledge on integration, it is important to recog-nise that the usefulness of the SNR is limited by issues common in longitu-dinal survey data; in particular, there is a high rate of attrition, meaning that the majority of interviewees had dropped out by the later waves. Still, despite data limitations, some patterns emerge. There are visible differences in terms of health and socio-economic situation between the worse-off populations of refugees, who are being dispersed—mainly to the North of England and to the Midlands—and those who are able to stay with friends and families, mainly in London and the South East.

Clearly, issues around asylum and refugees continue to be prominent in public discourse and policy, as shown by the frequency of legislative changes and variation in asylum trends. When it comes to actual recommendations, in order for the future debates and decision making to be best informed, further data collection and methodological approaches need to be considered. The potential usefulness of existing datasets could be enhanced through the development and application of data linkage methods. This is a relatively cheap and efficient way of creating additional information—for example, data that already identify asylum seekers or refugees may be linked to data (such as the census) that record extensive detail on individual characteristics.

Nevertheless, there are still many limitations and challenges—statistical as well as ethical—with data linkage methods. Therefore, the possibility of collecting additional data on asylum seekers and refugees—for example, by including a census question on the main reason for migration—would be an extremely welcome development for researchers, policymakers and practitioners looking to better understand the asylum process, the settlement experience of refugees and the associated policy impacts.

MIGRATION IMPACTS: MYTHS AND REALITY

In the early twenty-first century, international migration has become a crucial factor shaping the demographics of the United Kingdom. Since the enlargement of the EU in 2004, the increase of UK migration has led to many social concerns surrounding the issue, especially after the financial crisis of 2008–2009. However, the current debate on migration in the UK involves several myths and misconceptions, which relate to the uniqueness of the recent UK migration experience, as well as to the impacts of migration on various realms of social life.

As mentioned previously, net migration to the UK was mostly negative until the early 1980s. The migration levels after 2004, when the A8 countries joined the EU, have been indeed unprecedented. However, a large part of this migration growth was a result of a conscious policy decision to open the labour market for immigrants from the new member states fully, whilst most other countries (except Ireland and Sweden) introduced transitional restrictions on access. This decision has triggered a stepwise change in net migration to the UK. On the other hand, the financial crisis of 2008–2009 led to a relatively minor moderation of the inflows, curbing mostly the inflows from the A8 countries.

Since the second half of 2012, immigration is again on the increase, especially from the EU-15 countries and from Bulgaria and Romania (after their transitional restrictions expired in 2014). Even though immigration from outside of the EU has recently been relatively stable, if not contracting, the latest available data at the time of writing show the overall net migration to be at its highest recorded level, at 336,000 for the twelve months to June 2015 (ONS, 2015b). Still, the share of the foreign-born population in the UK has been increasing throughout much of the twentieth century, from around 2.6 per cent in 1931 to 7.3 per cent in 1991, and to 13.4 per cent in 2011 (Coleman, 2013).

A common problematic area related to the UK's international migration policy is the one of *net migration* as such, especially when it is used as a policy target, despite the idea being far from uncontroversial (Commons Library, 2015). In principle, government policy during the 2010 and 2015 Parliaments has aimed at reducing the *difference* between gross inflows and gross outflows to less than one hundred thousand people annually. However, since Article 12(2) of the International Covenant on Civil and Political Rights (ratified by the UK in 1976) states that 'everyone shall be free to leave any country, including his own', authorities have virtually no control over emigration, except for those who are allowed into the UK on temporary visas or residence and work permits. Further, only a partial control over flows of non-EU citizens can be imposed by restricting the total number of visas granted. Hence, in reality, meeting the *net migration* target may be a matter of pure chance.

Another misconception in the debate on the effects of migration is the presumed abuse of the British social welfare system by immigrants. This issue has been extensively analysed by Dustmann and Frattini (2013) in their study of the fiscal contribution of migrants who arrived in the UK between 1995 and 2011. This showed that migrants from the European Economic Area (EEA, comprising the EU, Iceland, Norway and Liechtenstein) and, more recently, from outside of the EEA have made a positive fiscal contribution, which amounts to a net gain of £8.8 billion (2011 equivalent). In fact, migrants who arrived after 2000 have been the most significant contributors. In percentage terms, EEA immigrants' payments were 4 per cent higher than their receipts via transfers and benefits (although Rowthorn, 2015, suggests that these estimates may be too high and may merely reflect the younger age structure of the new migrants). The native British as well as non-EEA migrant populations are, on average, net receivers of the public revenue. For example, native British contributed around £605 billion, which constituted 93 per cent of what they have received from the welfare system (Rowthorn, 2015).

George et al. (2011) further exposed the use of benefits. They demonstrate that the expenditures on personal social services (PSS) and health are higher for the native population than for migrants. These results reflect the fact that the average age of a British taxpayer was, in 2011, forty-one years, whereas both EEA and non-EEA migrants were around eight years younger, meaning that very few are in the age group that places the highest costs on social services—namely, sixty-five and over. As for specific welfare benefits, van der Wielen and Bijak (2015) have found that the A8 and A2 migrants have a slightly higher chance of claiming social benefits—particularly housing benefits—than British natives, but a lower one of claiming unemployment benefits or income support. This finding is not surprising given that many of these migrants work in low-paying sectors of the economy: their earnings are too high for them to qualify for income-related benefits, but it may not be sufficient to rent or buy housing without some level of state support. It also should be kept in mind that immigrants' access to welfare benefits has usually been restricted, at least temporarily.

As for education, a relatively young age of migrants may have led to larger expenditures on schooling for all children, including those in full-time education at age sixteen and seventeen, comparing to the relative size of their population. In 2009–2010, children of migrants received 15 per cent of the total of £74bn expenditure, whereas they accounted for 13 per cent of the total population (George et al., 2011). By contrast, at the tertiary level, the UK is the second largest market for international students with 12.6 per cent market share, only behind the USA with 16.4 per cent (Universities UK, 2014a). International students from outside of the EU contribute almost one-eighth of the Higher Education sector's income: in the academic year 2012–2013 a total of £3.5 billion, up from £3.2 billion in the previous year. It is worth noting that the higher-education sector in the UK has a significant impact on the entire economy, with 2.8 per cent contribution to the GDP in 2011–2012 (Universities UK, 2014b). In the same academic year it generated around £11 billion in export earnings, 36 per cent of which came from tuition fees and accommodation and another 32 per cent from off-campus spending of the non-EU students (Universities UK, 2014b).

One more myth related to immigration relates to employment and wages, especially the fear of immigrants taking the jobs and decreasing the wages of the native British labour force. Such discussion is remarkable when compared with the situation in the UK around 160 years ago, a time when Irish labour migrants built British railways and canals. Irish immigration posed a threat to the wages and living conditions of English workers and were 'driving the Saxon native out, taking possession in his room', as was argued by Friedrich Engels (Engels, 1845/1987; see also Castles and Miller, 2009). According to Devlin et al. (2014), the effect of a large increase in the UK's net migration in recent years might depend on the overall condition of the economy. During the economic boom prior to the economic crisis in 2008, immigration from the EU led to a slight decrease of wages in the bottom of wage distribution and an increase in the top, with a slight positive impact overall (Dustmann et al., 2008). Other, more recent, studies (Nathan, 2011; Lucchino et al., 2012) found little or no evidence of immigration impact on wages or unemployment of British natives, especially in the long term. Nathan (2011) concluded that the largest effect of immigration on native employment was for the low-skilled workers. However, a study by the Migration Advisory Committee (2012) revealed that, during the economic depression that ensued after the crisis, non-EU migrants who stayed in the UK for less than five years might have had a slight influence on the larger unemployment of the UK natives, whereas Rowthorn (2015) attributes some reduction in wages amongst the native unskilled workers to competition with new migrants. Nevertheless, these results cannot be extrapolated to the times when the economy is recovering. In other words, the reality of migration and its impacts is usually more complex than a simple narrative would imply.

DISCUSSION: FROM UNCERTAINTY TO KNOWLEDGE

To fully understand the causes and consequences of international migration and its impact on characteristics of the population in the UK, researchers and policymakers need to build a reliable, useful and understandable evidence base. However, available information and statistics on international migration in the UK are uncertain and have important limitations that need to be fully understood and taken into account if we are to improve our understanding of international migration to and from the UK (Disney, 2015). As mentioned above, the only source of comprehensive information on UK international migration is the International Passenger Survey (IPS), a sample survey conducted at ports and airports in the UK, originally designed primarily to measure expenditure on travel and tourism for the national accounts rather than for estimating international migration. The IPS is further adjusted to take into account asylum seekers, people who change their intended migration ('switchers') and migrants to and from the Republic of Ireland (ONS, 2012d).

In addition to the uncertainty associated with sampling variability, there are clear limitations, biases and problems with the coverage of the IPS, which lead to increased uncertainty surrounding UK migration estimates. The key limitations of the IPS are twofold. One is that, as it samples all travellers crossing UK borders, relatively few of whom are migrants (people intending to change their country of residence for at least twelve months), the survey is subject to a relatively large sampling error for the latter, which can be problematic especially when the data are broken down by age or citizenship. For example, the IPS estimate of immigrants entering England and Wales in 2014 with the 95% Confidence Interval is 537,000 ± 34,000 people, which is roughly ± 6 per cent. However, the number of immigrant children in the age group five to nine is estimated as 10,000 ± 4,000 people—± 40 per cent.

When we further break down this figure by region of destination (North West), the estimate is 2,000 ± 2,000—±100 per cent (ONS, 2016). The other problem with the IPS data is that the survey necessarily asks about migrants' intentions of length of stay rather than the actual length of stay in the UK, the latter not even for emigrants (Disney, 2015).

The uses of population data, and thus also of migration statistics, are wide ranging, going well beyond challenging the various myths listed above. Having reliable statistics on the size and demographic characteristics of the population is vital for the provision of equitable and good public services. The data, estimates and forecasts are used on a daily basis by policymakers, politicians, public health officials and planners—in both public and private sectors—to help inform important decisions (Boyle and Dorling, 2004), as well as by researchers to advance knowledge and to aid our understanding of society. Population statistics also influence the political process—for example, through establishing the boundaries for political constituencies. The numbers are also used in a more indirect way, providing denominators for many rate-based measures. As such, they are essential for improving the well-being, prosperity and legitimacy of modern democratic institutions and society alike.

In this context, trusted, independent and robust information about the size, structure and characteristics of populations is seen to be an essential underpinning of a modern society (Statistics New Zealand, 2011). It is thus vital that the users understand how the different statistics were compiled, how they relate to each other and what the uncertainty inherent in the estimates is. Given the importance of international migration in UK population change now, it is crucial to have a clear and documented account of how these statistics are arrived at, their strengths and weaknesses and the concepts and definitions they are based on.

Current migration estimates are based on population censuses, administrative records and random surveys, none of which provides a comprehensive picture of the UK migration. Hence, there is a need to combine the various data sources, through the means of statistical modelling, with measures of uncertainty reported to the users of data. This approach is in line with the provisions of the EU Regulation (EC) No. 862/2007 on Community Statistics on Migration and International Protection, Article 9 of which allows scientifically based and well-documented statistical estimation methods to be used to produce migration statistics.[6]

As stipulated by Willekens (1994), various existing sources of administrative data can be used to enhance the existing information on international migration—in this case, the IPS—and to piece together coherent estimates. This can be achieved through the use of statistical models that take into account the varying levels of coverage, definitions and accuracy of each data collection, which can come either from several UK sources (Disney, 2015) or from other countries (Raymer et al., 2013; Wiśniowski, in press). On the other hand, migration indicators can be added to other, routinely collected data sources, by way of migration 'mainstreaming' (Knauth, 2011).

A separate issue is related to the forecasting of international migration. Migration is the most unpredictable demographic component of change (for discussion, see Bijak, 2010), and the inherent uncertainty is only magnified by the imperfections in the data (Disney et al., 2015). However, migration foresights are indispensable for forecasting future population size and structure—again, crucial for planning and policymaking in many spheres of life. Hence, even if predicting migration is not possible, it is crucial to describe its uncertainty better and to convey this additional information to the users so that their policy or planning decisions are more prudent and more robust.

In terms of practical steps, in response to the Migration Statistics enquiry of the House of Commons Public Administration Select Committee, we proposed the following:

> We strongly recommend the use of alternative sources of data to aid the estimates of international migration. We suggest that, in the short term, alternative sources of data and statistical modelling should be utilised to help improve the UK international migration estimates. . . . In the long term, we recommend the fullest possible use of information available from the e-Borders scheme.[7] . . . When statistical modelling is used, we recommend that the results are reported together with a range of the associated uncertainty measures. An interactive engagement of the producers of the statistics with the users is suggested in order to help utilise this information fully, taking into account the decision context. We believe that an honest reporting of the imperfections of knowledge on migration will provide a prudent approach to the migration challenges facing the United Kingdom. (Bijak et al., 2013, § 26–28)

These proposals remain even more important in an increasingly migratory world. They were officially followed up by the UK Statistics Authority, which made a formal recommendation that 'ONS should make further improvements to the estimation of international migration statistics, including a greater use of international migration data collected by other countries to better understand the patterns of migration to/from the UK' (UK Statistics Authority, 2013: 25).

In our view, the research agenda surrounding international migration in the United Kingdom, especially for the next quarter of a century, should be similarly based on as broad an evidence base as possible, combining information on migration—and the associated errors—drawn from a range of different sources. Ideally, there should be also closer collaboration between the producers and users of migration estimates and forecasts, from academia, administration, policy and the private sector. Adopting such an approach will inform and facilitate policy and planning decisions being made under conditions of uncertainty about the true magnitude of the UK's international population exchanges and the likely future developments in them.

NOTES

1. Jakub Bijak and Arkadiusz Wiśniowski gratefully acknowledge the Economic and Social Research Council (ESRC) Centre for Population Change grants (RES-625-28-0001 and ES/K007394/1), and George Disney and Sarah Lubman their respective ESRC-funded PhD projects (ES/I032142/1 and ES/I026215/1). This chapter includes excerpts from the Response to the House of Commons Public Administration Select Committee (PASC) Call for Evidence on Migration Statistics (Bijak et al., 2013), reprinted by a kind permission of the Committee. The views, interpretations and recommendations presented in this document are the ones of the authors.

2. Commonwealth Immigrants Act 1962 c. 21, amended by the Commonwealth Immigrants Act 1968, c. 9, http://www.legislation.gov.uk/ukpga/1968/9/contents/enacted.

3. Immigration Act 1971 c. 77, http://www.legislation.gov.uk/ukpga/1971/77/contents.

4. Immigration and Asylum Act 1999 c. 33, http://www.legislation.gov.uk/ukpga/1999/33/contents; Nationality, Immigration and Asylum Act 2002 c. 41, http://www.legislation.gov.uk/ukpga/2002/41/contents; Asylum and Immigration (Treatment of Claimants, etc.) Act 2004 c. 19, http://www.legislation.gov.uk/ukpga/2004/19/contents.

5. *Convention determining the State responsible for examining applications for asylum lodged in one of the Member States of the European Communities—Dublin Convention* of 15 June 1990, OJ C 254, 19.8.1997, 1–12, http://eur-lex.europa.eu/legal-content/EN/ALL/?uri=CELEX:41997A0819%2801%29; *Regulation (EU) No. 604/2013 of the European Parliament and of the Council of 26 June 2013 establishing the criteria and mechanisms for determining the Member State responsible for examining an application for international protection lodged in one of the Member States by a third-country national or a stateless person*, OJ L 180, 29.6.2013, 31–59, http://eur-lex.europa.eu/legal-content/EN/ALL/?uri=CELEX:32013R0604.

6. *Regulation (EC) No. 862/2007 of the European Parliament and the Council on Community Statistics on Migration and International Protection*, OJ L 199, 31.07.2007, 23–29; http://eur-lex.europa.eu/legal-content/EN/TXT/?uri=CELEX:32007R0862.

7. The e-Borders scheme—later renamed Semaphore—is a system currently being designed to record arrivals into and departures from the UK, some elements of which can be used for measuring international migration. Detailed information can be obtained from ONS (2014c).

Chapter 5

Immigrants and Ethnic Fertility Convergence

Sylvie Dubuc[1]

As shown in Chapter 1, since the late 1990s net migration has overtaken natural increase in contributing to the UK population growth, largely driven by the decreasing number of births until 2001 but mainly by higher immigration since then. Moreover, the rise in the number of children per women of reproductive age since 2001 has been partly attributed—explicitly or implicitly— to immigration, bringing the fertility behaviour of immigrants into the wider public debate. This chapter examines the fertility of both immigrant and UK-born women of ethnic minority heritage in order to assess the contribution of their fertility to the overall rise. The chapter also sheds light on the extent to which fertility behaviours are converging and the role of intergenerational changes in this.

Childbearing 'choices' are arguably amongst the major and most consequential decisions shaping people's lives and are conditioned by multiple factors. Fertility behaviour is also an important dimension of the incorporation of immigrants and their children into their country of resettlement (Massey, 1981; Rumbaut, 2007). Often originating from high-fertility countries, immigrants in the UK and Europe more generally show higher fertility when compared with the norms and patterns in their host society,[2] although migration and fertility patterns are changing. Less well documented, however, is the fertility behaviour of the immigrants' children—second-generation migrants. In part this is a function of data in that vital statistics by the country of birth of women's parents are not available in the UK.

This chapter addresses the challenge of distinguishing between immigrants and women of the second generation in the UK by drawing upon fertility estimates derived from an alternative source. Until fairly recently, there were relatively few second-generation women aged thirty and over, but as

the children of those who migrated to the UK in the 1950s, 1960s and 1970s
have themselves reached childbearing age, their numbers have become large
enough for analysts to use survey data. Here Labour Force Survey (LFS) data
on people's ethnicity and country of birth are used together with the reverse
survival Own Child Method to distinguish within ethnic groups between
immigrant (i.e., foreign-born) women and UK-born (used as a *proxy* for
immigrants' children) women, as detailed in Dubuc (2009, 2012). In what
follows, we also refer to these two types of women, respectively, as the
'immigrant generation' and 'second generation'.

MIGRATION AND ETHNICITY: BACKGROUND AND DEFINITIONS

The majority of immigrant women belong to one or another of the various
ethnic minorities; according to LFS data averaged for 2002–2006, around
82 per cent of foreign-born women aged fifteen to forty-nine reported themselves as being from an ethnicity other than 'White British', and about a third
of ethnic minority women aged fifteen to forty-nine were born in the UK.
As Figure 5.1 shows, the vast majority of non-White minority ethnic women
who were born in the UK are aged below forty and therefore are likely to
be mostly of the second generation in the UK (i.e., the children of women
born abroad), although amongst those of Black Caribbean heritage there is
a substantial proportion of (young) third-generation women. The proportion
of UK-born women who are currently of childbearing age in each ethnic
group results from the combination of the level of past fertility and migration
history, as we now show.

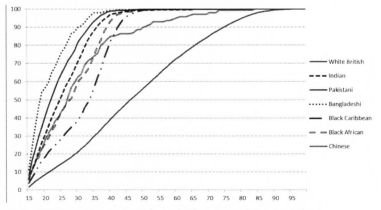

Figure 5.1   UK-Born Women by Selected Ethnicity and Age Distribution.
Source: Author's calculation.

Immigration to the UK since 1945

Postwar reconstruction and economic recovery in Britain created job opportunities and attracted immigrant workers, especially from New Commonwealth countries. Caribbean immigrants arrived mostly in the 1950s and 1960s and, despite an early wave of employment-related immigration by women (Byron, 1998), they were largely adult men (Foner, 2009). At the same time, temporary, mainly male, migrant workers arrived from the Indian sub-continent (Ballard, 1990; Brown, 2006), partly fuelled by the post-colonial Indian partition. Then, however, adoption of restrictive immigration laws in 1962 left workers with the choice of either returning to their place of origin with the risk of not being allowed back or settling in the UK. Many chose to settle, such that in the later 1960s the migration of dependants from the Caribbean (primarily children) and India (mainly women and children) dominated the immigration flow to Britain.

Since the 1970s, immigration from the Caribbean has dwindled, so that today and for some time past (as reflected in the height of both of their columns in Figure 5.2), the large majority of Black Caribbean women aged fifteen to forty-nine comprises the settled immigrants' children and increasingly grandchildren born in the UK. By contrast, at this time the Indian community grew further with the arrival of Indian immigrant families forced to leave East Africa by the insecurity and expulsions resulting from the post-colonial 'Africanisation' movement. These 'twice migrants', mainly from Gujarat originally, had formed the middle class in East Africa and were relatively highly educated and often wealthier than the India-born immigrants to the UK (Bhachu, 1985; Brown, 2006). Since 2000, Indian migration has recorded a new revival (in addition to family reunion migration), with an increase in work permits for highly skilled Indian nationals and the result of immigration policy increasingly favouring highly skilled non-EU immigrant workers (Salt and Millar, 2006).[3] As a result, first-generation immigrants still count for more than half of Indian women of childbearing age, with the UK-born women of Indian heritage mainly being second generation (Figure 5.2).

Family reunions started later for the Pakistani community and even more recently for the Bangladeshi community, as reflected in Home Office immigration data (Berrington, 1996). The Bangladeshis, along with Black Africans, were the fastest growing groups in the 1980s (Jones, 1993). Analysis of the 2002–2006 LFS data shows that the proportion of immigrant women that have arrived within the nine years prior to the survey varies widely between ethnic groups (Dubuc, 2012).[4] For the Pakistani and Bangladeshi groups, the relatively low recent migration and past high fertility combine to explain the rapid increase in the UK-born proportion, mainly second-generation women below thirty-five years old shown above in Figure 5.1. Immigration of Black

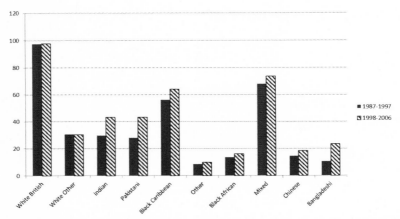

Figure 5.2   Change in the Proportion of UK-Born Women Aged 15–49 Within Ethnic Groups.
Source: Author's calculation.

Africans from a variety of countries has increased in recent decades (Daley, 1996; Mitton and Aspinall, 2010) and, as a result, the foreign-born Black African population still comprises the majority share of this ethnic group (Figure 5.2). The same also applies to the Chinese population in the UK, although London's Chinatown community first established itself back in the 1950s and 1960s. Early Chinese immigrants mainly originated from Hong Kong, but since the 1980s and the relaxation of emigration policy in China, they have come increasingly from Mainland China.

Most recently, immigrants to the UK have come from increasingly diverse countries of origin (Vertovec, 2007; see also Chapter 4), largely augmenting the ethnic group 'Others'.[5] Traditionally, non-British White immigrants were mainly from Europe, North America, Australia, New Zealand and South Africa. Since 2004, the ethnic and cultural plurality of the population of the UK has been diversified by substantial immigration flows from the European Union's newest members, especially from Poland (Vertovec, 2007; Tromans et al., 2009). The new EU migrants are mainly young workers enrolled in low-skilled jobs (Salt and Millar, 2006).

Combining Ethnic Categories and Country of Birth

Ethnicity is self-reported by survey respondents, but responses are shaped by a predefined nomenclature. The 2001 classification used here has two levels. Level 1 classifies individuals into five broad groups: 'White', 'Mixed', 'Asian or Asian British', 'Black or Black British', 'Chinese' and an additional group labelled 'Other'. Level 2 provides a finer classification nested within Level 1 and distinguishing sixteen ethnic groups as follows: The 'White' population is subdivided into White British, White Irish and White Other; 'Mixed' into White and Black Caribbean, White and Asian, White and Black African and Other mixed;[6] 'Asian British or Asian' into Indian, Pakistani, Bangladeshi and Other Asian and 'Black or Black British' into Black Caribbean, Black African and Other Black (with neither Chinese nor 'Other' being subdivided).

These ethnic categories largely reflect post–Second World War migration waves made up of the Caribbean, South Asian and Chinese diasporas. The recent trends and broader geographic origins of immigrants belonging to the 'Black African' ethnic category, however, complicate interpretations of their fertility estimates. Also, since 2001, in an attempt to capture new trends in migration, a category 'Other White' (notably for migrants from Eastern Europe) has been introduced, but the use of this category to approximate the second generation of 'White' migrants is problematic. For one thing, the nature of White migrants' flows has changed drastically over time, and UK-born 'White Other' women could be second or higher generations. Importantly, due to the racialized nature of the ethnic nomenclature, the daughters (and grand-daughters) of White migrants may identify with the group White British, whilst the daughters of Asian and Black migrants are more likely to identify with their parents' reported ethnicity, whatever their sense of being British is. Newcomers from Eastern Europe contribute to the high proportion of recently arrived women (aged fifteen to forty-nine) who identify with the ethnic category White Other, introduced in 2001. The UK-born White Other group is a much selected one, resulting from the 'statistical disappearance' of the children of White migrants who, as they grow older and self-report their ethnicity, identify with the White British ethnic category.

Postwar immigration has also resulted in the formation of mixed ethnicity populations. The age structure of the mixed ethnic origin population is very young, and the number of adult women remains low. Of those ethnically mixed women of childbearing ages in 1987–2006, 36 per cent identified as 'White and Black Caribbean', 25 per cent as 'White and Asian', 15 per cent as 'White and Black African' and 25 per cent as 'Other Mixed'. Altogether, nearly 74 per cent of the mixed groups were born in the UK. Amongst them the White and Black Caribbean, mainly UK-born, are thought to be predominantly third-generation descendants of immigrant Black Caribbeans (Layton-Henry, 2002). The rapidly increasing numbers of children of Mixed ethnic origin further challenge ethnic categorisation within the UK population, complicating research that aims to follow immigrants' descendants across generations in the future (see Chapter 9 for further detail). Despite these caveats, a fairly clear picture of ethnic convergence in fertility rates can be identified.

CONVERGING ETHNIC FERTILITY TRENDS

Differences in fertility by ethnic group in the UK are well documented (e.g., Large et al., 2006; Rees, 2008; Coleman and Dubuc, 2010). Relatively large differences in the estimated levels of fertility between major ethnic groups reflect specific fertility behaviour of immigrant populations and the different levels of fertility experienced in their home country. Fertility estimates from the late 1960s for ethnic groups originating from relatively high-fertility countries (e.g., South Asian and African countries) show a marked decrease in TFR over time (Coleman and Dubuc, 2010), indicating some convergence in process towards the lower UK average (Dubuc and Haskey, 2010).

Table 5.1 shows less variability in the level of the TFRs across ethnic groups in recent years compared with that in the 1990s, as measured by the decreasing coefficient of variation of TFR by ethnic group over time: from 0.36 in 1987–1997 to 0.27 in 1998–2006. Because White British women constitute the vast majority of women, their total fertility is very close to the UK average (1.8). Irish women have higher fertility (above 2). In contrast, White women who do not identify as either British or Irish have fertility below the UK average. Fertility differences across ethnic groups within the White

Table 5.1 TFR of the Major Ethnic Groups in the UK and Decreasing Inter-Ethnic Variability, 1987–1997 and 1998–2006

| | 1987–1997 | | 1998–2006 | | Inter-Period Change (%) | Total Sample Women |
	TFR	CI 95% (+/–)	TFR	CI 95% (+/–)		
White British	1.79	0.01	1.74	0.02	−2.9	2336617
White other	1.46	0.05	1.5	0.06	2.7	123584
Indian	1.75	0.08	1.67	0.09	−4.8	52955
Pakistani	3.16	0.15	2.89	0.15	−9.3	33108
Other	2.02	0.12	2.05	0.13	1.5	29858
Black Caribbean	1.94	0.11	2.04	0.14	4.9	29237
Black African	2.37	0.14	2.41	0.14	1.7	28210
Bangladeshi	4.12	0.29	3.15	0.24	−30.8	11164
Chinese	1.32	0.16	1.24	0.17	−6.5	11840
mean TFR	2.49		2.34			
Standard deviation	0.90		0.64			
Coefficient of variation	0.36		0.27			

Total fertility figures are generally consistent with data by Simpson (2013) using the child-women ratio based on census 2001 and 2011 data, although estimates appear much lower for the Caribbean group in comparison with estimates presented here, which can (at least partly) be explained by the limit of the child-women ratio method used in a context of increasing prevalence of children of mixed ethnic unions (as explained and detailed in Dubuc, 2009).

Note: The UK average TFR over 1987–2006 is 1.77.

Source: LFS 2001–2006; author's calculations based on LFS-OCM estimates in Dubuc and Haskey (2010) and Coleman and Dubuc (2010).

category are substantial. However, distinctions within this category were only introduced in 2001, limiting trend analyses.

What explains the fertility convergence across ethnic categories over time that is shown in Table 5.1? Women of the various minority groups were almost exclusively foreign born in the 1960s and 1970s. The key question therefore is as follows: Is convergence due to a change in the level of fertility over successive cohorts of immigrant women, or does it reflect the changing composition of these groups, with an increasing share of ethnic minority women being the second- and third-generation descendants of immigrants?

Global Fertility Transition and Immigrants' Decreasing Fertility

The pace of fertility convergence differs across ethnic groups. This is partly related to the differences in initial level of fertility as shown in Figure 5.3; the higher the number of children per woman initially, the stronger the reduction in fertility. Some differences across groups remain, partly linked to the different stage of the demographic transition experienced by international migrants' sending countries. However, those groups with an average larger family size in the 1970s experienced the most rapid fertility reduction. This reduction reflects the global fertility transition (toward replacement levels) taking place across many traditional countries of emigration. We further observe diverging trends for the Chinese ethnic group, where total fertility has fallen well below the UK average over the last three decades (Dubuc and Haskey, 2010), consistent with the trend in mainland China, Hong Kong and Chinese communities elsewhere.

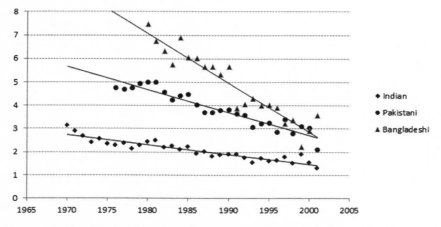

Figure 5.3 Trends in Total Fertility of the Main South Asian Ethnic Groups.
Source: Dubuc (2012); © John Wiley & Sons.

The decreasing fertility of immigrants not only reflects the demographic transition in their home country but also often tends to precede it. For instance, in the 1970s and 1980s, Indian and Pakistani immigrants showed fertility levels well below those in their home country. Such findings conform to other empirical evidence that immigrants from countries where the fertility transition has not been completed often have lower fertility than the levels in their countries of origin (e.g., examples from various receiving countries in Sobotka, 2008, and Dubuc, 2016). Many immigrants come from specific areas and social milieus, which may not represent the national-level fertility of their home country's population. For instance, Indian immigrants are largely members of the urban bourgeoisie, which is leading family and reproductive changes in India. Others belong to the highly educated high-middle class expelled from East Africa in the 1970s ('twice migrants'). By contrast, many Bangladeshi immigrants in the UK have rural origins, notably from the Sylhet region (Eade et al., 1996), where fertility is higher than the national average (Table 5.2), possibly explaining levels still around six children per woman observed in the early 1980s for the first wave of Bangladeshi female migrants. However, Bangladeshi women in the UK show the most rapid pace of fertility convergence, mirroring the rapid fertility decline in Bangladesh (especially in the last two decades). Differences between family size of immigrants and country of origin have further been attributed to the increasing impact of the receiving country in shaping the fertility of immigrants, with the duration of settlement being an important factor, notably for those who arrived in their childhood (e.g., Andersson, 2004; Sobotka, 2008).

Analysing trends in the fertility of immigrants over time and generations is further complicated by a potential change in the socio-demographic characteristics of successive waves of immigrants. Notably, restrictions on

Table 5.2   International Fertility Convergence Towards the UK Total Fertility (TFR)

Country/Place of Birth	1970–1975* TFR	1970–1975* Diff. with UK	1990† TFR	1990† Diff. with UK	2005–2006* TFR	2005–2006* Diff. with UK
Caribbean	4.6	2.3	2.9	1.1	2.4	0.6
India	5.4	3.1	4.0	2.2	2.8	1.0
Pakistan	7.1	4.8	6.1	4.3	4.1 (4.5 rural)	2.3
Bangladesh	6.1	3.8	4.4	2.6	3 (3.2 rural)	1.2
China	5.8	3.5	2.3	0.5	1.4	−0.4
Hong Kong	3.3	1.0	2.0	0.2	1.1	−0.7
UK‡	2.3		1.8		1.8	

*Population Division of the Department of Economic and Social Affairs of the United Nations (http://www.un.org/esa/population/), Table: Word fertility patterns, 2009. TFR for rural Pakistan and Bangladesh are shown when available because immigrants from these countries are mainly of rural origin.
†United Nations, UNICEF data (acceded July 10, 2010, at http://data.un.org/Data.aspx?d=SOW&f=in ID%3A127).
‡UK TFR: ONS FM1 Series no 8–37 (Years 1971, 1991 and 2005).
Source: TFR data for India, Pakistan and Bangladesh in Dubuc (2012).

immigration from non-EU members are increasingly selective in favour
of highly skilled immigration to the UK. For instance, the decrease in the
TFR of successive cohorts of immigrant Chinese women, from 2.39 in the
early 1970s to 1.26 over 1987–2006, partly reflects the changes in fertility
in the country of origin and partly results from a change in their composition, explaining their extremely low fertility, even below that of UK-born
Chinese women. Early waves of Chinese immigrants were largely from Hong
Kong and of peasant's background.[7] Because Hong Kong's TFR has reached
extreme-low levels in recent years, this is likely to impact on the TFR of
recent immigrants from Hong Kong, who are increasingly highly educated.
Additionally, since the late 1980s and the relaxation of the emigration policy
in China, relatively well-off Chinese students and highly skilled young professionals have come increasingly from urban Mainland China, where family
planning programmes and the One-Child Policy have also contributed to the
strong decrease in fertility since the late 1970s.

The Fertility of Immigrants and Second-Generation Women

To clarify the role of the second generation in explaining the fertility trends
of various minority ethnic groups in the UK, fertility estimates of the UK-
born are compared to those of contemporary immigrants for the main ethnic
groups in Figure 5.4. For the Pakistani, Bangladeshi, Black African and, to a

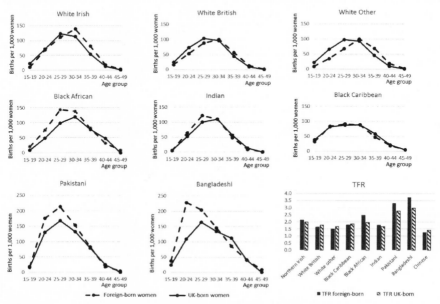

**Figure 5.4   TFRs and ASFRs of Immigrant and UK-Born Women Within the Main Ethnic
Groups.**
Source: Author's calculation.

lesser extent, the White Irish and Indian ethnic groups, the total fertility of the UK-born women is lower than that of first-generation immigrants. The difference is especially marked for the Pakistani and Bangladeshi groups. Although still over 40 per cent above the UK overall level, the difference in the total fertility of UK-born Pakistani and Bangladeshi women is less than half the difference recorded by immigrants from those countries.[8] Total fertility of UK-born Indian women has fallen to 1.5, well below that of the UK-born White British and overall national levels[9] (about 1.8 over 1987–2010). The TFR is now below the UK average for both immigrant and UK-born women belonging to the Chinese and White Other ethnic groups. In contrast, the total fertility of women of Black Caribbean heritage seems to have stabilised slightly above the UK average since the 1990s (see also Table 5.3) for both UK-born and foreign-born women.

The shape of the age pattern at childbearing of UK-born Pakistani and Bangladeshi women differs from the immigrant generation and has become closer to that of White British women (Figure 5.4). Notably, the much lower fertility of UK-born ethnic minority women below age thirty largely explains their lower total fertility. This includes a significantly lower ASFR amongst teenage UK-born Bangladeshi, comparable to the White British group. Because the fertility of immigrant Pakistani women has remained stable,[10] consistent with slow decline in Pakistan, the decreasing level of fertility at young age recorded by the Pakistani ethnic group since the late 1980s (Dubuc, 2009) appears to be due to the much lower fertility of young UK-born Pakistanis, whose proportion is growing. More generally, the difference in overall fertility between immigrant and UK-born Pakistani, Bangladeshi, Indian and Black African women appears to be due to lower fertility at young ages for the latter. Consequently, the age patterns of childbearing for the UK-born Indian and White British are very close to each other, except at very young age. In contrast to the White British group, teenage births are minimal amongst British Indian women, who also record lower fertility in their early twenties, explaining their overall lower TFR.

Although the age pattern of childbearing is similar for the UK-born White British and White Other women, levels are lower for the latter group, especially amongst women in their late twenties. For White Other women, the remarkable delayed childbearing profile of immigrants when compared to the UK-born generation contrasts with the very similar age pattern of childbearing amongst White British women, regardless of place of birth. In sharp contrast to most minority groups, more than 60 per cent of White British immigrant women are estimated to have come to the UK during their childhood, limiting both the potential disruption effect of migration on fertility and the impact of a foreign context of socialisation in shaping fertility behaviour. Traditional flows of White Other immigrants from Europe, North America and Australia are mainly motivated by study and highly skilled work experience, so more likely to delay childbearing. The recent wave of immigration from EU new members from Eastern Europe, where fertility has declined sharply (e.g., to about 1.3 in Poland), further contributes to this pattern (Waller et al., 2014). The low and strongly delayed childbearing of White Other immigrants suggests that migration for this group was not generally linked to family formation but was primarily motivated by work. The Chinese ethnic group is the most extreme example of delayed childbearing of all groups, with fertility largely occurring after thirty years old.[11]

Echoing the TFR results, the ASFRs of the Black Caribbean UK-born and foreign-born are close, showing an atypical age profile with a relatively high level of births to women at young ages and in their late thirties (Figure 5.4) instead of the more conventional peak-shape of fertility in the midrange ages. There was little significant change in the age pattern of the Black Caribbean women over time, either. For instance, in comparison with the White groups and the Indian UK-born women, the level of fertility for UK-born Black Caribbean heritage women aged thirty and over was already the highest of the four groups studied in 1987–1997 (Dubuc and Waller, 2014). Changes in ASFRs between 1987–1997 and 1998–2006 (data not shown) of the White British, White Other and Indian ethnic groups indicate a continuous decline in fertility amongst young UK-born women, coupled with some increase for those aged over thirty, indicating postponed childbearing. These trends are consistent with the overall increasing average age of women at childbearing in the UK to thirty (ONS, 2013b).

Immigration and National Fertility Change

Despite the global fertility transition and immigrants' fertility reduction, the overall number of births to foreign-born women is increasing, now contributing more than a quarter of all births in the UK (26.5 per cent according to ONS, 2013b). This is largely due to the younger age structure of immigrant women, with many being within the highest fertility range (twenty to forty), and their numbers are growing, as shown by 2001 and 2011 census data (Simpson, 2013). However, immigrants' family size has reduced. Whilst Tromans et al. (2009) show that immigrant women have produced the majority of the additional births in the UK, it is UK-born women who have contributed the greater part of the increase in total fertility since 2001 in the UK.

The extent to which the family size of immigrants remains higher than that of the UK-born needs some further clarification. In particular, classical Period TFR calculations[12] that are based on birth registrations may result in over-estimating the fertility of immigrants, resulting in misrepresentations of immigrants' average family size (Toulemon, 2004; Sobotka, 2008; Sobotka and Lutz, 2009; Parrado, 2011; Dubuc, 2012). This is explained by the association between resettlement and family formation resulting in post-migration high fertility (Andersson, 2004), especially within the few years following migration. In France Toulemon (2004) identified a boost in fertility, especially within four years following immigration, revealing how period fertility based on French birth registrations (i.e., solely capturing post-migration fertility) could overestimate the total completed fertility of immigrant women. In line with findings in France (Toulemon, 2004) and the USA (Parrado, 2011), in the UK post-migration fertility boost is balanced by depressed pre-migration fertility amongst immigrant women, observed for all ASFRs (Dubuc, 2012; Figure 5.5).[13] Similarly, the analysis of the fertility of Pakistani and Bangladeshi immigrant women both prior to and after arrival in the UK (Dubuc, 2012) indicated very distinct fertility levels, highlighting high post-migration fertility for women in their twenties. This is consistent with the idea that migration of women from Pakistan and Bangladesh is largely linked to marriage and family formation. Delayed childbearing through migration further contributes to the reduced teenage birth rate for immigrant women when compared to the very high levels in Bangladesh (Coleman and Dubuc, 2010).

Estimates in Figure 5.4 account for post-migration fertility as well as some of the pre-migration fertility history of immigrants, especially for those recently arrived and most susceptible to the effect of migration on their timing at childbearing,[14] likely minimising the overestimation of fertility levels of immigrants due to migration-specific tempo effects.[15] This probably explains why the overall LFS-OCM TFR of immigrant women is lower (1.94 on average over 1987–2006) than ONS estimates based on (post-migration) birth registrations in the UK, despite overall UK estimates from both methods being close (Dubuc, 2009; Coleman and Dubuc, 2010).[16]

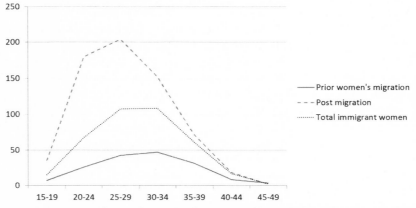

Figure 5.5   Age-Specific Fertility Rates of Women Before and After Migration to the UK, Average for 1987–2006.
Source: Dubuc (2012); © John Wiley & Sons.

In sum, the fertility of foreign-born women appears only slightly higher than that of the UK-born women (on average, 1.94 and 1.77, respectively, over 1987–2006, Dubuc and Haskey, 2010). Total fertility was declining for both UK-born and foreign-born women during the 1990s, after which the trend reversed for both (Dubuc and Haskey, 2010). The completed fertility and thus family size of immigrants and UK-born women are becoming more alike over time. Fertility of the second generation further contributes to the reduction of heterogeneity across ethnic groups. Changes across successive cohorts of migrants and generations support assumptions of overall converging trends in fertility across ethnic groups in population projection models, although the pace of convergence appears to vary across ethnic groups and in step with the stage of fertility transition experienced by the country of origin of the immigrant generation.

Intergenerational Fertility Convergence in Context

To what extent is immigrants' fertility behaviour transmitted to the second generation as opposed to the children of immigrants adopting UK childbearing behaviour? Taken together, there is much less variability in the TFRs across UK-born ethnic groups than foreign-born ethnic groups. This is illustrated by the coefficient of variation of TFR across ethnic groups of the two sub-categories, indicating that the diversity of fertility level measured between immigrant minority groups is considerably reduced (−43 per cent) when the second and subsequent British generations are considered.[17] The UK-born Pakistani and Bangladeshi women have fewer children at young ages compared to their immigrant counterparts. This is consistent with findings in the Netherlands for Turkish and Moroccan women (Alders, 2000; Garssen and Nicolaas, 2008). At the other end of the spectrum, the remarkably low total fertility of White Other and Chinese women—below the TFR of the White British—is even lower amongst immigrants, making the UK-born generations within these groups contribute to the overall closer reproductive behaviour (level and timing) of UK-born generations of ethnic minority groups compared with the differences across immigrant groups.

In Table 5.3, comparison of columns A and B shows the decreasing fertility of successive cohorts of immigrant women, reflecting in part fertility dynamics at their place of origin (as in Table 5.2). For instance, the decreasing level of TFR for the Indian immigrants at least partly reflects the progression of the demographic transition in India as previously discussed. Older cohorts of migrants (Table 5.3, column A) may be interpreted as a *proxy* for immigrant parents (first generation in the UK) of the UK-born women in 1987–2006 (Table 5.3, column C). The TFR of the second-generation women (column C) is lower than their *proxy* parent generation (column A) for all groups.

Table 5.3 Comparison of TFR of Selected Ethnic Groups in the 1970s, Contemporary Immigrants and UK-Born Women

Ethnic Groups	(A) TFR (1970s) All Ethnic Groups	(B) Immigrant Women	(C) UK-Born Women	(D) B - A	(E) C - A	(F) Immigrant Women B	(G) UK-Born Women A
		TFR (1987–2006)		Difference in TFR		Difference with overall UK TFR*	
Black Caribbean	2.12	1.93	1.95	−0.19	−0.17	0.16	0.18
Indian	2.47	1.90	1.67	−0.57	−0.80	0.13	−0.10
Pakistani	5.02	3.37	2.65	−1.65	−2.37	1.60	0.88
Bangladeshi	6.18	3.83	2.64	−2.35	−3.54	2.06	0.87
Chinese	2.39	1.26	1.45	−1.13	−0.94	−0.51	−0.32

LFS-OCM author's calculations; (A) values based on LFS-OCM estimates in Coleman and Dubuc (2010).
*Overall UK TFR over the period 1987–2006 was 1.77.
Source: Data for the Indian, Pakistani and Bangladeshi ethnic groups in Dubuc (2012).

For instance, the TFR of Pakistani women was 5.1 in the 1970s, about 3.1 above the UK average at the time. TFR of the second-generation Pakistani women have nearly halved compared to their (*proxy*) parents' generation. The intergenerational convergence is particularly striking for the Pakistani and Bangladeshi UK-born women who are driving the TFR of their whole ethnic group closer to the UK TFR over time—although the TFR of UK-born Pakistani and Bangladeshi women is still distinct from the national values in recent years.

Second-generation ethnic-minority women are leading the ethnic fertility convergence in the UK. Because their fertility is closer to that of the UK average, their increasing proportion within their ethnic group accelerates the pace of convergence between ethnic groups. Within groups, the fertility patterns of immigrants' children are closer to the UK average when compared to their contemporary immigrants' counterparts (i.e., same ethnic group) and suggests (1) ethnic minorities' intergenerational adaptation of fertility behaviour to the UK context and (2) the country of childbearing and socialisation strongly influence fertility behaviour (for both generations). Overall converging fertility of immigrants' descendants[18] is congruent with the intergenerational adaptation/assimilation hypothesis. Consistent with these findings, other studies on immigrants and their children's fertility have observed an inter-generational convergence in the USA (e.g., Parrado and Morgan, 2008) and Europe (e.g., Garssen and Nicolaas, 2008; Milewski, 2010). However, here and in other studies, potentially due to the short time span, trends have not yet reached full convergence and the social processes at play remain poorly understood.

Fertility and Education

Changes in fertility behaviour may be associated with, as well as indicate changes in, other spheres of people's lives and social characteristics. For instance, the much lower fertility of UK-born Pakistani and Bangladeshi women may reflect a greater involvement of the second generation in higher education compared to immigrant women.

We observe strong differences in fertility for all women in the UK by educational attainment. For instance, taking three broad categories, CGSE and below, A-level and higher education (degree), the average total fertility over the period 1987–2010 for overall UK women was, respectively, 2.12, 1.70 and 1.47 children per woman (using LFS 2001–2010). Unsurprisingly, we observe lower fertility at young ages and relatively high levels for women over thirty associated with higher educational attainment. Shifts toward later childbearing are commonly associated with the degree of education (e.g., Rindfuss et al., 1996; Mayer and Riphaln, 2000; in the UK: Rendall et al., 2005; Berrington and Pattaro, 2014).

The educational attainment of the daughters of post–World War II migrants is relatively high, above the UK average and the White British majority for most ethnic minority groups—with highest proportions of degree level for the second-generation Indian and Chinese women (Dubuc, 2015).[19] The high educational attainment of women of the second generation in the UK is associated with lower fertility, contributing to the fertility convergence across ethnic groups (Dubuc and Waller, 2014). For instance, the very significant lower fertility of young UK-born Pakistani and Bangladeshi women is consistent with their overall higher involvement in full-time education (30 per cent) in comparison to immigrant women (7 per cent; Dubuc, 2012) and their higher-educational attainment (Dubuc and Waller, 2014).

According to the minority status hypothesis (Goldscheider and Uhlenberg, 1969), higher segments of a minority population, aware of their disfavoured status, may reduce their family size in order to facilitate their socio-economic ascent and ensure a brighter future for fewer children. This may contribute to lowering the fertility of immigrant's children in the quest for upward social mobility. Indeed, Heath et al. (2008) analysing employment of the second generation found substantial ethnic penalties in the UK. Dustmann and Theodoropoulos (2010) also found that immigrants' children in the UK had much higher educational attainment than their parents, and often higher than White British, but the average employment probability and return of educational attainment in term of wages was lower for the UK-born ethnic minorities. The relatively lower fertility of many immigrants' daughters is associated with their high educational attainment; it remains unclear to what extent it can further be explained by the minority status hypothesis, calling for new research.

CONCLUSIONS

The distinctiveness of fertility across ethnic groups is reducing over time. This reflects both the global fertility transition and intergenerational convergence as second-generation UK-born women constitute a rising proportion of ethnic minority communities. The increasing number of births to immigrants in the UK is primarily the result of the young age structure of immigrant women and their increasing numbers. Over time, immigrants tend to have smaller families and, on average, the number of children immigrant women have is only moderately higher than non-migrant women, limiting their contribution to the increase in the overall TFR observed since 2001. Some new migrant groups, notably those from Eastern Europe and China, have remarkably low fertility, below the UK average.

Many women of the second generation in Britain have yet to complete their fertility life cycle. It remains to be seen how well current period total fertility measures are reflecting what the completed family size of young second-generation women will be, or if their current low fertility will eventually be compensated by higher childbearing at later age. To date, analyses of the effect of education on the completed family size of British women suggest that the postponed childbearing at younger ages amongst women with high educational attainment has not been compensated for by higher fertility at older ages (Berrington et al., 2015). Future research should clarify if and to what extent this will also apply to the daughters of immigrants in the UK. However, data on recent trends already suggest that the ageing population of Britain is unlikely going to be overturned by immigration in the long run, as immigrants and their daughters have increasingly less children themselves.

Despite signs of inter-ethnic convergence, the children of immigrants do, however, exhibit ethnic-specific fertility profiles that may reflect distinct social and cultural backgrounds, whilst their high educational attainment is in turn associated with lower fertility and delayed childbearing, reducing socio-demographic differences across ethnic groups. Very low fertility levels for some immigrant and ethnic groups, as well as atypical age patterns in childbearing, seem to depart from the overall converging trends. A better understanding of the socio-demographic processes behind these very low levels and the specific age patterns would help to refine current assumptions of fertility convergence toward the national average across ethnic groups in UK population projection models. For instance, projection of fertility by women's educational attainment may increasingly capture more heterogeneity within the UK population than ethnicity. Importantly, analysing inter-generational fertility changes of migrants and second generations through the lenses of ethnicity may hide major social factors of change, as suggested by the first findings on education. Social inequality may lead to large differences in reproductive behaviour across the UK population (Berrington et al., 2015), and analysing fertility convergence between ethnic groups may hide socio-demographic heterogeneity within ethnic minorities. To truly unravel the picture, further research would help to clarify how ethnicity and social inequalities intersect to explain changes in childbearing and family dynamics in the UK.

NOTES

1. The work reported in this chapter has been supported by grants from the ESRC, the British Academy and John Fell Awards from the Oxford University Press.

2. For the relevant literature on fertility of immigrants in Europe and emerging evidence for the second generation, see Alders, 2000; Garssen and Nicolaas, 2008; Scott and Stanfors, 2011; Milewski, 2010; Dubuc, 2012.

3. Professional and managerial occupations counted for 68 per cent of the employed Indian immigrants between 2000 and 2004 against only 39 per cent of their Pakistani and 38 per cent of their Nigerian counterparts (Salt and Millar, 2006; percentages were calculated by me based on counts in Table 12: International migration flows of employed migrants between 2000 and 2004).

4. More than half of immigrant women of Chinese, White Other and Other ethnic designation arrived less than ten years prior to the survey. In contrast, 30 per cent of Bangladeshi and Pakistani women and only 15 per cent of foreign-born White British arrived within the nine years prior to the survey (Dubuc, 2012).

5. For instance, LFS data from 2001–2006 show that about 67 per cent of women aged fifteen to forty-nine came within the nine years preceding the survey (Dubuc, 2012).

6. Due to small numbers, the four mixed-origin groups were grouped together to produce fertility estimates.

7. The lower socio-economic status of early Chinese immigrants is supported by a study by Dustmann and Theodoropoulos (2010), showing a lower level of full-time education and the wages of early immigrant Chinese when compared to their contemporary White natives (born between 1933 and 1954).

8. For instance, the average 1987–2006 Period TFR of the Pakistani and Bangladeshi UK-born women remained about 47 per cent higher than the UK-born White British, but the difference is about 88 per cent and 123 per cent when foreign-born Pakistani and Bangladeshi women were considered.

9. About four out of five of women of fertility age in the UK are White British, largely contributing to the overall UK TFR (1.8 over 1987–2006). Therefore, using the White British majority ethnic group, the UK average or all UK-born women as alternative benchmarks to evaluate ethnic fertility convergence in the UK leads to similar results, although conceptually the choice of benchmark does make a difference.

10. Fertility of Pakistani immigrants recorded only a small decrease at older age between the periods 1987–1998 and 1998–2006.

11. ASFR decomposed by migrant status are not reported in Figure 5.4; perhaps due to small numbers, the differences in ASFR between the UK-born and immigrant generations of Chinese women were not large enough to be statistically significant.

12. Period total fertility estimates the average family size a woman would have if she experienced the age-specific fertility rate in that year across her entire reproductive lifespan. This provides estimates of recent trends but with some uncertainty, notably due to the changes in the timing (tempo effects) in childbearing behaviour.

13. Consistently, exploring Longitudinal Study data (LS-ONS), Robards et al. (2012) observed a peak of fertility for migrant women shortly after arrival in the UK.

14. Based on reverse survival techniques, LFS-OCM estimates comprise maximally fifteen years of fertility history of immigrant women, including fourteen years prior to the survey and independently of their arrival date in the UK (see Dubuc, 2012, on this and Dubuc, 2009, for an assessment of the LFS-OCM method).

15. A cohort analysis by ethnic or immigrant groups of women who have completed their fertility (above forty-five) would provide a good alternative to estimate the fertility of immigrants free of migration-specific tempo effect, providing the fertility

history of immigrant women is documented and numbers are large enough. However, such an approach would not allow the analysis of recent fertility patterns (including comparing with fertility of contemporary second-generation women).

16. The TFR for all immigrants (defined as overseas-born) estimated by the Office for National Statistics based on birth registrations (i.e., post-migration births) was 2.3 in 1991, 2.2 in 2001 (ONS, 2009). These estimates are useful for UK population projections, but they probably tend to overestimate immigrants' family size. In addition, the impact of immigrants' children left behind in the country of origin, which could impact on LFS-OCM fertility estimates, was estimated to be very small (overall only 0.2 per cent of the children arrived more than four years after their mothers; see Dubuc, 2012).

17. The coefficient of variation of TFR across ethnic groups of the two sub-categories (UK-born versus foreign-born women) was, respectively, 0.21 and 0.39 over 1987–2006. This holds true when excluding the White British from the analysis.

18. Early developments of the linear assimilation theory hypothesised a convergence in social profile towards the White British group taken as the 'reference group' and the 'mainstream', with the assumption that social convergence would follow cultural assimilation. Later developments relaxed this assumption, however, and the segmented assimilation theory (Portes and Zhou, 1993) identified additionally to the mainstream scenario, a downward path and an upward path of social assimilation.

19. Other studies (e.g., Rothon, 2005; Heath et al., 2008) have also provided evidence for high educational attainment of the children of Asian migrants to the UK.

Chapter 6

Children's Changing Family Context

Ursula Henz[1]

Over the last four decades, the place of children in the British population has changed considerably and their families have become more diverse. In 2011, 10.5 million children under the age of sixteen lived in Britain, constituting 19 per cent of the British population (ONS, 2015p), down from just over one-quarter in 1971 (ONS, 2010a). At the same time, the second demographic transition has unfolded in Britain, associated with declining fertility rates, increased numbers of children born outside marriage and greater levels of non-marital cohabitation and partnership breakdown, to name just a few aspects (Lesthaeghe, 1995). Children's lives have also been affected by the rising levels of qualifications amongst their parents, along with new labour-market opportunities, particularly for mothers.

These types of changes are already well documented on the household and family levels, but it is also important to see how family changes are reflected in children's family contexts. First, trends in children's families can differ from trends documented for parents, families or households. For example, the proportion of lone-parent families of all families is not the same as the proportion of children living with a lone parent if lone-parent families tend to have fewer children than couple families. Similarly, the proportion of mothers having three or more children differs from the proportion of children living in families with three or more children. Secondly, the experience of childhood has become more heterogeneous as families have become more diverse. This increasing diversity refers both to structural features and to diversity in the characteristics of parents, such as their age, ethnicity and labour-force participation.

Yet, with some honourable exceptions (Haskey, 1998; Clarke, 1992, 1996; Clarke and Joshi, 2003), few studies have described these transformations from the perspective of the children themselves. This is the primary aim of this chapter, as well as exploring trends in the diversity of contemporary childhood. It goes beyond the previous studies by addressing more recent changes and also by analysing a longer time period. It presents trends in children's family context during the past four decades, taking advantage of the accumulation of thirty-eight years of data from the General Household Surveys (GHS) and General Lifestyle Surveys (GLF) that span the years from 1972 to 2011. These repeated cross-sectional surveys are used to study trends over historical time as well as changes between children's birth cohorts.

Focussing on core demographic processes that can be addressed with the GHS/GLF data, the chapter examines three aspects of children's families: the size of the sibling group; living with a lone mother; and mothers' labour-force participation. After a separate section describing the data sets and the methods used to analyse them, the chapter takes each of the three topics in turn and examines the findings, giving particular emphasis to the changes that have been observed over time and between birth cohorts. The concluding section summarizes the main findings and discusses policy implications.

STUDYING CHILDREN'S FAMILY CONTEXT

As just mentioned, this chapter looks at three aspects of children's family context using the combined data of the annual General Household and Lifestyle Surveys from 1972 to 2011.[2] These hold information about 977,008 individuals, of whom 222,866 were aged fifteen or under at the time of the respective survey[3] and are henceforth referred to as 'children'. Children are coded into five birth cohorts: 1961–1970, 1971–1980, 1981–1990, 1991–2000 and 2001–2010.

The information on these five cohorts varies in its completeness. That for the 1971–1980 and 1981–1990 birth cohorts is most complete: the data represent children born during each of these calendar years for each year of age from zero to fifteen, with one small exception of children born in 1971 who are not observed during their first year of life. For the later birth cohorts, the data include children born during each of these calendar years, but for some cohorts it was not possible to cover the whole age range from zero to fifteen as data were not available.[4] The GHS/GLF assigns each individual household member to a 'family unit', which is either a married or cohabiting couple on their own or a couple or a lone parent with their never-married children, following the standard ONS definition of a family. Anyone who cannot be allocated to such a family is assigned to a separate 'non-family unit'. One household can consist of several family and non-family units. Three-generation families are divided into two separate family units according to the above definitions—the middle generation with children constituting one family unit and the oldest generation forming another family unit. Adopted and stepchildren belong to the same family unit as their adoptive or step-parents, respectively, whereas foster children constitute separate non-family units.

In what follows, family units constitute the basis for identifying children's parents because the information is consistent for all years and applicable irrespective of the size and complexity of the household. Parents are identified as living in the same family unit and being at least fourteen years older than their children. Whereas parents and children can be reliably linked in this way over the forty years, it is not possible to distinguish between biological, step and adoptive parents. Only since the 1996 survey is it possible to separate marital from non-marital cohabitation, so to ensure consistency since 1972 the paper does not distinguish between married and cohabiting parents, instead using de facto marital status. Lone mothers are mothers who are not married and do not live with a partner in the family unit.

Changes in the coding of educational levels over the survey years make it difficult to derive a fully consistent measure for educational attainment over the whole time period. The variable 'Mother's Education' has three categories: low level of education (being qualifications that generally do not give access to upper secondary education), medium level of education and degree. Over the study period the distribution of mothers' level of education has profoundly changed: in 1972 the vast majority of mothers, 85 per cent, had a low level of education, 8 per cent had a middle level of education and 7 per cent had a degree, whereas the respective figures for 2011 were 14 per cent, 46 per cent and 40 per cent.

Finally, it should be noted that, whilst the vast majority of children live with their parents, some do not. Out of the children covered by the data set, more than 99 per cent lived with at least one parent: 84.5 per cent with both a father and a mother, 13.4 per cent with a lone mother and 1.3 per cent with a lone father. About 0.4 per cent of all children lived with a grandparent, and about the same proportion lived with neither a parent nor a grandparent.[5] Also, not living with one's parents becomes more prevalent as children grow older. Whereas only 0.14 per cent of children under age one lived with a grandparent, this proportion increased to 0.62 per cent amongst fifteen-year-olds. Similarly, 0.21 per cent of children under the age of one lived neither with their parents nor their grandparents, increasing to 0.78 per cent amongst children aged fifteen. The percentages displayed in the figures below refer to all children who lived with at least one parent (Figure 6.1) or their mother (Figures 6.2–6.7).

The next three sections deal successively with the three selected aspects of family context—number of siblings, living with a lone mother and living with an employed mother—looking at trends over historical time, differences by mother's level of education and age-cohort trends.[6]

NUMBER OF SIBLINGS

The number of siblings with whom children grow up matters in many ways. First of all, the number of siblings affects the future structure of the collateral kin network; smaller sibling groups will reduce the future number of family relationships. In addition, the number of siblings is a good indicator for one's own number of children because children from large families tend to have more children themselves. The number of siblings also has implications for individual well-being. Children who grow up in larger families must share their parents' time and material resources with more siblings. This 'resource dilution' is regarded as one reason for the lower educational attainment of children from larger families (Downey, 1995; Conley and Glauber, 2008). From this perspective, a decline of larger sibling groups might be beneficial for children, whereas an increase would be seen as detrimental.

Whether sibling groups become larger or smaller over time depends first and foremost on fertility rates, which have fluctuated considerably over the past forty years. The UK's total fertility rate (TFR) was 2.4 in 1971, declined rapidly to 1.69 in 1977, then stayed around 1.8 before dropping further in the late 1990s to a minimum of 1.63 in 2001, before rising to 1.91 by 2011 (ONS, 2014d). The TFR, however, is also influenced by the level of childlessness, which dropped from about 13 per cent amongst women born in the early 1930s to 11 per cent for those born in the early 1940s and 9 per cent in the 1946 birth cohort, steadily increasing thereafter to reach 20 per cent for those born in the 1960s (ONS, 2012f; see also Table 2.2 in this volume's Chapter 2). Because of increasing levels of childlessness, lower fertility rates do not necessarily imply that the average child lives in a family with fewer children. Levels of childlessness only affect the rates of first birth. If the higher-order birthrates were to remain unchanged, children's number of siblings should not change, either. Some higher-order birthrates for England and Wales have, however, fallen (Frejka and Sardon, 2007). We now examine how the combined changes of fertility rates have played out for children.

Analysis of the GHS/GLF data set reveals that, over the last four decades, the average number of co-resident children (aged fifteen or under) in families has decreased from 2.0 to 1.7—that is, families with co-resident children have shrunk on average by 0.3 children over the study period. This decrease was smaller than the decrease in the average number of siblings experienced during the same period, which dropped from 1.5 to 1.0.

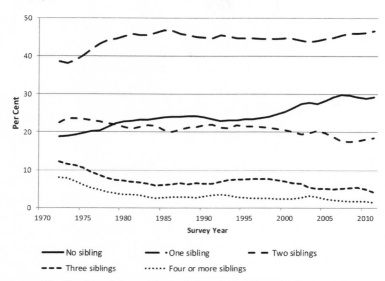

Figure 6.1a Distribution of Co-resident Siblings in Family Unit, by Survey Year.
Source: General Household/Lifestyle Surveys, own calculations.

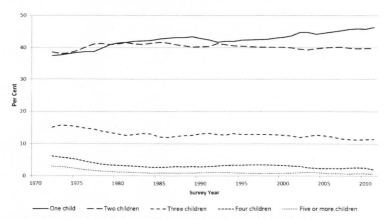

Figure 6.1b Distribution of Co-resident Children in Family Unit, by Survey Year.
Source: General Household/Lifestyle Surveys, own calculations.

Figure 6.1a displays the distribution of the number of siblings aged under sixteen who lived with the child in the same family unit at the time of the survey. In all years, living with just one sibling was by far the most common configuration, with more than 40 per cent of all children living with one sibling since the late 1970s. The proportion of children who were the only child in a family unit (from now on 'only children') amongst all children has increased over the last four decades from 19 per cent in 1972 to 29 per cent in 2011. Most of the rise occurred either prior to 1985 or between 2000 and 2008. Since 1979, being an only child was the second most common sibling configuration. The proportions of children living with two, three or four or more siblings have declined over the observation period from 43 per cent to 24 per cent, though with a moratorium during the 1990s.

This picture contrasts with trends at the level of families (shown in Figure 6.1b). In 1972, the two largest types of family were families with two children and those with one child, contributing 39 per cent and 37 per cent, respectively, of all families. Larger families were considerably less common, with families with three, four and five or more children constituting 15 per cent, 6 per cent and 3 per cent, respectively, of all families. By 2011, one-child families had become the most common family type, with 46 per cent of families falling into this category. The proportion of families with two children remained quite stable around 40 per cent, whereas the other types declined to 11 per cent, 2 per cent and 0.7 per cent, respectively—a distribution similar to that of dependent children reported by ONS (2015r). Altogether, the most common family type in recent years was the one-child family, whereas the most common sibling configuration was living with one other sibling, illustrating the value of the children-focussed perspective taken in this chapter.

The number of siblings with whom a child lives can vary over the child's life course and is often lower than the total number of children of the mother. Looking at all children in the data set (not shown here), 24 per cent of them were only children, but as many as 42 per cent were an only child when they were born, dropping to 39 per cent when they were one year old, 29 per cent when they were two years old and 13 per cent when they were seven years old. From this age onwards, the proportion of only children increased again to 24 per cent at age twelve and 42 per cent at age fifteen. Correspondingly, the proportion of children who lived with two or more siblings was 22 per cent amongst children aged under one, rising to 40 per cent amongst eight-year-olds and decreasing to 24 per cent amongst fifteen-year-olds. These variations in the number of co-resident siblings should correspond to a variation in the resources that parents can provide for each child at least as far as time resources are concerned. Thereby, the negative effects of large sibling groups on child development might apply differently to each child in a family.

How does the number of siblings vary between families from different socio-demographic groups? Figure 6.2a compares the average number of siblings by mothers' educational attainment. In all survey years, children whose mother had a low level of education tended to have more siblings than children whose mother had attained a higher level of education. In 1972, children of a mother with a low level of education had on average about 1.6 co-resident siblings, whereas children from mothers with a degree had about 1.4 siblings and children of mothers with a medium level of education

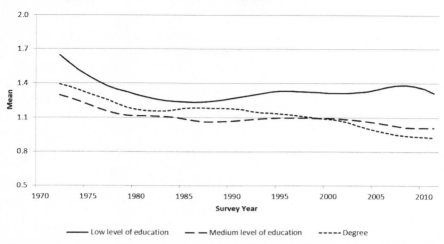

Figure 6.2a   Average Number of Co-resident Siblings, by Survey Year and Mother's Level of Education.
Source: General Household/Lifestyle Surveys, own calculations.

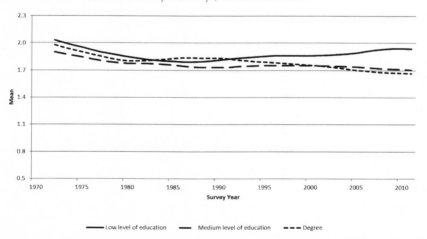

Figure 6.2b   Average Number of Co-resident Children, by Survey Year and Mother's Level of Education.
Source: General Household/Lifestyle Surveys, own calculations.

had only about 1.3 siblings. Following a decline in the number of siblings during the 1970s, which affected all educational groups, the differences in the number of siblings between the three groups were at their lowest, with a maximum gap of 0.2 around a total average of 1.15 siblings.

After a period of stability during the 1980s, opposite trends emerged from the early 1990s onwards. In the late 2000s, the number of siblings increased amongst children born to mothers with a low level of education to a high of 1.4, whereas it decreased slightly for children of mothers with a medium level of education to 1.0 and more strongly to 0.9 amongst children whose mothers had a university degree. Interestingly, only since about 2000 do the children of mothers with a university degree have fewer co-resident siblings than other children. The increasing gap between children of mothers with a low level of education, on the one hand, and those of mothers with medium or high educational qualifications, on the other hand, corresponds to the increasing selectivity of the group of mothers with a low level of education, which switched from the majority group to a rather small minority amongst all mothers.

The differences by mother's level of education were more modest if they are examined at the family level (Figure 6.2b). Before the year 2000, mothers with different levels of education differed by no more than 0.12 in their average number of children. This small gap increased to about 0.25 at the end of the study period.

Overall, the figures demonstrate considerable change in the number of co-resident siblings. Children are less likely today to live in large sibling groups than they were in the past. Whereas 43 per cent of children lived with two or more siblings in the early 1970s, their proportion has dropped to 24 per cent in recent years. However, they still constitute a sizeable group. The number of siblings varies considerably during the course of childhood. Differences in sibling size by mother's level of education were modest, but they increased towards the end of the observation period, pointing to somewhat larger siblings groups amongst children from low-educated mothers.

CHILDREN LIVING WITH LONE MOTHERS

Lone motherhood was a key focus of Kiernan's chapter on family change in Joshi's volume, reflecting the growth in lone-parent families in Britain during the 1970s and 1980s (Kiernan, 1989). Lone-parent families have grown from a small minority of 8 per cent of families in 1971 (ONS, 2010a) to just over a quarter (26 per cent) in 2011 (ONS, 2012g), though with little of this change occurring in the last ten years. The increase was associated with the rising trend of childbirth outside marriage and increasing divorce rates. Since the 1960s, the proportion of children born outside marriage has risen from 5.4 per cent in 1960 and 8.4 per cent in 1971 to 47.2 per cent in 2011 (ONS, 2015g). Although many of these children were born into cohabiting unions, they still had a higher risk of living with a lone mother at some point of their childhood than children born in marriages because of the lower stability of non-marital unions compared to marriages (Clarke and Jensen, 2004). But even the latter were growing less stable, with divorce rates starting to rise in the 1960s, increasing strongly in the 1970s and remaining at a high level during the 1980s and 1990s before decreasing in the new millennium (ONS, 2011a). About half (49 per cent) of couples divorcing in 2011 had at least one child under age sixteen living in the family, but down from 62 per cent in 1970 (ONS, 2011a).

Children growing up with a lone mother have stood out as a particularly vulnerable group in virtually all Western societies. In the UK, they are twice as likely to be severely materially deprived as children living with both parents (ONS, 2014e). Family income in childhood is a strong predictor for future disadvantage. In addition, poverty is often related to higher levels of stress in families, which can in turn affect child development.

The higher levels of poverty in lone-parent families are due to lower levels of employment and lower levels of state transfers to support lone parents. Since 1998, the UK government's 'New Deal for Lone Parents' has encouraged employment amongst lone mothers, for example through tax credits (Gregg et al., 2009). Although the policy was successful, the difficulties of combining paid work and caring responsibilities still limit lone mothers' access to the labour market and to well-paid jobs (Millar, 2010).

Many lone-parent families get established due to a divorce. A large body of research has identified increased risks of psychological, behavioural and health problems for children after divorce (see Klett-Davies, 2016, for a review). However, recent, more complex, statistical analyses have suggested that many of these problems might not be caused by parental divorce itself but by pre-existing conditions and that many effects of divorce are only temporary (Amato, 2010; Härkönen, 2014). Even if the effects that can be attributed to divorce are more modest than presumed earlier, there is little doubt about the increased levels of vulnerability of children who grow up in lone-parent households.

The results of analysing the GHS/GLF data are broadly consistent with the official statistics mentioned above, with the proportion of children living with lone mothers steadily increasing during the last three decades of the twentieth century from 5 per cent in 1972 to 22 per cent in 2001. They differ, however, in their post-2001 trajectory, with the GHS/GLF data indicating a gradual decrease thereafter, down to 19 per cent in 2011, in contrast to the stability of the ONS data. This is perhaps not surprising, given Haskey's (2002) observation of considerable disparities when using different surveys to estimate the number of children living with lone parents with different surveys, and it is beyond the scope of this chapter to resolve this issue.

Figure 6.3 depicts the percentage of children living with a lone mother by children's age and comparing the five birth cohorts. For each successive ten-year birth cohort, a higher proportion of children lived with a lone mother during their first year of life. The first full estimate is available for the 1971–1980 cohort, where about 6 per cent of children lived with a lone

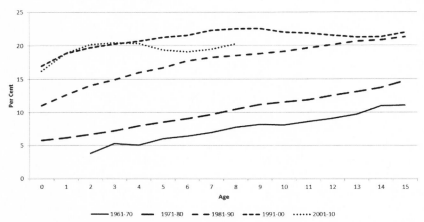

Figure 6.3   Per cent of Children Living with a Lone Mother, by Child Age and Birth Cohort.
Source: General Household/Lifestyle Surveys, own calculations.

mother during their first year of life. In the 1981–1990 cohort, the proportion had increased considerably to 11 per cent and further to 17 per cent in the 1991–2000 cohort. There was no further increase in the youngest cohort.

As children aged, some of them moved between lone-mother and two-parent families through their mothers' separation, re-partnering or, in a few cases, widowhood. Figure 6.3 documents how the proportion of children living with a lone mother increased as children aged, reaching about 11 per cent amongst fifteen-year-old children in the 1961–1970 cohort, 15 per cent in the 1971–1980 cohort and 21 per cent in the younger cohorts. The cohort comparison suggests that, in each subsequent cohort except the youngest, a higher proportion of children was affected by parental divorce. The large gap between the 1971–1980 and 1981–1990 cohorts indicates a particularly strong change taking place during the childhood of these children. This might be related to divorce behaviour, as during those years parents started to separate more often than before when younger children were involved.

The lines for the youngest birth cohorts suggest that the increase in the proportions of children who live in a lone-mother family has come to a halt or even reversed. A halt would correspond to the overall trends reported by the ONS about no change in the percentage of children living with a lone mother. The evidence for a reversal should be treated as tentative because it occurs in those calendar years when the GHS/GLF surveys report a drop in children living with lone mothers in contrast to the statistics published by the ONS.

Children of lone mothers have a high risk of living in poverty because lone mothers experience more difficulties in accessing the labour market. Figure 6.4a shows the percentage of children who live with an employed

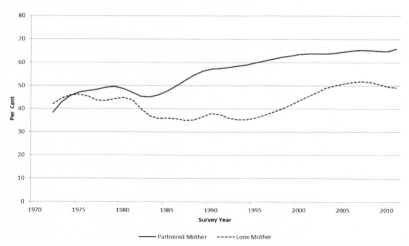

Figure 6.4a Mothers in Employment, by Survey Year and Mothers' Partnership Status: Per cent of Children Living with a Mother in Employment.
Source: General Household/Lifestyle Surveys, own calculations.

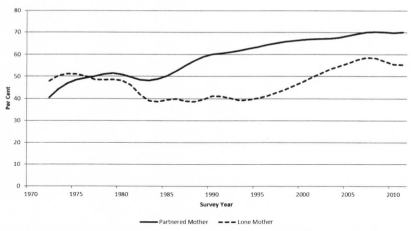

Figure 6.4b Mothers in Employment, by Survey Year and Mothers' Partnership Status: Per cent of Mothers in Employment.
Source: General Household/Lifestyle Surveys, own calculations.

mother—one in paid work for at least one hour per week—separately for partnered and for lone mothers. In the mid-1970s, about 45 per cent of children had an employed mother, irrespective of whether the mother was partnered or not. A gap between the two groups of children emerged during the 1980s, when a higher proportion of children of partnered mothers had a mother in employment than children of lone mothers. In the early 1990s, only 35 per cent of children of lone mothers had a mother in employment compared to about 58 per cent of partnered mothers. However, from the mid-1990s onwards, the increase in having a mother in paid work was stronger amongst children of lone mothers than amongst children of partnered mothers, leading to a narrowing of the gap to about 15 per cent in 2011.

Figure 6.4b shows the percentage of mothers in employment, separately for partnered and lone mothers. A comparison of Figures 6.4a and 6.4b shows that the proportions of children with mothers who are in employment are lower than the proportions of mothers who are employed. For example, only 35 per cent of children of lone mothers had an employed mother in the late 1980s, whereas 39 per cent of lone mothers were employed. By 2011, the mothers of 49 per cent of children of lone mothers were employed compared to 55 per cent of lone mothers. These differences reflect the well-known negative relationship between women being in paid work and their number of children. In other words, increases in mother's employment rates do not directly translate into increases in the proportions of children living with employed mothers. It is also noteworthy that the decrease in the employment rates amongst lone mothers in the early 1980s coincides with a marked increase in the proportion of younger children living with a lone mother (cf. Figure 6.3), which might have contributed to the decrease in lone mothers' employment. The increase in the late 1990s has been related to welfare reforms, particularly the introduction of the Working Families Tax Credit and the New Deal for Lone Parents (Gregg et al., 2009), though the exact temporal link is difficult to pin down with the smoothed GHS/GLF data.

Finally, what relationship is there with the educational level of the mother? Figure 6.5 shows that, whereas the differences between educational groups were small in the early 1970s, they grew strongly thereafter. By the mid-1980s, a child of a mother with a low level of education was twice as likely to live with a lone mother as children of mothers with a university degree (13 per cent versus 7 per cent), and the gap further increased over the later decades. The latter was partly due to the onset of the decline for children of a mother with a degree, which preceded the decline for those with low-education mothers. In the 2000s, up to a third of children of mothers with a low level of education had a lone mother compared to less than a quarter amongst children whose mother had a medium level of education and, at most, a sixth of children whose mothers had a degree.

In sum, this section has shown, first, that living with a lone mother has become more common for all ages of children, including the very youngest. Secondly, the newest cohort does not show any further increase in the proportion of children living with a lone mother. Thirdly, over time, the increase in children living with a lone mother is seen to have been most pronounced in

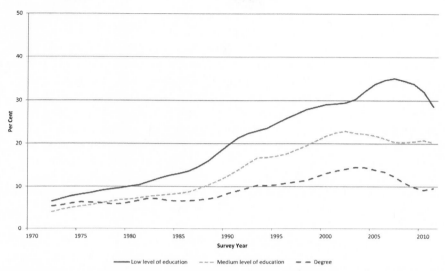

Figure 6.5 Per cent of Children Living with a Lone Mother, by Survey Year and Mother's Level of Education.
Source: General Household/Lifestyle Surveys, own calculations.

families in which the mother had a low level of education. Finally, children of lone mothers more often live with a mother who is not employed than children living with a partnered mother, but this gap has narrowed in recent years.

CHILDREN LIVING WITH EMPLOYED MOTHERS

This section focusses in more detail on mothers' employment status, as the increased labour-force participation of mothers has also altered children's family context. As Joshi highlighted in her own chapter in the previous volume, women's increasing economic independence was a key feature of the 1970s and 1980s (Joshi, 1989b). Women's labour-force participation rose from 53 per cent in 1971 to 67 per cent in 2013 (ONS, 2013c). Meanwhile, the gap in employment rates between mothers and childless women has nearly closed in recent years, with 66 per cent of mothers and 67 per cent of childless women being employed in 2010 (ONS, 2011b). Amongst the reasons for this narrowing are the rising age of motherhood and the decline of employment amongst younger women during the recent recession (ONS, 2011b).

Mothers' labour-market participation affects children's lives in a number of ways. Most important, children can profit from the additional financial resources of the family, which might improve their health and life prospects. Mothers' employment has also been associated with changes in couples' division of household work and increases of fathers' involvement in child-care. As a result, less traditional gender role ideals might be transmitted to children. On the other hand, mothers' paid work can lead to a decline in the time that parents spend with their children. In fact, according to time-use research on the USA (Sayer et al., 2004), the relationship between mothers' employment and time in childcare is more complex than this. Whereas full-time mothers spend less time in childcare than part-time mothers, the decline in childcare hours due to overall trends in mothers' employment has been compensated by a general trend of parents spending more time in childcare. Therefore, concerns about mothers' involvement in paid work have shifted to concerns around parents' stress from combining paid work and childcare and its possible effects on children. Increasing hours of mothers' employ-ment also means that more parents rely on an informal network of family and friends for childcare or on formal childcare.

According to the GHS/GLF data set, the proportion of children with a mother in employment has increased pretty steadily, rising from 38 per cent in 1972 to 50 per cent in 1980, dropping down to 42 per cent in 1982 fol-lowing the 1980–1981 recession and then increasing again to 64 per cent in recent years. These figures include the many mothers working for less than fifteen hours per week; without these, the proportions drop by nearly 20 per cent before the early 1990s and 10 per cent during the 2000s. Only a small minority of children had a mother who worked more than thirty-five hours per week—stable at around 10 per cent up to the mid-1980s and then rising slowly to about 16 per cent in 2011. These figures emphasize that most children have grown up in families where parents displayed traditional or neo-traditional gender roles and that change towards a less traditional gender division of paid work has been slow.

Figure 6.6 shows how the experience of growing up with a mother in employment (paid work for at least one hour per week) has changed over the course of childhood for children in different birth cohorts. According to Figure 6.6a, mothers' employment rate has increased with the child's age in all birth cohorts. Whereas in the 1971–1980 cohort only about 12 per cent of children had an employed mother during their first year of life, this figure increased to 70 per cent by the time the child reached fifteen years of age. Figure 6.6a also shows a dramatic increase in mothers' employment rates in the first year of life of the child over the different birth cohorts, rising from about 12 per cent in the 1971–1980 cohort to about 48 per cent amongst chil-dren born in the new millennium. The increase was particularly large between children born to the 1981–1990 cohort and those to the 1991–2000 one. Care is needed in interpreting the decline of the proportion of children living with an employed mother around age six in the youngest birth cohort because of the limited time span so far available for this group.

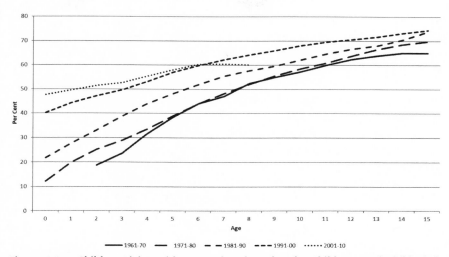

Figure 6.6a Children Living with an Employed Mother, by Child Age and Child Birth Cohort: Per cent of Children Living with a Mother Who Is in Paid Work for at Least One Hour Per Week.
Source: General Household/Lifestyle Surveys, own calculations.

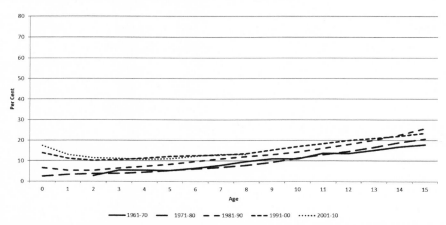

Figure 6.6b Children Living with an Employed Mother, by Child Age and Child Birth Cohort: Per cent of Children Living with a Mother Who Is in Paid Work for More than Thirty-Five Hours Per Week.
Source: General Household/Lifestyle Surveys, own calculations.

Changes in the proportion of children with an employed mother at age fifteen were comparatively modest, rising from 65 per cent in the 1961–1970 cohort to 74 per cent in the 1991–2000 cohort. Another way of describing the trends is by looking at the age by which half of all children in a birth cohort had a mother in employment. This occurred between age seven and eight in the 1961–1970 and 1971–1980 cohorts; dropping to between age five and six for the 1981–1990 cohort and between age three and four for the 1991–2000 one. In the 2001–2010 cohort, the proportions for ages one and two were very close to the 50 per cent threshold.

The effects of mother's labour-force participation on children's lives depend on the number of hours that the mother was in paid work, growing with the hours worked. If one counts only children whose mother worked for at least sixteen hours per week, the increase over children's age and cohorts was less pronounced than that shown in Figure 6.6a. The proportion of children with a mother working for at least fifteen hours in the child's first year of life increased from 7 per cent in the 1971–1980 cohort to 40 per cent in the 2001–2010 cohort, but amongst fifteen-year-old children the percentage increased from 50 per cent in the 1961–1970 cohort to 62 per cent in the 1991–2000 cohort (figure not shown). The changes in having a mother who worked full time were much more modest (cf. Figure 6.6b). In the 1971–1980 birth cohort, the proportion of these children increased from less than 3 per cent in their first year of life to about 21 per cent at age fifteen. In the later cohorts, the share of children with full-time employed mothers decreased over the first two years of the child's life because mothers on maternity leave still count as employed. At age two, the share of children with a full-time employed mother was about 5 per cent in the 1981–1990 cohort and increased to between 10 and 12 per cent in the younger cohorts. At age fifteen, about 26 per cent of children in the 1981–1990 cohort and 23 per cent of children in the 1991–2000 cohort lived with a full-time employed mother.

Children in different socio-economic positions differ in their experience of living with an employed mother, as shown in Figure 6.7. In all survey years, children were most likely to have a mother in employment if the mother had a degree. In this group, the proportion of children with an employed mother was above 50 per cent in all survey years and has reached proportions of 75–80 per cent since the mid-1990s. The trends for children of mothers with a medium level of education closely followed the trend for children of mothers with a degree, but at a 10–15 per cent lower level. In contrast to these trends, the propensity of having a mother in employment did not increase amongst children whose mothers had a low level of education; it even decreased from the 45–50 per cent levels of most survey years up to 2003 to below 40 per cent.

It is therefore clear that changes in mothers' employment, albeit in terms of part-time rather than full-time work, have also served to alter children's family context, in this case with particular impact on the early years of childhood. Also evident is that the effects are likely to be greater for the children of highly educated mothers than those of less educated mothers.

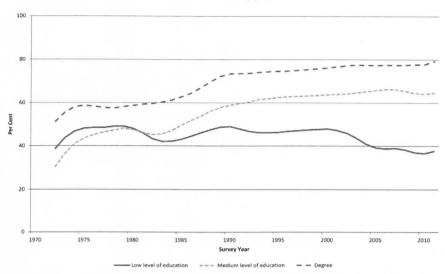

Figure 6.7   Per cent of Children with an Employed Mother, by Survey Year and Mother's Level of Education.
Source: General Household/Lifestyle Surveys, own calculations.

CONCLUSION

This chapter has explored selected changes that have taken place in the family context of children during the past four decades. In one way or another, all the three topics studied can be linked to precarious living circumstances for children, with implications for their financial, social and emotional well-being, both in childhood and in later life. Children in large families, children of lone mothers and children of mothers who are not employed are at a higher risk of poverty than children in other types of families. Two of these circumstances are less common today than they were forty years ago, which indicates improving conditions under which children have grown up. In contrast, the third circumstance—living with a lone mother—has become more widespread.

The general trend to smaller family size has reduced the pressure on parental resources and might lead to more opportunities for development amongst children, but it also results in a decreasing availability of lateral kin and shrinking family networks, meaning that future adults will have to rely more than previous generations on friends for support. This is of concern because, for example, friendship networks tend to be less involved than family members in providing care to frail or elderly people.

Lone-mother families are exposed to high risks of poverty (Klett-Davies, 2016). Over the last four decades, increasing proportions of children have grown up in lone-mother families. Whereas in older birth cohorts the prevalence of living with a lone mother increased strongly with children's age, more recent birth cohorts also experienced high levels of living with a lone mother from birth. As research evidence about the importance of the early years of life for future life chances is accumulating, the large number of young children who live in a lone-mother family needs particular support. This should take the form of financial support where needed, as well as high-quality childcare like that provided in the Sure Start children centres.

The increase in the percentage of children who live with a lone mother has come to a halt in the most recent birth cohorts. This can be regarded as positive for children's well-being, but it is most likely related to increased levels of re-partnering amongst lone mothers. Although the risk of material deprivation is lower in stepfamilies than in lone-mother families, recent research suggests that family instability (Osborne and McLanahan, 2007) and living in a stepfamily (Sweeney, 2010) might also be associated with depressed levels of child well-being.

This chapter has shown that, over successive birth cohorts, children lived at an increasingly younger age with a mother in employment; for nearly half of all children in the latest cohort, their mother was employed during the child's first year of life. On the other hand, only a minority of mothers was employed full time even when children were in their teens. Despite lower household incomes, it might actually be advantageous for pre-school children if their mother works less than full time, as it tends to be associated with better cognitive skills and educational attainment (Ermish and Francesconi, 2001; Han et al., 2001; Hansen et al., 2006; Heinrich, 2014). Whether mothers work full time or part time, the availability of affordable high-quality childcare becomes a major concern.

The expansion of early education and childcare including free childcare for the three-to-four-year-olds has provided children from all backgrounds with access to high-quality childcare. However, the quality of formal childcare tends to be lower for children in disadvantaged areas, at least according to Ofsted assessments (Gambaro et al., 2013). Mothers' increased labour-force participation has been accompanied by increased involvement of fathers in childcare. The extension of parental leave policies has supported British parents in their efforts to combine their worker and parent roles, but many parents still struggle with inflexible workplaces. If fathers are expected to further increase their involvement in childcare and make up for mothers' rising labour-force participation, work-life policies should be developed that are tailored towards both parents' needs (Daly and Hawkins, 2008).

In sum, when looking across the last forty years at the three aspects examined in this chapter, one notices a widening gap in family circumstances between children of mothers with a low level of education and other children.

For the former, the key features are a larger number of siblings and a greater likelihood of living with a lone mother and living with a mother who is not employed. At the other end of the spectrum, children whose mother has a university degree are more likely to have a co-resident father figure, a mother in employment and fewer siblings. Policy interventions should target children of mothers with a low level of education to improve their life chances. Existing policies for giving mothers access to better qualifications should be further expanded as a sustainable way for improving their access to stable jobs.

NOTES

1. Acknowledgements: The Office for National Statistics (ONS) conducted the General Household Surveys 1972–2007 and the General Lifestyle Surveys 2008–2011. The data was accessed through the UK Data Service (UKDS). Neither ONS nor UKDS bear any responsibility for the analysis and interpretation of the data. The research has received funding from the Suntory and Toyota International Centres for Economic and Related Disciplines. I thank Professor Yaojun Li for his valuable support with upgrading the GHS/GLS Time Series Data set.

2. There were no GHS surveys in 1997 and 1999. The GLF stopped being a household survey in 2012 and was discontinued after 2012. The data analysed in this chapter extend the GHS Time Series Data from 1972–2004 provided by the ONS (ONS, 2007).

3. By limiting the analyses to children under the age of sixteen, the reported trends are not affected by the profound changes in educational enrolment and labour-market entry that took place during the study period.

4. In the 1961–1970 birth cohort, the data hold information about children born in all years from 1961–1970 for ages eleven and older, but observations for younger children tend to be drawn from children born in the later years of 1961–1970. Similarly, the data represent children from all birth years for the 1991–2000 birth cohort for children up to age eleven, but the sample of older children does not include children from the latest birth years. Finally, for the 2001–2010 birth cohort, information about older children is provided only in the earlier years. The under-representation of particular birth-year-age combinations in some cohorts means that the estimates for the affected ages in these cohorts are biased towards the adjacent cohort in the data set.

5. Grandparents and their grandchildren should normally not belong to the same family unit except when the grandparent is responsible for looking after the grandchild.

6. The findings displayed in the charts are based on smoothed data, meaning that it is not possible to provide standard errors.

Chapter 7

Household Composition and Housing Need

Ann Berrington and Ludi Simpson[1]

After a century of falling household size that stimulated rates of house-building over and above those of population growth (see Murphy, 1989, in Joshi's book), that trend has subsequently stalled, with average household size remaining steady in the twenty-first century so far. As we show in this chapter, the increase in number of households is now outpacing the volume of new housebuilding. Population growth and population ageing have been adding to demand for extra housing and will continue to do so, but the supply-side response has been deficient. As a clear sign of the increasing pressures on the housing stock, young adults have been less likely to form independent households—a process that started in the 1990s, well before the 2007 banking crisis and subsequent recession. The extent to which this reduction in household formation is structural or temporary is still impossible to identify, but the main unknown to future housing needs continues to be change in population numbers.

This chapter examines how changes in population and household composition are influencing housing demand in the UK. The chapter is aimed not only at students of demography but also at analysts and policymakers grappling with issues relating to housing the current and future UK population. We draw on data published in the most recent, 2012-based, household projections produced by the Department for Communities and Local Government (DCLG, 2015a). Household projections show household numbers that would result if the assumptions based in previous demographic trends in the population and rates of household formation were to be realised in practice. Household projections can be criticised for the way in which they can encourage circularity in planning: lower recent headship rates due to economic recession and lack of availability and affordability are projected forward as reduced housing need. Thus, fewer houses will be built, leading to further pressures on availability and affordability (Bate, 1999). Nevertheless, these projections provide a useful basis from which to explore past and future trends in household formation.

The chapter begins with definitional matters and by briefly reviewing the current housing context. The following section examines the role of demographic factors in increasing housing demand. Then we apply a simple decomposition technique to quantify the relative importance of demographic factors and household structure. Finally, we consider the evidence of single people and families being 'concealed' within households, some of whom would wish to have separate housing. We have provided UK figures where possible, but because of the different approach to household projections by each of the national statistical agencies, later discussion focusses on England, and London within it.

BACKGROUND

The Nature of the Evidence

Data sources differ in their definition of a *household*, but here we will generally be using the 2011 Census definition that is consistent across all countries of the UK—that is, 'one person living alone, or a group of people (not necessarily related) living at the same address who share cooking facilities and share a living room or sitting room or dining area' (ONS, 2014f). *Household composition* classifies households according to the relationship between members of a household. A household might consist of just one person, or more than one in a family or multiple families, and with or without others not in a family. The distribution of households according to their composition is affected by numerous factors including age structure of the population, average number of children per family, levels of partnership formation and dissolution and the likelihood that multiple families live together within a complex household. The likelihood of forming a household is captured by the *household representative rate*, measuring the number of households per person in the *household population*, which excludes those in communal establishments like care homes and student halls of residence. Thus, an average household size of 2.0 equates to an overall household representative rate of 0.5. Household representative rates are generally calculated for separate age groups to identify the likelihood of being in an independent household rising with increasing age. They require the identification of a household 'head', 'reference person' or 'representative', which in UK statistics is not self-identified but dependent on age, sex and sometimes economic activity. Household representative rates are the same indicator as the more common 'headship rate', a term that has been avoided in this chapter because of its implication of responsibility within the household. Representative rates reflect the preferences and constraints facing individuals in forming a separate household.

To facilitate forward planning in the public and private sectors, the DCLG makes regular *projections* of the future likely number of households for England and its local authority districts. The devolved administrations for Wales, Scotland and Northern Ireland make similar projections. These household projections are trend-based, informed by the projected population and projected household representative rates (broken down by age and sex) and by Census and Labour Force Survey data. They are therefore driven by assumptions both on future levels of fertility, mortality and migration and on future patterns of household formation behaviour relating to the way that this population groups into household units as measured by household representative rates (Welsh Government, 2011; DCLG, 2015a).

Household projections form the starting point for the objective assessment of future need for housing, as set out in government guidance (DCLG, 2015b), but the need for housing is different from the household projections for a number of reasons. The number of *dwellings* needed is not the same as the number of households they accommodate. Some households share a front door (the main criteria for a separate dwelling or unit of accommodation), whilst there are always some dwellings that are unoccupied—vacant or being used as second homes or holiday homes. This adjustment between future households and need for housing is small in comparison with the likely underestimation of housing need by household projections due to 'suppressed' demand. Because household projections are based on recent trends, they reflect only the 'effective demand' (Planning Advisory Service, 2014), a market-driven concept that relates to the 'quantity and quality of housing which households will choose to occupy given their preferences and ability to pay (at given prices)' (Bramley et al., 2010: 25). Evidence for suppressed demand, which is not included in the effective demand that official projections measure, can be seen in the growing numbers of both young adults remaining in the parental home (Berrington and Stone, 2014) and multiple families within a household (Smith, 2014), as is examined in more detail later in the chapter.

The Housing Crisis

The current housing crisis can best be seen as a mismatch between need for housing and its provision. We have already indicated that official household projections are an underestimate of housing need. Figure 7.1 indicates that, nonetheless, the rate of housebuilding in the UK in the first four years of the

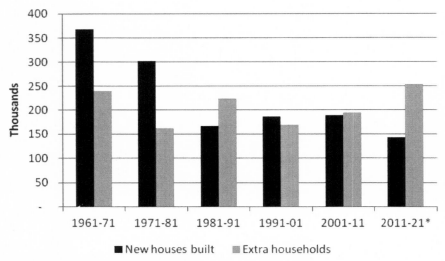

Figure 7.1   Change in Number of Households and Housebuilding, Annual Averages for Decades 1961–2021, England.
Note: 2011–2021: households as projected in DCLG annual average (2015b), housing completions annual average 2011–2014.
Source: DCLG live tables of households, household projections and housing completions.

2010s was 100,000 per annum lower than the demand indicated by household projections. By contrast, in the 1960s and 1970s, housebuilding exceeded demand partly because a lot of old sub-standard housing was demolished, but it is also associated with fewer families having to share accommodation; after that, until the 2000s, housebuilding more closely matched changes in the number of households.

The UK housing crisis of the late 2000s and early 2010s has a number of dimensions—too few, too expensive, in the wrong places or of poor quality (Moore, 2015). These aspects are inter-related, but their relative importance for an individual will differ depending on geographical locality, income group, life course stage and so forth—different segments of the population facing different problems. Just as there are many features of the housing crisis, multiple factors are responsible: often these are presented as a list (Chu, 2014; Moore, 2015), with their relative importance being a matter of debate (Dorling, 2014). Key issues are the shortage of available housing and lack of affordability.

Housing Availability

Figure 7.2 shows the total number of new houses built in the UK each year from 1920 to 2013, with a breakdown into those built by the private sector (for rent as well as for sale) and the contribution made by the public/housing

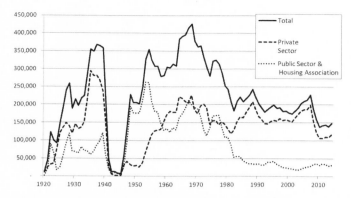

Figure 7.2 Annual Numbers of New Houses Built, UK, 1920–2014.
Source: From 1946: DCLG live tables of housing completions. Earlier: Scottish Government (2014, chart 3) and Holmans (2005); Northern Ireland, less than 5 per cent of UK total, included only from 1948.

association sector (nowadays commonly referred to as 'social housing'). Following World War II, housebuilding increased, peaking in the late 1960s before declining through to the early 1980s; the number was then roughly stable until 2008, when building dropped dramatically to a new low.

Reasons for the more recent lack of new build include the global financial crisis, land supply and the cost of land, as well as planning regulations (Shelter, 2015). Wilcox et al. (2015: 8) argue that 'greater supply of land with planning permission is generally acknowledged as a key factor in boosting supply'. However, planning regulations insist that Local Plans permit an amount of land for housing at least as great as the household projections indicate, unless any shortfall is made up by neighbouring local authorities (DCLG, 2015b). The regulations bind the government Planning Inspectors' approval of Local Plans and thus ensure a supply of land commensurate with or greater than the projection. Thus, lack of housebuilding appears to also result from an inability, unwillingness or lack of resources to build, rather than from the supply of land. Whitehead and Williams (2011) highlight implications of global economic uncertainties on the number of housing starts together with the changes in the National Planning Policy Framework and moves towards a localised community-planning control regime. Whitehead and Williams (2011) believe that a considerable number of planning proposals have been abandoned as a result of the removal of output targets for local authorities.

Housing Affordability

There are a number of reasons why housing has become less affordable, especially for young adults (Kennett et al., 2013). These include the faster increases in house prices than earnings, especially for first-time buyers (Whitehead and Williams, 2011; McKee, 2012). Over and above house-price inflation, it has been access to credit that has been a key factor: following the global financial crash in 2008, lenders have been less willing to provide mortgages with a high loan-to-value ratio. Large mortgage deposits are required, which are generally unaffordable for young adults without assistance from others, usually parents (Kemp, 2015). At the same time, cuts to welfare benefits have meant that lower-income households are also finding it more difficult to cover their housing costs. Post-recession austerity measures include the reduction in the value of the Local Housing Allowance, the overall welfare cap and the restriction of the value of housing benefits for single people aged under thirty-five to a level required to rent a room in a shared property (Rugg et al., 2011; Berrington and Stone, 2014; Tunstall, 2015).

For some population sub-groups (e.g., wealthier couples who are both in work), affordability of owner occupation has actually improved in recent years—at least outside of London—primarily as a result of reduced interest rates (Wilcox et al., 2015). Government interventions have also targeted first-time buyers (FTBs): in 2014 around one-third of the 311,000 FTBs were helped on the 'housing ladder', a further third were supported by parents and just a third made it on their own (Wilcox et al., 2015). Whilst there is some evidence that the buying propensity of young adults recovered a little in 2014 except for the very youngest age groups (Clarke, 2015), government-funded schemes such as Help to Buy 'risk making matters worse by increasing purchasing power without resulting in a commensurate increase in the supply of new homes. Hence, the average house price-to-income ratio for FTBs will remain at very high levels for the foreseeable future' (Kemp, 2015: 14).

Lack of affordability and residualisation of the social housing sector means that low-income families are increasingly looking to the private rented sector (Kemp, 2011). Figure 7.3 shows the proportion of household reference persons renting privately by age in 2001 and 2014. Renting privately was always commonplace amongst those in their early twenties, but this century's increase has affected older adults: today around one-half of household representatives in their late twenties and over one-third in their early thirties are renting. This is the life-course stage when having children and insecurity of tenure can become a serious issue (Kemp, 2015).

Whilst there have been previous housing crises—for example, in supply during the immediate postwar period or of affordability due to high mortgage interest rates (Malpass, 1986; Bramley, 1994)—new elements of the current crisis include inter-generational inequalities in housing as a result of the retirement of cohorts who own their own homes and the rising importance of the private-rented sector in response to the lack of affordability of owner occupation and the residualisation of the social-rented sector. Property has become an 'attractive speculative investment', leading to buy-to-let (Dorling, 2014).

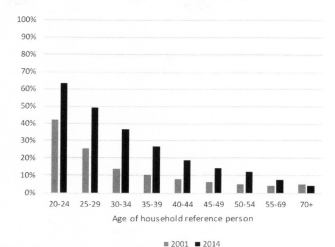

Figure 7.3   Percentage Private Renting by Age of Household Reference Person, 2001 and 2014, UK.
Source: Authors' analyses of Labour Force Survey.

Private landlords have benefited from the increased reliance on private-rented accommodation that has resulted from the lack of affordability to buy.

DEMOGRAPHIC CHANGES AND HOUSING NEED

In this section, we focus on the measurement of housing demand based on past numbers of households and on projections into the future, as well as evidence of additional need for housing from individuals and families not in independent households.

Population Growth

Since 2004 the UK population has grown much faster than previously, by around 450,000 per year as compared with around 150,000 a year in the 1990s. Much of this acceleration is associated with an increase in the level of net migration to the UK (see Chapters 1 and 4). Since 1998 the rate of natural increase has also risen, in part an indirect effect of the fertility of recent immigrants (see Chapter 5), but also due to an increase in the level of fertility amongst UK-born women during 2002–2012.

The precise impact of increased international migration on housing demand is difficult to quantify since immigrants to the UK tend to be young and live in larger, more complex households (Whitehead, 2011; Holmans, 2013). One simple estimate of the percentage of the future number of households that are due to projected net international migration assumes that the household representative rate of that extra population is the same as the overall population. Using the 2011-based DCLG household projections and an ONS projected net migration figure of around 122,000 a year, Heath (2014) calculated that 27 per cent of England's extra households is due to immigration. Using a different approach, with foreign birthplace to represent all the surviving residents who have ever immigrated to the UK, ONS have estimated that the increase in foreign-born household reference persons is equivalent to around 66 per cent of the 1.96 million increase in households that took place in the UK between the 2001 and 2011 censuses (Migration Watch, 2015). However, any international migration is bound to change the balance of foreign-born and UK-born householders, so that a faster-growing number of foreign-born householders is to be expected. The 2012-based DCLG household projections (DCLG, 2015c) suggest that net migration will account for one-third of household growth between 2012 and 2037.

The housing careers of immigrants in the years following arrival in the UK are likely to be different from those of the UK-born as a result of both constraints and preferences regarding living arrangements (Stone et al., 2011; Holmans, 2013). However, we do not have enough empirical evidence to know what the medium- and longer-term impacts will be (Robinson et al., 2007). Furthermore, their concentrations in particular geographical localities mean that the impact on local housing markets can be quite different from the overall impact (Whitehead, 2011).

Population Ageing

The UK population is ageing and will continue to do so for the first half of this century (see Chapters 1 and 2). On Census day in 2001 there were 1.01 million people aged eighty-five or over. By 2011 this had increased by a quarter to 1.25 million, accounting for 2.2 per cent of the whole population, compared with 1.9 per cent in 2001. Older people tend to live in smaller households: 59 per cent of the population aged eighty-five-plus in England and Wales lived alone in 2011, as compared with just 10 per cent of those aged twenty-five to thirty-four (ONS, 2014g). Household representative rates are therefore higher at older ages, with the result that population ageing increases the number of households for a given overall population size, as we discuss further below in the context of projections.

Changing Household Composition

Average Household Size

Average household size in both England and Wales, as well as in Scotland, declined almost continuously from 4.8 per household in 1851 to around 4.3

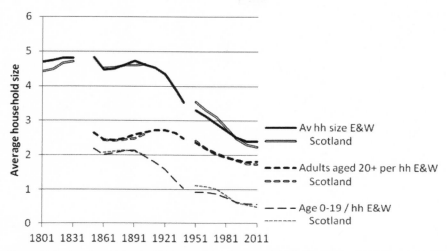

Figure 7.4   Average Household Size and Adults Per Household, 1801–2011, for England and Wales and Scotland.
Source: 1801–2001 censuses and 1939 population registration analysed by Holmans (2005), and 2011 Census analysed by authors.

in 1921, 3.5 in 1939, 2.7 in 1981 and 2.4 in 2001. As can be seen in Figure 7.4, up until the mid-1950s, the majority of this reduction in household size was due to declining fertility that reduced the average number of residents aged under twenty. However, from the 1920s there was also a decline in the number of resident adults in each household, indicating a spreading out of the adult population between more households.

This trend to smaller households is associated with both the ageing of the population and higher household representative rates at most ages. Both act to increase the proportion of one- and two-person households, which rose dramatically over the half century to 2011 (Figure 7.5). For example, in Scotland the percentage of households that consisted of just one or two persons increased from around two-fifths (41 per cent) to over two-thirds (69 per cent). The continuously upward trend is also seen in Wales, England and Northern Ireland.

Household projections made before the 2011 Census made assumptions that continued the decline in average household size (DCLG, 2010a), but in fact the decline stalled with average household size in 2011 being 2.24 in Scotland and 2.40 in England and Wales, having been 2.31 and 2.41, respectively, in 2001. Reasons for this misalignment between the projected decline and the observed stability include the projections over-estimating household representative rates for young adults and an unanticipated increase in concealed households (Holmans, 2013). We can also see from Figure 7.5 that the

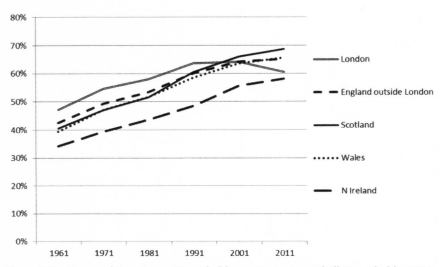

Figure 7.5   One- and Two-Person Households as a Percentage of All Households, 1961–
2011, for London, England, Outside London, Scotland, Wales and Northern Ireland.
Source: Authors' analyses of national Census results.

upward trend towards more one- and two-person households has slowed in
the past decade and actually reversed in London after stabilising in the 1990s.

Household Representative Rates

In order to understand more closely what is happening to household composition, it is instructive to look at household representative rates for each age
and sex, shown in Figure 7.6. For these official projections, the eldest male
is taken as the household representative; hence, if a woman is in a couple,
she will have a household representative rate of zero. As in most countries,
men's representative rates rise sharply between the fifteen-to-nineteen and
thirty-to-thirty-four age groups and then increase more slowly to reach a
maximum close to one for men aged in their sixties and early seventies. For
women, we typically see representative rates increase through their early
and mid-twenties as young women leave the parental home and establish
independent households, some living outside a couple. The rate then remains
fairly constant until women reach their sixties, when representative rates rise
significantly, often as a result of widowhood.

What is of particular interest are the deviations from this general pattern
observed in England over the period 1991–2011 (Figure 7.7). Over these
twenty years, household representative rates amongst women have increased
in young adulthood, and especially in midlife, but have declined for those aged

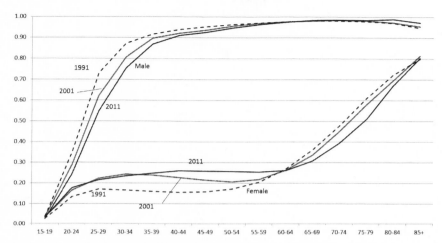

Figure 7.6   England Household Representative Rates, 1991, 2001 and 2011, for Males and Females by Age.
Source: DCLG (2015d).

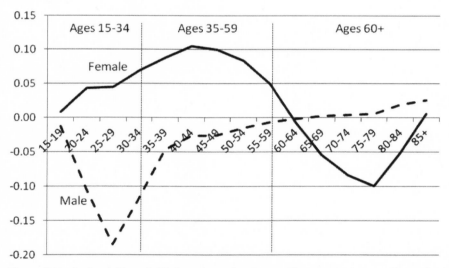

Figure 7.7   England Household Representative Rates, Change 1991–2011, for Males and Females by Age.
Source: DCLG (2015d).

in their seventies and early eighties. Amongst men, we observe a steep decline in representative rates, especially amongst those aged in their late twenties. These trends reflect both period and cohort changes in the household composition. First, in young adulthood, women are nowadays less likely to leave home to form a co-residential partnership but are more likely to be living alone or sharing accommodations (Stone et al., 2011)—hence the increase in their household representative rates. Furthermore, men especially are increasingly likely to remain in the parental home in their late twenties (Berrington and Stone, 2014).

In midlife, the rise in representative rates for women results from increased partnership dissolution and lone parenthood (Demey et al., 2011). However, women currently aged in their seventies and early eighties (who were born in the late 1920s and early 1930s) are more likely to be living in a couple household than those born previously. This is due to several factors: increased longevity (especially for males), being far more likely to have married (they were part of the golden age of the family in the post-war 1950s economy) than those born ten years earlier, and not experiencing the rise in divorce of subsequent cohorts (Murphy, 2011). As there appear to be three main age ranges at which change appears to have occurred—fifteen to thirty-four, thirty-five to fifty-nine and sixty-plus)—we use these three age groups within our decomposition in the next section, where we quantify the extent to which overall change in household numbers results from population increase, population ageing, the changing relationship composition of the population and representative rates conditional upon age group and relationship status.

UNDERSTANDING THE DRIVERS OF HOUSEHOLD GROWTH

In this section, we use a simple decomposition to quantify the relative importance of each driver of household growth. We examine observed growth from 1991 to 2011 and then the growth projected in the 2012-based DCLG household projections (DCLG, 2015d). The DCLG projections are for England only, and we focus on England because the different methods of projection used for each country that makes up the UK preclude an amalgamated dataset. London is shown separately to investigate its special pressures as already highlighted in Figure 7.5, but we do not show data for the rest of England as its patterns are very similar to those for England as a whole. In what follows, we first describe the technical calculations that inform Table 7.1 below, then describe the drivers of observed population growth from 1991 to 2011 and finally examine the future contributions to household growth in the period 2011–2037, according to the DCLG projections.

The Decomposition Method

The overall number of households can be written as $\Sigma_{a,s,r}$ (household population x representative rate), where 'a', 's' and 'r' correspond to age, sex and relationship status. Changes in the household population can result from

(a) overall population growth; (b) changes in the age and sex composition; and (c) changes in the distribution by 'relationship' status, which in the DCLG work identified whether each person was in a couple and, if not, whether they had been divorced, separated or widowed.

To examine the role of changing representative rates amongst adults, as mentioned above we use three broad age groups: young, fifteen to thirty-four; middle, thirty-five to fifty-nine; and older, sixty-plus. To obtain the impact of total population growth, we apply the age and relationship-specific household representative rates from the start of the time period to the new population total without changing the age structure. To obtain the impact of changes in age structure and relationship status composition, we repeat the exercise using the starting population's household representative rates, the new population total, the new age composition and then relationship status composition at the end of the time period. Adding these together provides the total change in the number of households due to population change, the 'all population impact' in Table 7.1.

Next, we apply the new household representative rates for the end of the time period to the old population as at the start of the period. The sum of the effects for our three broad age groups is the total effect of changes in household representative rates, the 'all rates impact' figure in Table 7.1. Finally, the interaction effect represents the way in which the impacts of population and the household representative rates are interrelated: for example, the growth of a population group that has relatively high household representative rates will further boost the household change.

Drivers of Past Household Growth, 1991–2011

Table 7.1 shows the results of the decomposition for England as a whole and for London separately. Looking first at the results for England (first two data columns in the top panel), we can see that during the period 1991–2001 an average of sixty-two thousand additional households were formed annually simply because the population grew in total size. A further fifty-nine households were created due to a shift in age-sex composition—mainly the baby boom generation born during the 1960s coming into older adult ages when almost all are in couple households. Between 2001 and 2011 the number of households grew at a faster rate than the previous decade, with 152,000 extra households being formed per year as a direct result of total population growth and a further 37,000 as a result of changes in age composition—this time towards a more elderly population where households tend, more than at any other age, to consist of just one or two adults. In both decades, shifts in the proportions in each relationship status, particularly a reduction of elderly women living alone, led to a reduced number of households.

Table 7.1   Decomposition of Observed and Projected Household Change, 1991–2037, for England and London

| England | Thousands Per Year | | | |
	1991–2001	2001–2011	2011–2021	2021–2037
Total population	+62	+152	+161	+135
Age-sex composition	+59	+37	+59	+66
Relationship status	−9	−8	−18	−9
All population impact	+111	+181	+201	+192
Rates 15–34f	+6	−6	+3	+3
Rates 15–34m	−10	−24	−3	−5
Rates 35–59f	+6	−2	+5	+4
Rates 35–59m	+3	−2	+3	+3
Rates 60-plusf	+8	+6	+3	+2
Rates 60-plusm	+1	+1	+1	+1
All rates impact	+14	−27	+13	+7
Interaction	+10	+4	+5	+4
Total household change	+136	+158	+219	+204

| London | Thousands Per Year | | | |
	1991–2001	2001–2011	2011–2021	2021–2037
Total population	+21	+37	+44	+35
Age-sex composition	+3	−1	+11	+14
Relationship status	+2	+1	−0	+0
All population impact	+27	+36	+54	+49
Rates 15–34f	−1	−3	−0	+0
Rates 15–34m	−4	−7	−2	−1
Rates 35–59f	+1	−1	+1	+1
Rates 35–59m	+0	−1	+0	+1
Rates 60-plusf	+1	+0	+1	+1
Rates 60-plusm	+0	−0	+0	+0
All rates impact	−3	−11	+0	+2
Interaction	+0	−1	+1	+1
Total household change	+24	+24	+55	+52

Source: Authors' calculations using DCLG's 2012-based household projections detailed data.

Changes in household representative rates had less impact on the number of households. During the 1990s, an increase in the number of young (aged fifteen to thirty-four) women-headed households was matched by decreases amongst men. In the 2000s, whilst there was just a slight decline in the propensity of young women to form their own households, representative rates amongst young men fell dramatically, effectively reducing household growth by twenty-four thousand each year. Amongst those aged thirty-five to fifty, household formation increased for both men and women, partly due to delayed partnership formation but also increased partnership instability and a growth in the number of lone parents. During the 2000s, these trends are not so apparent. For both decades, the older population, given their relationship status, exhibit more independent living with higher representative rates.

For London (lower panel of Table 7.1), the number of households grew by 24,000 a year in both 1991–2001 and 2001–2011. Almost all of this growth was due to an increase in total population. Changes in the population age structure and relationship composition had only a minimal impact on household growth, whilst in both decades household representative rates, especially for those aged under thirty-four, declined.

Drivers of Future Household Growth, 2011–2037

The 2012-based projections (DCLG, 2015a) estimate that the number of households in England will reach 27.5 million in 2037, up from 22.3 million in 2012—an average annual growth of 210,000 per year, even greater than that seen for 2001–2011. Table 7.1 (last two data columns) indicates that over two-thirds of this household growth is projected to result from increases in the total population, whilst changes in population age structure (primarily the ageing of the large 'baby boom cohorts' born in the 1960s) will also significantly add to household growth. It is noticeable that the projections assume that changes in household representative rates will have little further impact on the future growth in the number of households in England as a whole, increasing slightly for women but reducing slightly for young men, reflecting the view that the recent decrease in household formation amongst young adults will not be reversed over this period. Future population ageing means that the proportion of one- and two-person households will increase, which explains why the projections suggest that the number of households will increase faster than the household population, and, as a result, average household size in England is projected to fall from 2.35 to 2.21 (DCLG, 2015a).

Turning to London, the lower panel of Table 7.1 shows that annual projected household growth is twice that seen in 2001–2011. Annually, more than fifty thousand extra households are estimated to require accommodation, more than one-quarter of all the projected increase in demand for England. This growth is being driven almost entirely by population growth and changes in the population age composition. If not all this growth can be accommodated in London, some must be converted into migration to areas outside London if the capital's housing pressures are not to become even greater (see Chapter 8).

Since the calculations in Table 7.1 were made, updated national population projections show a slightly more rapid increase, mainly due to upwardly revised projections of international migration, amounting to 534,000 more people in 2037 (ONS, 2015k). This translates into approximately a further five to ten thousand households per annum. It emphasises that the growth in population and the uncertainty in that growth are the major factors in assessing overall need for housing.

FURTHER EVIDENCE OF CHANGES IN
LIVING ARRANGEMENTS, 2001–2011

The 2011 UK Census results suggested that there had been unanticipated changes in household composition over the previous decade, halting the century-long decline in average household size. Two key changes are discussed below: the tendency for increased co-residence between adult children and their parents, and an increase in the number of multi-family households.

Young Adults' Living Arrangements

An increasing proportion of young adults are co-residing with their parents (Figure 7.8). The trend for increased co-residence predates the economic recession (Berrington and Stone, 2014), but it is likely to have been accentuated by it, especially amongst young men. The vast majority of those living with their parents do not have a family of their own, but between 2000 and 2014 there was an increase, especially for women in their twenties, in the proportion living with either a partner or a child in a multi-generational household. Institutional changes, including increased participation in higher education, change to the youth labour market and delay in the age at which family formation occurs, mean that young men and women are nowadays less likely to leave home upon partnership formation. Those who leave the parental home for reasons other than family formation are more likely to return home, the so-called Boomerang Generation. Evidence from longitudinal data suggests that young people return when they require support, such as after finishing full-time education, ending a job or through partnership dissolution (Stone et al., 2014).

To some extent, the changing living arrangements of young adults result from the delay in family formation to later ages. The likelihood of being married by age thirty has declined dramatically in England and Wales: over half (59 per cent) of men born in 1962 were married by age thirty compared to just over one-third (36 per cent) of men born in 1972 and one-quarter (24 per cent) of those born in 1982 (ONS, 2014h). However, the increase in cohabitation means that the proportion living in a couple has remained steady at ages twenty-five and above, although there has been a decline for those aged under twenty-five associated with a concomitant increase in the proportions either

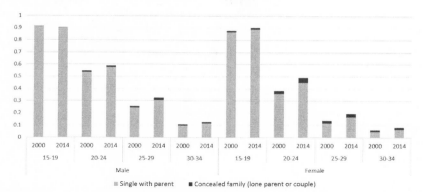

Figure 7.8 Percentage of UK Young Adults Living with at Least One Parent, by Whether Single or Living as a Concealed Family.
Note: The term *parent* includes grandparents, stepparents and foster parents. Students living in halls of residence during term-time and living with their parents outside term-time are counted as not living with their parents.
Source: Authors' analysis of ONS Special Table of UK Labour Force Survey.

living with their parents or sharing accommodations (Berrington and Stone, 2014). The proportions of young adults living with their parents vary across the UK, most notably with higher co-residence in Northern Ireland.

The postponement of family formation and decrease in rates of household formation are both associated with the changing nature of the transition to adulthood, which is becoming more protracted and non-linear. The drivers of young adults' living arrangements are diverse. Some are more structural and long-standing, including cultural shifts in expectations for the age at family formation, institutional shifts in the proportions attending higher education and increased economic uncertainty resulting from globalization and the changing nature of the youth labour market. Others are associated more obviously with the global recession of the late 2000s, such as restrictions on access to credit, increased austerity and reductions in the generosity of welfare (Berrington and Stone, 2014). It is thus difficult to predict whether the depressed household formation will continue.

The Rise in Concealed Families

Concealed families are used as an indication of potential extra housing need. They are defined as a second family living in a household that does not include the representative of the household. The concealed family may be a married or cohabiting couple with or without children, or a single-parent family. Thus, concealed families are different from and extra to the single adults in their parental home discussed above.

Table 7.2 Households and Concealed Families, 1951–2011, for England and Wales

Year	Households (Thousands)	Concealed Families (Thousands)	Households Plus Concealed Families (Thousands)
1951	13,259	935	14,194
1961	14,724	702	15,426
1971	16,871	426	17,297
1981		No census data	
1991	20,213	273	20,486
2001	21,825	170	21,995
2011	23,740	289	24,036

Source: Censuses analysed by Holmans (2014: 4).

As shown in Table 7.2, concealed families have been measured by the Census since 1951, and their more than halving in number over the next twenty years has been taken as an indicator of the success of housing policy then. However, for England and Wales the sharp increase to 289,000 in 2011 suggests that it would be useful to reintroduce the category in future projections so as to provide planners with an indication of unmet need for housing. Prior to 2008, concealed family representative rates had provided projections of the number of concealed families for this reason (DCLG, 2010b).

Concealed families are particularly common amongst young adults. The 2011 Census for England and Wales shows 13 per cent of all families with a reference person aged under twenty-five are concealed in other households (16 per cent in London). Not all concealed households represent unmet need, and the proportion that does represent unmet need varies with cultural norms. For example, a larger number of adults per household in the Asian communities is partly a reflection of desired household arrangements (Smith, 2014; Catney and Simpson, 2014).

CONCLUSION

Until the mid-2030s, housing demand in England is projected to increase even faster than in recent decades, largely as a result of the increasing size of the population resulting from both natural increase and sustained net immigration, the latter now projected to be 170,500 per year (ONS, 2015s). Given that net international migration was estimated to be over 330,000 for the year ending March 2015, some have questioned whether the impact of international migration on future household growth is underestimated (McDonald and Whitehead, 2015). Any uncertainties in migration projections therefore feed into uncertainties in housing projections, not only at the national level but also at the local level. There are also uncertainties about assumptions regarding the types of households that future immigrants are likely to form.

Furthermore, there are a number of reasons why trend-based projections—which essentially project forward recent behavioural trends—are only the starting point for planning to meet housing need. First, they do not take account of physical limitations such as crowded urban areas or of planning restrictions such as the green belt around urban areas. Secondly, the projection assumes that recent levels of household formation will continue into the future, including the significantly lower rates of household formation amongst young adults. Whilst this may seem reasonable in the short term, the projections are predicated on past effective demand and exclude suppressed demand represented by delayed partnerships and concealed families, which could usefully be re-introduced into projection outputs to help estimate a more complete picture of the need for housing. Thirdly, the mismatch between the need for and the supply of housing is, above all, due to a lack of appropriate housing at the lower end of the income range.

There is a problem of low supply of housing driving up prices for homebuyers, putting pressure on social housing and driving up the cost of private renting. Additionally, there is a mismatch between the price of housing including rents and the available incomes, especially for younger people. The mismatch can probably be tackled only by investment in social housing, given that initiatives to encourage home buying or expand housing supply have been successful only at the margins. As noted by McDonald and Whitehead (2015), recent rates of housebuilding for the four years 2011–2012 to 2014–2015 have been sufficient to supply only half the homes identified in the DCLG projections for England. This means that more houses would have to be built in the forthcoming years to reach a target that is already likely to be unachievable. This probable deficit of housebuilding is likely to be highest in London and the South East, where the growth in the number of households is anticipated to be largest.

The lack of housing availability may well act to reduce household formation to levels lower than that predicted in the 2012-based projections. Whilst this would reduce the demand for housing, a less obvious housing crisis could emerge—one where poorer standards were the expectation. The Royal Institute of British Architects (RIBA), using government guidelines for minimum reasonable standards, noted that 'more than half of the new homes built today are not big enough to meet the needs of the people who buy them' (RIBA, 2015: 3).

Planning for housing need in the UK would benefit from greater investment in household statistics and their analysis. Different and changing approaches to housing projections in each country of the UK make the time series difficult to construct, but the more serious problem that assessments of housing need must face is incomplete data. For example, household projections for England rely on incomplete analysis of the Census, which may affect both the projections and our decomposition of change (Simpson and McDonald, 2015). Furthermore, estimates of England's household numbers between 2001 and 2011 are linearly interpolated rather than estimated directly, making the impact of the economic shock of 2008 more difficult to trace.

The biggest unknown, arguably, is the nature of the reduction in effective housing demand that has taken place since the turn of the century. Although more of a halt in overall rates of household formation than a real reduction, the increased number of those remaining in parental or shared households who would previously have found separate accommodation is real enough for those affected. Having indicated the variety of causes in this chapter, further work should be focussed on understanding the long-term structural changes that may be involved and on developing scenarios that indicate how the current housing crisis may best be overcome.

The level of overall population growth is by far the biggest driver of housing demand. Revisions to national population projections that acknowledge the long-term increase in net migration to the UK emphasise this driver. This, however, will not strongly affect the confident projection of an ageing population that also increases housing demand. Behavioural changes do have some impact that differs between age groups. Judging by Scandinavian standards where over 40 per cent of households are of one person compared to the UK's 30 per cent (Jamieson and Simpson, 2013), the currently stalled average household size discussed in this chapter has not reached a lower limit. Whilst small in their impact compared to population growth and ageing, behavioural changes in living arrangements are legitimate targets of social policy. Governments can help to maintain the currently tight relationship between income and independent living amongst new generations, or they can find ways of subsidising affordable housing. These policies will determine whether housing is mainly geared to monetary demand or to satisfying wider aspirations to adequate housing for all.

NOTE

1. The authors thank the Department of Communities and Local Government, who provided advice about data sources, and the Family Team within the Office for National Statistics (ONS) for their advice on data sources and for producing a special table from the UK Labour Force Survey. The editors provided helpful comments on a draft version of the chapter, and comments on presentations to the British Society of Population Studies and the British Academy were valuable stages in the chapter's development. The ONS and Northern Ireland Statistics and Research Agency carry out the UK Labour Force Survey. Data were made available with permission of the UK Data Service. The UK Census is Crown Copyright.

Chapter 8

Internal Migration and the Spatial Distribution of Population

Tony Champion

This chapter examines the changing spatial distribution of the UK population and the drivers of this, with a particular focus on internal migration. In doing this, it compares the latest trends with those of the 1970s and 1980s documented by Champion (1989) in Joshi's book. It is able to identify elements of both continuity and change. Back then, the key themes were seen as the North-South divide, the exodus from the cities and the inner-city problem, all associated to some extent with increasing social polarization. That review had also felt the need to start by justifying the inclusion of a chapter devoted to sub-national patterns as well as bewailing the inadequacy of data on local area populations, especially as it had been written eight years after the most recent Census—a period of great turbulence following the recovery from the 1980–1981 recession and the various shocks instigated by Thatcherism.

A quarter of a century on, there is no need to make the case for examining regional and local variations, not least given the devolution trend under New Labour and the subsequent focus on localism and for combined-authority agreements in England. There have also been some substantial improvements in the scope and quality of data relevant to this chapter, especially on migration, traditionally the least well measured of the demographic components. As regards the principal dimensions of spatial redistribution, the North-South divide is still a source of national concern, but the drivers of this have changed, as shown in the next section. Secondly, although there is still net migration out of cities, there has been a major urban recovery since the 1980s, with city-centre population growth tending to upstage inner-city issues. In the third section, the chapter probes a newly recognized development concerning the declining frequency with which most types of people are moving home, which is becoming more apparent now that four decades of data are available.

THE NORTH-SOUTH DIVIDE

The 'North-South drift' has been a key dimension of population redistribution in the UK since the peaking of its Industrial Revolution over a century ago, and it was thus a central theme of Champion's (1989) review. This remains the case, but as this section shows, the faster growth of the South is no longer driven by net migration from the North but by its greater attraction of international migration and its stronger natural increase. Though the balance of migration between the two parts of the UK fluctuates over time principally in line with the business cycle, the long-term trend since the 1970s has been for the attenuation of the southward flow, to such an extent that the average for 2001–2014 was a small net flow northwards. Nevertheless, the much larger gross flows behind the latter are still serving to further unbalance the UK economically because of their selective nature, with the southbound migrants tending to be more concentrated on young adults, the high skilled and no doubt the ambitious than the reverse flow.

The long-term trend in regional growth can be seen from Table 8.1. The five regions making up the South can be seen to have accounted for the

Table 8.1   Population Change, 1971–2011, by Country and English Region

Country and English Region	Population (000s)			Population Change Rate (% for Decade)			
	1971	*2011*	*Change*	*71–81*	*81–91*	*91–01*	*01–11*
UK: Total	55928.0	63285.1	7357.1	0.77	1.92	2.91	7.06
Northern Ireland	1540.4	1814.3	273.9	0.17	4.17	5.07	7.43
Scotland	5235.6	5299.9	64.3	−1.06	−1.87	−0.38	4.65
Wales	2740.3	3063.8	323.5	2.67	2.11	1.29	5.28
North East	2678.5	2596.4	−82.1	−1.58	−1.87	−1.81	2.22
North West	7107.8	7056.0	−51.8	−2.36	−1.40	−1.02	4.18
Yorkshire & Humberside	4902.3	5288.2	385.9	0.33	0.36	0.82	6.26
West Midlands	5146.0	5608.7	462.7	0.79	0.83	0.98	6.21
North: Total	29350.9	30727.3	1376.4	−0.45	−0.20	0.25	5.11
East Midlands	3651.9	4537.4	885.5	5.50	4.12	4.44	8.30
East	4454.3	5862.4	1408.1	9.00	5.48	5.46	8.55
London	7529.4	8204.4	675.0	−9.62	0.36	7.22	12.05
South East	6829.7	8652.8	1823.1	6.05	5.33	5.17	7.84
South West	4111.8	5300.8	1189.0	6.61	6.95	5.44	7.23
South: Total	26577.1	32557.8	5980.7	2.11	4.20	5.66	8.96
South's share (%)	47.5	51.4	81.3				
South's premium				2.56	4.40	5.41	3.85

Note: English region is the former Government Office Region. South's premium refers to % point excess of South over North.
Source: Calculated from ONS midyear population estimates; Crown copyright data.

lion's share of the UK's overall population growth over the forty years since 1971, contributing almost 6 million out of the 7.4 million, or 81 per cent. This was greatly in excess of its 47.5 per cent share of the UK's total population in 1971 and served to raise this share to 51.4 per cent in 2011, this on less than one-third (32.8, not shown in the table) of the UK's land area.

Table 8.1 also shows that the South East region was the largest contributor to UK growth over this four-decade span, accounting for a quarter (24.8 per cent) of national population growth, followed by the East of England with just under one-fifth (19.1 per cent). These are the regions that together surround the Greater London Authority (GLA) area and include not only part of the capital's labour market area but also some of its suburbs. The GLA's 'under-bounding' of London explains why, on this statistical definition, its share of national growth was less than one-tenth (9.2 per cent). Yet that is only part of the explanation: in the earlier part of this period, London was in the doldrums in terms of population trend, dropping by almost 10 per cent between 1971 and 1981, but since then it has staged a remarkable recovery, with its decadal growth rate rising progressively (see the right-hand columns of Table 8.1). Its 12 per cent growth rate for 2001–2011 represents an increase of 882,000, or over one-fifth (21.1 per cent) of UK growth for this decade, hugely above its 0.7 per cent share of the UK's land area.

The corollary of the South's strong growth is that the North punches below its weight. This has been the case throughout the period shown in Table 8.1, but was most noticeable in the first two decades when it experienced overall decline, this due to losses for Scotland and the North East and North West regions of England. These three most northerly parts of mainland Britain continued their decline into the 1990s, but since 2001 there has been a marked uplift in growth rates across the North. In fact, the acceleration in growth then occurred nationwide, but the degree of uplift was greater in the North than the South, despite London's strong showing then. The upshot of this is that the South's growth premium over the North reduced to 3.9 per cent points in 2001–2011, after progressively rising over the three previous decades.

These trends raise questions about the drivers of both the South's long-term supremacy, especially the role of North-South migration, and the more recent recovery of the North, including whether it survived the economic recession of 2008–2009. Direct answers are provided in Table 8.2, which splits down the 2001–2014 overall growth rates for North and South into pre- and post-recession periods and also distinguishes between its three major demographic components. The story cannot be taken back before 2001 because the split between international and within-UK migration components is not available then, and even after 2001 there is an element of migration that cannot be divided between these two at the sub-national level. Nevertheless, the main elements of the picture are clear. Over the full period from 2001 to 2014, the

Table 8.2 **Population Change and Its Main Components, 2001–2014, for the UK's South and North**

Area	Total Change	Natural Increase	International Migration	Within-UK Migration
2001–2014				
UK	0.68	0.29	0.37	0.00
South	0.88	0.39	0.49	0.00
North	0.48	0.19	0.25	0.00
South-North	0.40	0.20	0.24	0.00
2001–2008				
UK	0.64	0.22	0.39	0.00
South	0.80	0.32	0.52	−0.04
North	0.48	0.12	0.26	0.04
South-North	0.32	0.19	0.26	−0.09
2008–2014				
UK	0.73	0.37	0.35	0.00
South	0.98	0.48	0.46	0.05
North	0.48	0.26	0.24	−0.05
South-North	0.50	0.22	0.22	0.09

Note: Data refer to per cent per annum, compound rate. North and South are as shown in Table 8.1. The three components do not always sum to the total change rate partly because of rounding but also because the latter includes 'Other changes', which mainly comprise unexplained change arising from the comparison of 2011 Census results with the population estimates rolled forward from 2001.
Source: Calculated from ONS midyear population estimates and components of change; Crown copyright data.

South's faster growth was due to a combination of a higher rate of net immigration from abroad and stronger natural increase. By contrast, net within-UK migration played no part in this, because in addition to the rate being zero for the UK as a whole by definition, it was also zero for both its parts.

As regards the difference between before and after the onset of recession in 2008 (shown in the two lower panels of Table 8.2), it is found that nationally the annual average growth rate rose somewhat between the two periods, up from 0.64 to 0.73 per cent. This can be seen to be entirely due to the South's growth strengthening from 0.80 to 0.98 per cent, as the North's rate stayed at 0.48 per cent, this leading to the renewed widening of the North-South divide. The primary cause of the South's acceleration was the substantial uplift in natural change between the two periods, but this also occurred in the North to almost the same degree. The main reason for the rise in the South's growth premium after 2008 was a switch in the within-UK migration balance in favour of the South in contrast to the net flow being towards the North in the previous seven years.

The longer-term context of migration between North and South is shown in Figure 8.1, reinforcing the point that net 'drift' to the latter is now but a pale shadow of its former self. Whilst its most obvious feature is the short-term fluctuations that are largely associated with the way in which cycles of boom

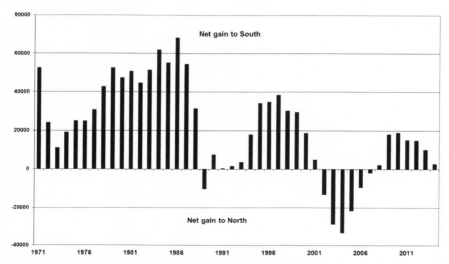

Figure 8.1   Net Migration from North to South of UK, 1971–2014.
Note: See Table 8.1 for definition of North and South.
Source: Calculated from NHSCR-derived migration data provided by ONS; Crown copyright.

and bust have impacted on regional economic differentials, the longer-term trend is of a slackening in the rate of southward movement since the 1980s, if not the 1960s (though annual records are not available for then). Dividing the period shown into three sections, the net gain to the South averaged 41,350 a year up to 1986 and then almost halved to 20,850 in the fourteen years to 2000, finally swinging round into a 1,550 annual average gain for the North in 2001–2014. In parallel, the peaks of the South's migration gain have fallen back with each cycle from 68,250 in 1986 to 38,450 in 1997 and 18,900 in 2010.

It remains to be seen whether this long-term attenuation of North-South migration will continue into a sustained reversal in favour of the North, because the factors behind it have not yet been fully researched. One potential explanation is that the acceleration of immigration from overseas, with its particular concentration on London (see next section), has led to shrinkage in the types of job vacancies that have traditionally been filled by migrants from the North. Partly related to this perhaps but also driven by the general pressures of growth in the South is the progressive widening of the regional divide in the availability and cost of housing, especially between London and the rest of the UK (see Chapter 7). This would be a particular deterrent for lower-skilled people, especially families with children, who might well find themselves financially worse off after moving into the high-cost South, especially if taking up low-paid and possibly insecure work. Even before the

house-price differentials became so wide, research recognised that unemployed people living in the UK's periphery might do better to stay close
to family and community support networks in their home area where their
welfare benefits would also go further (Kitching, 1990).

At the same time, however, it should not be thought that people have
ceased moving between North and South: the gross flows remain substantial.
For instance, in the year to June 2014 (the latest year shown in Figure 8.1),
the net 2,680 gain to the South was the outcome of 562,000 people moving
between the two: 264,350 southwards and 261,670 northwards. Moreover,
whilst some of these were moving relatively short distances between the
counties abutting the North-South boundary, the majority moved further. Of
those moving southwards, nearly two-thirds (153,610) went to the Greater
South East (including the East and South East regions) and more than two-
fifths of these (65,840) to London. As London's outflow to the North was
59,440, the capital made a net gain of 6,400 people. Whilst the latter figure
fluctuates over time alongside the overall North-South balance shown in
Figure 8.1, the total exchanges between London and the North remain fairly
constant over time, staying at around the 125,000 mark recorded for 2014.

Yet even if the flows between North and South now tend to balance out in
numerical terms across a business cycle, the outcome is not neutral because
the composition of the two migration streams differs considerably. In particular, the southward movers, especially those heading for London, are on
average younger than those moving the other way. This is no new phenomenon, being well documented ever since reliable records on internal migration became available in the 1960s (see, for instance, Stillwell et al., 1992).
Moreover, the southward flow is also the more positively selected in favour of
more highly qualified and skilled people, most notably in terms of graduates
from provincial universities being attracted to the capital (Champion et al.,
2007). According to Gordon (2013), these migrants are also more ambitious, which fits well with the 'escalator region' model proposed by Fielding
(1989, 1992). Initially tested by tracking people between the 1971 and 1981
Censuses, this demonstrated that south-eastern England drew in people at the
early stage of their careers wanting to take advantage of the faster promotion prospects there, followed by their departure later in their working lives
or at retirement. Subsequent studies indicate that this process has continued
and even intensified (Fielding, 2012; Champion et al., 2014), but they have
also modified its details, notably showing that many of those moving to the
escalator region seem to settle permanently (Champion, 2012).

In sum, it would therefore seem that the North-South divide is just as wide
now as when documented by Champion (1989), with rather similar policy
issues arising. Even in the 1980s, Hughes and McCormick (1987) were
able to show that the South's net migration gains were entirely composed

of non-manual workers (see also Champion, 1989, Table 8.3). Despite the volume of net southward migration shrinking to virtually zero since then, in qualitative terms it still favours the South, with that effect now being reinforced by the latter's greater attraction for immigrants and higher rate of natural increase than the North. The policy issues are nearly as much to do with relieving inflationary pressures on the South as with better harnessing the underutilised resources of the North. Initiatives like the Northern Powerhouse (Osborne, 2014) and the quest for a stronger Scotland (Scottish Government, 2015) would, however, seem to face an uphill struggle in trying to counter the London effect, judging by the gulf between the capital and northern city regions in the strength of their 'escalator' function (Champion et al., 2014; Gordon et al., 2015) and their economies more generally (Champion and Townsend, 2013). Nevertheless, as the next section shows, in recent years there has been a widespread urban resurgence that might possibly provide the springboard for such a regional rebalancing.

URBAN POPULATION RECOVERY

Since Champion's (1989) review, there has been a major change in spatial redistribution trends at the urban scale, with a switch from widespread city decline to almost universal growth. This section documents the extent of the turnaround over this period and then gives more detail about the post-2001 underpinnings of this, with a particular focus on the role played by changes in within-UK migration. For this purpose, it uses the physically based definition of cities adopted by the *State of the English Cities* report (DCLG, 2006) as extended to the whole UK by the Centre for Cities (2015; see also Champion, 2014), including updating to the best fit of post-2009 local government areas. As such, urban Britain comprises sixty-four Primary Urban Areas, referred to below as Cities, which are classified by size into Major, Large and Small. The remainder of the UK is subdivided into two categories based on the 2001 population size of its main centre—namely, Large Towns (with an urban area of at least fifty thousand people) and Small Towns and Rural.

The scale of the urban recovery, as measured on this geographical basis using data from the official midyear estimates, is impressive and dates from around the start of the new millennium. In the two decades before then, over one-third of the sixty-four cities experienced population loss, twenty-six between 1981 and 1991 and twenty-four in 1991–2001, but there were only three cases of shrinkage in the next few years leading up to the onset of recession in 2008 and just two in 2008–2014 (2014 being the latest year for which data were available at the time of writing). Perhaps most impressive, all the Major Cities were absent from the list of declining cities by this time, which

is in stark contrast to the 1980s when just Belfast and London gained population. Even by 1991–2001 only Leeds had joined these two, with the other
six Major Cities—Birmingham, Glasgow, Liverpool, Manchester, Newcastle
and Sheffield—still contracting. The remaining cities in decline at this time
were spread across the other two size groups roughly in proportion to their
total numbers of cities, comprising in both 1981–1991 and 1991–2001 six
of the nineteen Large Cities and a dozen of the thirty-six Small Cities. By
contrast, the only two cases of shrinkage remaining in 2008–2014—Blackpool and Dundee—were both Small Cities, providing further evidence of a
reversal in the role of city size.

The transformation in the relationship between population growth rate and
urban status over the past quarter of a century is reinforced by Figure 8.2's
portrayal of the change rates for the five size groups. The three City categories all saw a progressive uplift in growth rate from the 1980s, with just the
one exception of the slowing of growth for the Small Cities in the 1990s.
Moreover, the percentage point extent of the rise is found to be greatest for
the Major Cities, with their switch from being the only declining group in
the 1980s to becoming the strongest growing in 2008–2014, seemingly unaffected by the recession then. The rise over the period shown in Figure 8.1
becomes steadily less substantial with falling size, such that the least urban
group of Small Towns and Rural posted a growth rate in the final period
that was little different from its 1980s level. As a result, the clear 'counter-
urbanisation' relationship at the outset, when growth rates generally rose with
reducing urban status, had by 2008–2014 been replaced by an 'urbanisation'
one, with the Major Cities outpacing the two lesser city sizes that in turn grew
faster than the two non-city categories.

How has this urban resurgence come about? Part of the answer can be seen
from Figure 8.2's final panel, which shows a progressive uplift in the UK's
overall rate of population growth. Its particularly strong uplift in 2001–2008
is reflected in all five levels of the urban hierarchy, but it is most pronounced
for the three city categories and especially the Major Cities group. Also
impressive is that the increase in growth rate between before and after 2008
was above the national shift for all three, with the extent of uplift rising with
urban status. Clearly the national surge in growth rate has impacted British
cities more than its countryside or, conversely, it is the cities, and especially
the larger ones, that have led the country's accelerating growth—a remarkable change of fortunes since the well-documented downward trajectories
of most of the larger cities in the period leading up to Champion's (1989)
review, though presaged there (123) in terms of Greater London's decline
bottoming out in the mid-1970s.

The demographic drivers of this growth are shown in Table 8.3. Looking
first at the seven years leading up to the onset of recession in 2008, at the

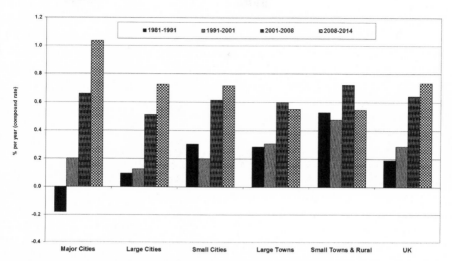

Figure 8.2 Population Change, 1981–2014, for the UK and Its Urban Status Types.
Source: Calculated from ONS midyear population estimates and components of change;
Crown copyright data.

Table 8.3 Overall Population Change and Its Components, 2001–2014, for the UK and Its Urban Status Types (Per cent Per Annum, Compound Rate)

Urban Status Type	Period	Natural Increase	International Migration	Within-UK Migration	Overall Change
Major Cities	2001–2008	0.48	0.76	−0.63	0.66
	2008–2014	0.69	0.65	−0.32	1.03
Large Cities	2001–2008	0.25	0.41	−0.19	0.51
	2008–2014	0.43	0.41	−0.14	0.73
Small Cities	2001–2008	0.23	0.36	−0.08	0.61
	2008–2014	0.40	0.34	−0.07	0.72
Large Towns	2001–2008	0.12	0.18	0.31	0.60
	2008–2014	0.24	0.17	0.15	0.55
Small Towns & Rural	2001–2008	0.00	0.15	0.57	0.72
	2008–2014	0.09	0.13	0.33	0.55
UK	2001–2008	0.22	0.39	0.00	0.64
	2008–2014	0.37	0.35	0.00	0.73

Note: The three components may not sum to 'Overall change' because the latter includes 'Other changes'. The latter mainly comprises unexplained change arising from the comparison of 2011 Census results with the population estimates rolled forward from 2001, which given the very accurate data on births and deaths is assumed to be unrecorded migration that cannot be split into its international and within-UK components at the sub-national level.
Source: Calculated from ONS midyear population estimates and components of change; Crown copyright data.

national level (where internal migration is a zero-sum game by definition) it was net immigration from abroad that played the primary role, generating three-fifths of the UK's growth then. Similarly, for all of the five urban levels, international migration made a larger contribution to their growth than did the surplus of births over deaths. Both of these components display a clear 'urbanisation' relationship, with their rates becoming progressively lower down the urban hierarchy. For within-UK migration, by contrast, the opposite pattern holds, with the highest rate of net loss being for the Major Cities (−0.63 per cent a year) and a progressive switch down the urban levels to the gain of 0.57 per cent for the Small Towns and Rural category. Indeed, this internal migration is clearly the principal driver of growth for the two non-city types in 2001–2008, contributing more to their overall growth than the other two components combined.

Table 8.3 also shows what changed after 2008 to further boost the urban recovery. The rise in the national growth rate that has contributed to this (see above) is entirely due to the rise in the natural increase rate from 0.22 to 0.37 per cent a year, given that the international migration rate fell back from 0.39 to 0.35 per cent. All five urban status types share both trends, though with the degree of absolute change (in percentage-point terms) generally reducing with urban status. Impressively, by this time the contribution of natural increase had overtaken that of net immigration in all but the least urban category. The biggest change from the pre-2008 picture, however, is shown to be the slowing of internal migration's role in redistributing population between the five levels. The net out-migration rates of the three city types became less negative and the net in-migration rates of the two non-city ones became less positive, with the range across the urban hierarchy almost halving from 1.20 percentage points in 2001–2008 (the difference between −0.63 and +0.57) to 0.65 points (−0.32 to +0.33) in 2008–2014.

As with the issue raised earlier about the fading of net North-to-South migration, this reduction in the pace of net migration from more to less urban places poses a key question: Will it continue to slow as a result of long-term factors pushing in this direction and further boost the urban population recovery, or is this merely a temporary phase associated with the economic recession? A preliminary answer can be obtained from Figure 8.3, which shows the rates for the five size groups since 2001 on an annual basis. The impact of the 2008–2009 recession is clear from the marked narrowing of the range between the Major Cities at one end of the scale and the Small Towns and Rural at the other. At the same time, it can be seen that this convergence started back in 2004–2005, which suggests that migration behaviour was anticipating the recession (or else is due to other factors that may be longer term). However, post-2009 it is also evident that the rates have started to diverge again, albeit more slowly than the previous contraction. This difference could well be due

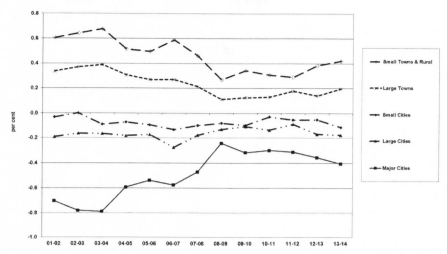

Figure 8.3 Annual Rate of Net Within-UK Migration, 2001–2002 to 2013–2014, UK, by Settlement-Size Group.
Source: Calculated from data provided by ONS; Crown copyright.

to the slowness of the economic recovery due to the credit squeeze and associated austerity policies, but there is also a regional dimension to it. Migration data for the Greater London Authority area (Champion, 2015) show that the capital's net out-migration to the rest of the UK, which had dropped to twenty-eight thousand in 2008–2009, had by 2013–2014 bounced back to sixty-six thousand, close to its long-term average. By contrast, the other Major Cities in aggregate had seen no significant rebound by this time.

Taking a contrary viewpoint, there are some grounds for suggesting that the urban exodus may not return to its previous high levels, some of which relate to points made elsewhere in this book. It could be that the 2008–2009 recession and the policy responses to it may be producing a very different context for migration behaviour through the impact on housing and labour markets—for instance, making it harder to enter owner occupation and more attractive for children to stay on longer in the parental home, as noted in Chapter 7. Another is the growth of the ethnic minority population documented in Chapter 9, which, although showing some convergence with the behaviour of the White community in terms of urban dispersal (and also fertility; see Chapter 5), has traditionally been much more 'city-loving' than the latter. Also, planning restrictions on building on greenfield sites are arguably now at their tightest ever, with the continuing 'urban renaissance' programme ushered in by the Rogers Report (1999) being reinforced by the 'localism' agenda of the 2010–2015 Coalition and the associated strengthening of NIMBY (Not in My Back Yard) syndrome in more rural areas.

Certainly, it is not just that there has been a revival of the larger cities; this process is particularly evident in the population rejuvenation of the more central and inner parts of these cities. This is not a new phenomenon, dating back to gentrification in the 1960s and the docklands-type redevelopments of the 1980s, but it accelerated in the 1990s (Nathan and Urwin, 2005). Inner London led the way then, with its population rising by 10 per cent between 1991 and 2001, up from its 2 per cent rate for 1981–1991, but other Major Cities have followed, most notably Manchester where the two central local authorities of Manchester and Salford saw their combined population rise by 15 per cent between 2001 and 2011, far outpacing the growth rate for the rest of the urban area (Champion, 2014). The precise geography of this growth is well demonstrated by Rae's (2013) study of the 2001–2011 change in the number of Output Areas (areas of roughly equal population size designed for the release of census data) in a selection of cities. Waterfronts feature commonly, as do the part of cities dominated by higher education establishments. A similarly fine-grained analysis by Thomas et al. (2015) found that the city-centre areas of England and Wales grew by 37 per cent over this decade, compared to 8 per cent for the suburban population, and that this increase was driven primarily by students (their numbers more than doubling in city centres over the decade) but also people in work (up by 53 per cent), with young professionals—no doubt including many former students—featuring most strongly.

In sum, there has been a remarkable turnaround in the population fortunes of urban Britain since the 1980s, mainly since the turn of the millennium. Natural increase and net international migration have been major drivers of the urban upsurge since the 1990s, but it is the changes in within-UK migration that have been primarily responsible for the further acceleration of city growth since 2008. Can this urban resurgence be expected to continue? Much depends on what the future holds for births, deaths and international migration at the national level, which in its turn depends on recent trends in these components and how their drivers are altering—topics that are covered by other chapters in this book.

As regards the internal migration component, it is probably wise to separate the immediate future from the longer term. The latest evidence presented above suggests that recovery from the 2008–2009 recession is being accompanied by accelerating out-migration from cities as the housing market frees up, following the pattern of previous business cycles. In this context, Berrington and Simpson (Chapter 7 in this book; see also Simpson and McDonald, 2015) are correct in attaching a health warning to the latest (2012-based) population and household projections that use the recession-affected average of 2007–2012 for their within-UK migration assumptions and, as a result, suggest much stronger population retention by London and other big cities than now looks likely.

Longer-term, the jury is still out, according to the review above. On the demand side, it may be that the balance of residential preferences across the UK population is shifting in favour of city living, as encapsulated in the 'café society' underpinning much of the thinking set out in the Rogers Report (1999), though a large-scale survey of people's attitudes by Thomas et al. (2015) suggests that city centres, suburbs and rural hinterlands each hold a strong attraction, albeit for different groups of people. On the supply side, there are issues about the availability and cost of development land countrywide, but given the 'housing crisis' described in Chapter 7, government policy now seems to be shifting away from an agenda focussed on (mainly urban) brownfield sites to encouraging the release of any suitable sites that can be found.

MIGRATION SLOWDOWN?

Previous sections have indicated that some elements of within-UK migration have become less pronounced in recent years, notably with the apparent cessation of net (but not gross) migration from North to South and the reduction in migration (gross as well as net) out of cities. Does this mean that there is a long-term trend towards lower migration intensities—are people tending to move home less frequently now than in the past? If so, this would parallel the experience of the USA and some other countries as documented by Cooke (2011) and Bell et al. (2015), amongst others. This observation has been greeted with mixed feelings because, though it might suggest greater satisfaction with current arrangements, alternatively it could arise from people being less able to move when they want to do so. More commonly, however, migration slowdown is viewed in negative terms because of its perceived disadvantages for economy and society—for instance, in slowing the labour-supply response to the changing geography of jobs and leading to a more sclerotic housing market with greater mismatch between household and dwelling types. Given these potential implications, this section examines the situation in the UK, with the main focus being on England and Wales because of data availability and the ability to draw on two new studies (Champion and Shuttleworth, 2016a, 2016b).

As there is no single source of migration data that provides a comprehensive picture of long-term trends in migration intensities here, it is necessary to patch together the insights derived from two separate datasets—the National Health Service Central Register (NHSCR) and a dataset derived from the Population Census. Looking first at the NHSCR, this allows the continuous monitoring of migration between health areas and provides a record back to the 1970s for England and Wales. When the data are adjusted for changes

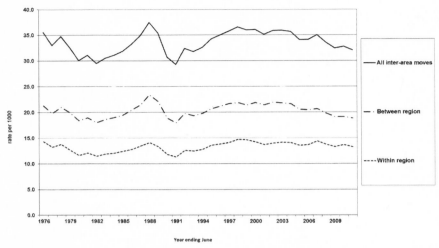

Figure 8.4   Migration Rate, 1975–2011, for All Inter-Area Moves and Between-Region and Within-Region Separately.
Source: Calculated from data provided by ONS; Crown copyright.

over time in the geography of these areas, the resultant pattern (shown in Figure 8.4) is one that appears to be dominated by business-cycle effects, with troughs during the recessions of 1980–1981, 1990–1991 and 2008–2009 and higher rates during the intervening years of recovery. This is the case both for 'between-region' migration (mainly long-distance moves between the former Government Office Regions of England and Wales, though there will also be an element of boundary crossing between adjacent regions) and for 'within-region' migration (which, as mentioned, are restricted to moves between a standardised geography of health areas). In terms of the long-term picture, neither type of migration seems to have shared the US experience of declining migration intensity, with the rates for the latest years falling broadly within the range of those for the earlier part of the thirty-six-year period shown.

A more precise test, which averages across the two halves of the 1975–2011 period, is shown in Table 8.4, also breaking the population into broad age groups that traditionally have distinctive migration behaviour. This shows that the overall rate of inter-area migration was actually higher in the second half, especially so for moves between areas within regions. At the same time, clearly this was not the case for all the age groups, with the main push behind the rise in overall rate coming from sixteen-to-twenty-four-year-olds. There was also some increase for twenty-five-to-forty-four and forty-five-to-sixty-four-year-olds, but a substantial fall in rates for those aged

Table 8.4 Comparison of Average Annual Migration Rates for 1975–1993 and 1993–2011, by Type of Move and Age

Age Group	Between-Region Moves			Within-Region Moves			All between-Area Moves		
	1975–1993	1993–2011	% Change	1975–1993	1993–2011	% Change	1975–1993	1993–2011	% Change
All ages	19.9	20.7	+4.4	12.6	13.9	+9.6	32.5	34.6	+6.4
0–15	16.4	15.2	−7.1	11.3	11.8	+4.5	27.7	27.0	−2.4
16–24	43.7	59.7	+36.8	22.4	27.1	+20.9	66.1	86.8	+31.4
25–44	25.2	25.9	+3.1	18.1	20.8	+14.6	43.3	46.7	+7.9
45–64	9.5	9.6	+1.7	6.2	6.9	+11.3	15.7	16.6	+5.5
65+	9.0	7.0	−21.7	5.4	4.9	−8.6	14.4	12.0	−16.8
All except 16–24	16.1	15.7	−2.1	11.1	12.2	+9.6	27.2	27.9	+2.7

Note: Rates of between-region moves and within-region moves may not sum exactly to rates of all between-area moves due to rounding.
Source: Calculated from NHSCR-derived data supplied by ONS (see text); Crown copyright.

sixty-five and over and a small one for the under-sixteens. The increase in the sixteen-to-twenty-four's rate is particularly high for between-region migration, which is consistent with the increase in numbers leaving the parental home for university as higher-education participation rates have been rising. If this age group is omitted (as in the bottom row of Table 8.4), there was only a very small increase in the overall inter-area rate between before and after 1993 and a small fall in the between-region rate, with the increases for those aged twenty-five to sixty-four being offset by the generally lower rates at both ends of the age spectrum.

A rather different picture, however, is found for the shorter-distance address changing that is largely omitted from the data on migration between health areas. The source most commonly used for studying all distances of move is the Population Census, but by itself this provides information on only one year in every ten through its question on address one year ago and with the additional drawback that the reference year tends to occur at varying points in the business cycle. In this case, the best way of minimising the effect of the latter is to examine ten-year migration by comparing the same people's address at one census with that at the previous one, which is possible back to 1971–1981 via the Longitudinal Study of England and Wales (LSEW). According to this approach (as adopted by Champion and Shuttleworth, 2016b), there has been a progressive fall in the ten-year address-changing rate since then, dropping from 55 per cent for the 1970s to 53.0 in the 1980s and 49.8 in the 1990s and ending up at 45.3 for 2001–2011, adding up to a decline of 9.7 percentage points and a relative decline of 17.7 per cent.

This result, however, is not incompatible with the evidence of Figure 8.4 and Table 8.4 because the distance of move variable available in the LSEW indicates that virtually all this reduction in the ten-year rate is accounted for by short-distance migration. The proportion of people changing address by less than 10 kilometres between successive censuses fell by 9.4 percentage points between the 1970s and the 2000s, down from 36.9 to 27.5 per cent, a relative decline of almost a quarter. Additional information on the types of people contributing most to this fall (see Champion and Shuttleworth, 2016b) gives a contraction in rate by a half or more for people aged sixty-five and over and by over one-third for ages fifty to sixty-four, as well as the sick, unskilled workers, immigrants and all marital statuses except single. By contrast, the proportion of people moving at least 50 kilometres fell by just 2.6 per cent, consistent with the between-region change noted above. Similarly, this small change represents the balance between a big increase in rate for student age groups and some substantial falls (by at least one-fifth) for several other groups, including people with degrees, professional occupations, owner occupiers, part-time workers and the armed forces.

Combining the results derived from both sources, the main message seems clear: whilst longer-distance migration rates seem fairly stable over time aside from short-term fluctuation, there has been a substantial fall in the intensity of short-distance migration in England and Wales since the 1970s. Much less clear (and perhaps not surprising given the newness of this research topic) is what is driving the various changes adding up to this overall picture, as well as what the policy implications may be. The rise in migration rates for sixteen-to-twenty-four-year-olds must be largely to do with widening participation in higher education, though over shorter distances it may also be linked to younger adults more generally becoming increasingly reliant on the high-churn private-rented sector (Champion and Shuttleworth, 2016b). The large reduction in migration rates for the oldest cohorts, especially over shorter distances, is likely to reflect the substantial increases in owner occupation and healthy life expectancy in recent decades (see Chapter 1), but there is at least anecdotal evidence of empty-nester households becoming slower to downsize because of the lack of suitable properties and tax disincentives (House of Lords, 2016; see also Chapter 7). The large reductions in rates of longer-distance migration for higher-qualified people and the unemployed are likely to be seen in negative terms as they suggest a less flexible labour market that may also be related to the high cost and limited availability of housing in growth areas such as London and south-eastern England.

CONCLUSION

Looking at the latest trends in migration and population redistribution compared with a quarter century ago, there is clear evidence of both continuity and change. Much attention is still being given to the UK's North-South divide, but nowadays, unlike previously, within-UK migration seems to be playing only a small part in the faster growth of the South. Since the 1980s, there has been a remarkable turnaround in urban population trends, with a full-scale switch from a negative to a positive relationship between growth rate and settlement size. In this case, however, the net exodus of people from large cities to more rural areas continues, albeit slowing markedly in the mid-2000s but beginning to pick up again, especially out of London. On both of these scales, it is the international migration component that is now dominating change, contributing disproportionately to the growth of the South and to that of the larger cities, with London being the common denominator.

Policy issues abound, as has been mentioned at several points in the chapter. Whilst it is impressive that virtually no cities have seen absolute population decline in recent years, even in the former industrial heartland of northern England, their improved performance may be difficult to sustain in the long term, given its initial reliance on massive programmes of public investment followed by the boost of strong immigration and the post-recession slowdown in the urban exodus. In an era of austerity policies, strong anti-immigration feeling and sustained, albeit slow, economic recovery, old weaknesses may well become more evident along the lines documented by Pike et al.'s (2016) study of the UK's struggling cities. At the other end of the spectrum lie the challenges posed by the strength of recent growth, especially in terms of accommodating large numbers of extra people, especially in and around the national capital, as highlighted by the London Housing Commission (2016).

It is also important to keep a close eye on what is happening to migration longer term, most notably in terms of the frequency with which people move home. As pointed out in the previous section, it is only recently that it has been noticed that rates of address changing have been declining for most types of people, perhaps not surprisingly, as internal migration remains by far the most important of the four main demographic components in numerical terms. According to the 2011 Census, fully 6.9 million people were then living at a different UK address from that twelve months before, which is ten times as many as had moved from outside the UK and is of the same order of magnitude larger than the 811,000 births and 556,000 deaths registered in the UK in the year to June 2011. Yet, by the same token, even a small percentage decline in the address-changing rate would involve a considerable absolute number of people, so there should be policy interest in the causes and consequences of such a trend and which aspects should be viewed positively and which negatively. Some pointers to this can be gleaned from Smith et al.'s (2015) major review of British research on internal migration, as well as from Fielding (2012), but the topic merits more systematic investigation than has been the case thus far.

Chapter 9

Ethnic Diversity

Nissa Finney[1] and Gemma Catney[2]

Ethnic diversification has been one of the most significant changes to Britain's population over the past two decades, prompting consideration of the meaning of ethnicity for demography. This is important because it raises questions about how population patterns and processes vary between population sub-groups; it helps population scientists to understand and comment upon broader social debates about inequalities; and it enables us to challenge misconceptions about populations as defined by ethnicity. Considering the ethnic dimensions of population change reminds us that population issues not only affect individuals at the most intimate level but also are political and of policy relevance.

Ethnicity is an aspect of personal and collective identity, incorporating elements of race, nation and culture (Parekh, 2008). Britain's ethnic diversity has origins in its history of immigration, particularly in the first three decades after World War II, when people arrived in Britain from former colonies and the Commonwealth, settling and building lives as set out in Diamond and Clarke's (1989) chapter in Joshi's book (see also Chapter 4 of this book). Today, it is their grandchildren who form a large part of Britain's ethnic diversity; demographic momentum means that the majority of ethnic minorities have been born in Britain.

Ethnicity as a marker of difference does not operate independently; it intersects with other aspects of identity including gender, class and religion. Indeed, this is said to be a time of super-diversity (Vertovec, 2007). Yet ethnicity remains a useful concept for population scientists, as it allows the examination of two important social phenomena. First, as a result of immigration, there are processes of integration and adaptation, where the mixing of different systems of beliefs and practices alter the circumstance and behaviours of migrants (and their descendants) and of longer-term residents. This includes demographic behaviours to do with fertility, living arrangements, health, caring and residential mobility. Secondly, there are processes of racism and discrimination whose long history and contemporary expression affect the demography of ethnic groups—for example, in terms of health and residential location.

This chapter comprises six sections. The first outlines how ethnicity is measured in UK population datasets, whilst the next describes the ethnic diversity of Britain and how it has changed since 1991. The third section examines the population dynamics of ethnic groups, focussing on differences between the groups in age structure, fertility, partnership and mortality. Then two sections are devoted to the geographies of ethnic diversity, dealing with segregation and mixing and with the migration of ethnic groups within the UK. Both present new analyses in addition to drawing on the existing literature. These geographical themes are given prominence partly because they reflect our own research interests and partly because they represent the largest bodies of scholarship on population change and ethnicity in Britain over the last twenty-five years. The chapter concludes with comment on ethnic diversity becoming the norm for the population of Britain and discusses the extent to which ethnicity, as a marker of stratification, will continue to be useful in population studies.

DEFINITIONS OF ETHNICITY IN UK DATASETS

The social significance of ethnicity has resulted in considerable debate amongst population scholars and other social scientists about its measurement. Some have argued that the illusive and dynamic nature of the concept renders reliable measurement impossible, whilst others maintain its measurement as important for monitoring population change, disadvantage and discrimination (see Finney and Simpson, 2009). Despite many efforts at the time, a question on ethnicity was not approved for inclusion in the 1981 Census, forcing Diamond and Clarke's (1989) analysis of demographic patterns amongst Britain's ethnic groups to focus on groups defined by their world region or country of origin: the New Commonwealth, Pakistan, Africa and Asia. A question on ethnic-group identity was asked for the first time in the 1991 Census (Coleman and Salt, 1996). The introduction of an ethnicity question in the Census constitutes a landmark, giving recognition of the significance of ethnicity for British society and providing a means of shaping understandings of ethnicity and ethnic groups in terms of their behaviour and experiences.

The construction of ethnic-group questions in UK censuses has been contested. This has resulted in differences between England, Wales, Scotland

Table 9.1   Ethnic Group Category Response Options to 'What Is Your Ethnic Group?' on UK 2011 Census Forms

England and Wales	Scotland	Northern Ireland
A: White	**A: White**	White
English/Welsh/Scottish/ Northern Irish/British	Scottish	Chinese
Gypsy or Irish Traveller	Other British	Irish Traveller
Any other White background (write in)	Irish	Indian
B: Mixed/Multiple ethnic groups	Gypsy/Traveller	Pakistani
	Polish	Bangladeshi
White and Black Caribbean	Other White ethnic group (write in)	Black African
White and Black African	**B: Mixed or Multiple ethnic groups**	Black Caribbean
White Asian	Any Mixed/Multiple ethnic group	Black Other
Any other Mixed/Multiple ethnic background (write in)	(write in)	Mixed ethnic group (write in)
C: Asian/Asian British	**C: Asian, Asian Scottish or Asian British**	Any other ethnic group (write in)
Indian	Pakistani, Pakistani Scottish or Pakistani British	
Pakistani	Indian, Indian Scottish or Indian British	
Bangladeshi	Bangladeshi, Bangladeshi Scottish or Bangladeshi British	
Chinese	Chinese, Chinese Scottish or Chinese British	
Any other Asian background (write in)	Other (write in)	
D: Black/African/ Caribbean/Black British	**D: African**	
Caribbean	African, African Scottish or African British	
African	Other (write in)	
Any other Black/African/ Caribbean background (write in)	**E: Caribbean or Black**	
E: Other ethnic group	Caribbean, Caribbean Scottish or Caribbean British	
Arab	Black, Black Scottish, Black British	
Any other ethnic group (write in)	Other (write in)	
	F: Other ethnic group	
	Arab, Arab Scottish or Arab British	
	Other (write in)	

Notes: In all cases, respondents were required to select one ethnic group from the options provided. In Wales the first option in the 'White' category read 'Welsh/English/Scottish/Northern Irish/British'. Forms in Wales were available in Welsh. Census ethnic group questions from 1991, 2001 and 2011 for UK countries are compiled at http://www.ethnicity.ac.uk/research/outputs/briefings/dynamics-of-diversity/related-documents/. An ethnic group question was asked in England, Wales and Scotland in the censuses of 1991, 2001 and 2011 and in Northern Ireland in 2001 and 2011. The ethnic group categories considered comparable between 1991, 2001 and 2011 for England, Wales and Scotland are White, Indian, Pakistani, Bangladeshi, Chinese, Black Caribbean, Black African, Other (Jivraj and Simpson, 2015).

and Northern Ireland in the questions asked, in changes to the ethnic-group categories and their order between the 1991, 2001 and 2011 censuses, and in the addition of ethnic groups to the list of tick-box responses. Most notable in this regard is the disaggregation of the White category in 2001, as well as the addition of 'Mixed/multiple ethnic group' options in 2001 and 'Gypsy and Irish Traveller' and 'Arab' in 2011. Additions to ethnic-group categories can never fully accommodate the population's ethnic diversity, and the write-in 'Other' options (the alternatives to the more specific tick-box choices) constitute collectively the largest ethnic-group affiliation, aside from the White British majority. Between 2001 and 2011, the fastest growth of all ethnic groups was for the Other groups (taken collectively), which grew by 133 per cent on their 2001 population (and 284 per cent from 1991). The ethnic-group categories offered in the 2011 Censuses are presented in Table 9.1; these represent, in various combinations, racial, national and geographic dimensions of identity. These Census classifications have become commonplace for the monitoring of ethnicity in surveys and administrative data and, arguably, have shaped societal perceptions of ethnic identities.

In the following sections, we make use exclusively of Census data on ethnic group. For more in-depth discussion about the measurement of ethnic groups in the UK, we refer you to Jivraj and Simpson (2015). It is worth noting at the outset that some of the results presented below are for England and Wales and some are for the UK, depending on availability of Census data and their (in)consistencies between its constituent countries. Consequently, the ethnic groups to which we refer vary. Where we make comparisons over time, we follow Simpson et al. (2015) in using those groups considered to retain coherence across the three censuses: White, Indian, Pakistani, Bangladeshi, Chinese, Black Caribbean and Black African. Sabater and Simpson (2009) have made population estimates comparable over time for ethnic groups and small areas, which take account of minority undercount in the 1991 and 2001 censuses (available from the UK Data Service), and where possible we use these estimates.

ETHNIC DIVERSIFICATION SINCE 1991

This section considers the extent of ethnic diversification since ethnicity was first measured in the Census, focussing primarily on England and Wales. The period 1991–2011 experienced significant changes to the ethnic composition of the population and signified a new era in ethnic diversity and mixing. It was a time of growth in inter-group contact at several levels: the individual, the home and—as illustrated in the later sections—not least the neighbourhood. Table 9.2 shows the growth of each of the seven ethnic groups as defined on a consistent basis (see above), plus a residual category, across the 1991, 2001 and 2011 censuses of England and Wales. The White population, as a proportion of the total population, decreased from 94 per cent in 1991

Table 9.2   Ethnic Group Populations, 1991–2011, England and Wales

Ethnic Group	1991 Population in 000s (% of Total)	2001 Population in 000s (% of Total)	2011 Population in 000s (% of Total)	1991–2011 Change (%)
White	47,429 (93.5)	47,747 (91.2)	48,209 (86.0)	1.6
Indian	892 (1.8)	1,053 (2.0)	1,413 (2.5)	58.4
Pakistani	495 (1.0)	728 (1.4)	1,125 (2.0)	127.2
Bangladeshi	177 (0.3)	287 (0.5)	447 (0.8)	152.8
Chinese	173 (0.3)	233 (0.4)	393 (0.7)	127.0
Black African	255 (0.5)	495 (0.9)	990 (1.8)	287.6
Black Caribbean	570 (1.1)	572 (1.1)	595 (1.1)	4.4
Other	757 (1.5)	1,245 (2.4)	2,904 (5.2)	283.6
Total	50,748 (100.0)	52,360 (100.0)	56,076 (100.0)	10.5

Notes: Only comparable ethnic groups from 1991 to 2011 are shown. The Other group is included for completeness, but note that there are issues of comparability over time for this group.
Source: 2011 Census, Table KS201EW (Crown copyright), and complete population estimates based on the 1991 and 2001 Censuses (Crown copyright); authors' own calculations.

to 91 per cent in 2001 and to 86 per cent in 2011, with the minority ethnic populations growing to 14 per cent of the total.

At this national level, ethnic minority groups grew via two main mechanisms—more immigration than emigration and more births than deaths—and the relative importance of these varies between groups according to their migration history, fertility, life expectancy and age structure. The relative contributions of international migration and natural change to the growth of each ethnic group between 2001 and 2011 are explored in depth in Simpson and Jivraj (2015). They show that, for minority groups with a long history of immigration to the UK, immigration generally contributed less to their growth than did the excess of births over deaths over this decade. This was the case for the Pakistani and Bangladeshi groups, which both grew by around 50 per cent, and also for the Black Caribbean group, which grew by under 5 per cent. In contrast, despite its established history in the UK, the Indian group grew more through immigration than births.

As regards other groups, Simpson and Jivraj (2015) show that both immigration and births were responsible for the considerable growth of the Black African, Chinese and Other White groups between 2001 and 2011 (the latter is merged with White in Table 9.2). The White Irish group (also merged with White in Table 9.2) decreased in size due to mortality (given its relatively elderly age structure), net emigration and a transfer of ethnic-group affiliation to the White British group. Shifts in ethnic-group self-categorisation over time are an additional mechanism of ethnic-group change, and Simpson et al. (2015) explore the impact of this instability and its implications for ethnic-group comparability over time.

A category of ethnic-group identification introduced in the 2001 Census provided insight into the numbers of people identifying with four Mixed or Multiple ethnic groups—namely, White and African, White and Caribbean, White and Asian and Other Mixed (these are all included in the 'Other' category in Table 9.2). The proportion of people in England and Wales affiliating with a Mixed group nearly doubled over the subsequent decade, reaching 1.2 million or 2.2 per cent of the population by 2011. These groups have very young age structures, with just 4 per cent aged sixty-five or older, and double the national-level proportion of children aged under fifteen (Simpson and Jivraj, 2015), typically being composed of the children of parents with different ethnic-group affiliations. As such, the growth of this group might be interpreted as an indicator of increasing ethnic-group social interaction and greater opportunities for mixing, or perhaps used as a barometer for wider social acceptance of mixed ethnic identities, which encourages mixed ethnicity self-identification. Given their youthful age structures, growth of the Mixed groups is set to continue into the future (Rees et al., 2013).

This increase in ethnic mixing in England and Wales can also be seen at the household level, thanks to data from tables UV069 and QS202EW of the 2001 and 2011 censuses, respectively. The number of ethnically mixed multiple-person households (those where at least one other person in the household had a different ethnic-group affiliation) grew by nearly 650,000 over the decade, accounting for over 12 per cent of multiple-person households in 2011 compared to just over 9 per cent in 2001 and equating to roughly two million households. Censuses identify the various ways in which people of different ethnicities may come together under one roof. In 2011, mixed ethnic-group partnerships accounted for the largest share of the growth in mixed-ethnicity households; in 2011, over one million households contained a mixed-ethnicity couple, making up around half of the multiple ethnic-group households. Around 3 per cent of households of two or more persons (around a quarter of multiple ethnic-group households) comprised mixed ethnic groups between generations. The remainder of mixed ethnicity households comprised other combinations of mixing, including non-relatives such as students.

The data presented in Table 9.2 are for England and Wales only because of differences in ethnic-group categorisation between the UK Censuses (see Table 9.1), but significant growth in ethnic diversity was also experienced in the other two countries of the UK. In Scotland, by 2011 the ethnic minority population had increased to 16 per cent (850,000 people, up from 600,000 in 2001), and some groups more than doubled their population between 2001 and 2011 (Smith and Simpson, 2015). Scottish Census data revealed several commonalities with England and Wales, including a significant growth in ethnic diversity; an increase in the number of people identifying with 'Other' groups since 2001 despite additions to ethnic-group categorisations in the Census; and a growth of mixed ethnic group affiliation (Smith and Simpson, 2015). In Northern Ireland, issues around diversity differ from the British case and have tended to focus on religious/community background groupings (Shuttleworth and Lloyd, 2009). However, whilst its ethnic minority populations remain numerically and proportionately very small, its ethnic diversity also experienced a significant increase. The minority population as a whole more than doubled between 2001 and 2011, with its population share rising from 0.8 to 1.8 per cent (based on Tables KS006 and KS201NI of Northern Ireland's 2001 and 2011 censuses, respectively).

ETHNIC DIFFERENCES IN DEMOGRAPHY

The immigration history of Britain's ethnic minority groups means that their demographic foundations—the age-sex structure of their populations—are distinct from those of the longer-resident White British majority. This, in its turn, has implications for fertility and mortality: if there are larger proportions of young people than in the population overall, there is a higher proportion of ethnic minority groups 'at risk' of having children and a lower proportion 'at risk' of ill health and death. In this section, we focus first on the age differences, then on the fertility differences and associated characteristics and finally on mortality.

As regards age structure, as has already been noted for Mixed ethnic groups, minority groups in Britain are younger than the population overall. This is because immigrants tend to arrive as young adults. For example, migrants from the Indian sub-continent predominantly arrived in the 1960s and 1970s, which means that in the 2010s these first-generation migrants are entering their seventies, with relatively few Pakistanis, Indians and Bangladeshis being above this age yet. An even more striking example is provided by the Other White group, which is largely made up of people arriving since the mid-2000s from the new European Union member countries, particularly Poland, and so still having a very high proportion aged in their twenties and thirties. The population pyramids in Figure 9.1 clearly demonstrate the younger age structures of these minority groups—Indian and Other White—compared to the White British group.

Turning to fertility, ethnic differences have lessened since the 1970s, primarily as a result of the decrease in the total fertility rate of Bangladeshi and Pakistani groups from around 6 and 5, respectively, in the late 1970s (Coleman and Dubuc, 2010). For the period 2001–2005, the average period total fertility rate (TFR) was lowest for Chinese (1.24), Other White (1.5) and Indian (1.64), with Black Caribbean (1.94) slightly higher than White British

White British

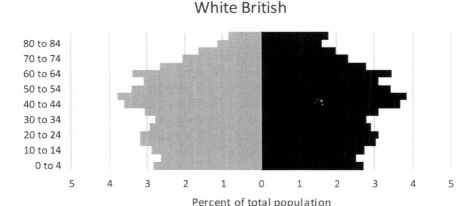

Percent of total population

■ Females ▣ Males

Figure 9.1a   Population Pyramids Showing the Age and Sex Distribution of Ethnic Groups in England and Wales, White British.
Source: 2011 Census, Table DC2101EW (Crown copyright); authors' own calculations.

Indian

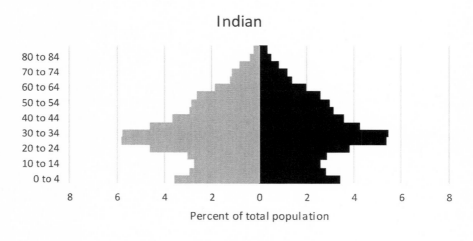

Percent of total population

■ Females ▣ Males

Figure 9.1b   Population Pyramids Showing the Age and Sex Distribution of Ethnic Groups in England and Wales, Indian.
Source: 2011 Census, Table DC2101EW (Crown copyright); authors' own calculations.

(1.71), though still below replacement level. Black African (2.32) had a TFR above replacement level, but the highest TFR remained for Bangladeshi (2.97) and Pakistani (2.79) ethnic groups (Coleman and Dubuc, 2010). All ethnic groups have seen a delay in the timing of births (i.e., women having

Other White

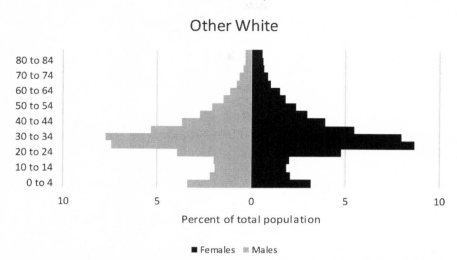

Figure 9.1c Population Pyramids Showing the Age and Sex Distribution of Ethnic Groups in England and Wales, Other White.
Source: 2011 Census, Table DC2101EW (Crown copyright); authors' own calculations.

children at a later age), with this tempo shift particularly evident for the Indian ethnic group.

Ethnic minorities in the UK have lower fertility than the populations of their countries of origin. In the case of Pakistani women, Coleman and Dubuc (2010) demonstrate that UK-born women have lower fertility rates than migrants from Pakistan, but the decline in total fertility rate between 1970 and 2000 is observed for Pakistani-born women in the UK *and* UK-born Pakistani women. Coleman and Dubuc's comparison of the fertility of migrants from particular origins in different destination countries leads to the suggestion that 'the effect of the host country's environment on first-generation immigrants may play a lesser role in influencing family-size choices than do influences and norms from within the ethnic group itself' (Coleman and Dubuc, 2010: 36; see also Dubuc, 2012). On the overall question of fertility convergence, Coleman and Dubuc (2010: 35) write, 'If some minorities remain concentrated in lower occupational groups, with poor educational attainment and high levels of unemployment and economic inactivity, birth rates are unlikely to converge to national norms. Specific cultural or religious or minority-status effects are additional factors'. (For further details on ethnic fertility convergence, see Chapter 5.)

In addition to socio-economic and cultural reasons for differing fertility, the nature of partnership should be considered. Hannemann and Kulu (2015) compare the partnership trajectories of immigrant groups in the UK and the

British-origin majority and find certain distinctions. For example, people of European and Caribbean origin have high cohabitation rates, whereas cohabitation is rare for those of South Asian origin; those from the Caribbean and their descendants have higher divorce rates than the British-origin population, whereas divorce rates are low for South Asians. Although differences between the partnership trajectories of immigrants and their descendants were found, these did not clearly demonstrate a convergence to a common experience. Rather, ethnic/migrant differences in partnership formation and dissolution persist in the UK (Hannemann and Kulu, 2015).

Similarly, Catney and Simpson (2014) show persistence in ethnic differences in household composition. Although they find a general reduction in household size, including for those (Asian) ethnic groups that have traditionally formed large households, they conclude that this is largely a result of a reduction in the number of children in a household, which is consistent with reduced fertility. They find persistence in the number of adults in a household, with a continuation of inter-generational adult households amongst some minority groups in the UK.

A stark marker of social group differences is mortality, often expressed in terms of life expectancy or healthy life expectancy. For example, Wohland et al. (2015) report that in England and Wales in 2001 there was a difference of 10.5 years for men and 11.9 years for women in healthy life expectancy at birth between ethnic groups, with Chinese having the highest and Bangladeshi (men) and Pakistani (women) the lowest. It has been suggested that such inequalities are largely to do with socio-economic differences between ethnic groups, together with differences in dietary, smoking and physical activity behaviours (Mindell et al., 2014).

Tracking the demography of ethnic groups is not straightforward. Aside from issues of changes to ethnic-group categories and changes to individuals' ethnic-group affiliations that can result in an alteration of the characteristics of ethnic groups (Simpson et al., 2015), the statistics on births and deaths are not statutorily recorded by ethnic group. Considerable methodological ingenuity has been deployed for providing the above picture of the demography of ethnic groups. The difficulty in correctly estimating demographic differences and trends for ethnic groups is well illustrated by Rees et al.'s (2013) ethnic-group population projections. The challenge of data and estimation will persist and perhaps grow as interest gathers in the ageing of minority groups, prompting research to focus on the initially small elderly ethnic minority populations. What the work on ethnic-group demography in the UK has already shown, however, is that such endeavours bear fruit in terms of identifying demographic differences between ethnic groups, whilst also raising questions about their meaning, causes and consequences.

GEOGRAPHIES OF ETHNIC DIVERSITY, SEGREGATION AND MIXING

Paucity of data is a particular challenge for studying ethnic differences at the local scale and the processes of residential mobility and longer-distance migration that are the main drivers of change in these. Yet thanks primarily to the detail available from the censuses, the last two decades have seen growing attention being paid to matters of geography. Debate has been fierce in the academic, policy and political discourses about ethnic residential segregation and the patterns of internal migration that are changing the population landscape.

The geographies of ethnicity and ethnic diversity constitute an important theme of research for two main reasons. The first relates to the potential for understanding better the highly charged debates that surround issues of integration and for shedding light on the social myths that are associated with them. Interest in the extent to which ethnic groups live together or apart gained policy and media prominence in the early 2000s, following the 'race riots' in several northern cities. A review of the debates and sometimes controversial policy interventions that ensued is provided in Finney and Simpson (2009), Phillips et al. (2014) and Catney (2015a). Although integration has lessened in policy import in recent years, it continues to be a concern of government (COMPAS/DCLG, 2015), such that debate about inter-group relations and the (local) impacts of immigration and diversity are a nearly daily feature in the national and local press.

The second major reason that residential patterns are worthy of attention is their relationship with ethnic inequalities. Whilst the attractiveness of certain neighbourhoods, and attachment to place, act to retain residents in certain locales (for example, see Phillips et al., 2007), constraints on housing and neighbourhood choice are powerful forces that can limit opportunities. Socioeconomic inequalities can hinder spatial mobility, whilst direct and indirect racism and prejudice can result in spatial inequalities if some areas are rendered 'out of bounds' for certain groups.

Ethnic diversity is typically an urban phenomenon. Attractive to immigrants and their descendants, cities provide labour and housing market opportunities, ethno-cultural services and supportive familial and social networks. As such, as with other immigration-receiving countries, the UK's metropolitan areas have traditionally been home to by far the largest share of ethnic minority populations. In 2011, whilst 78 per cent of the White British population of England and Wales lived in urban areas, at least 90 per cent of each ethnic minority group were urban based—with the sole exception of the White Gypsy/Irish Traveller group, at 75 per cent (Catney, 2016). Historically, settlement has favoured urban areas with specific labour demands, and the cities of Birmingham, Leicester, Manchester, Liverpool, Glasgow, Bradford and especially London are some of the largest UK 'gateway' places.

Although the urban bias of ethnic diversity is still observable for UK cities, new evidence from the 2011 Census suggests that the geographical patterning of diversity is becoming more intricate (cf. Neal, 2002). Indeed, new forms of ethnic mixing, and not just between people but also between places—and in new places—has accompanied the significant growth in ethnic minority populations. Figure 9.2 is a map of the 1991–2011 change in the population affiliating with ethnic groups other than White, for a consistent set of ward boundaries (for more details, see Catney, 2015b). Growth of these groups was highest in London and other large cities with a history of diversity, including Birmingham, Bradford, Leeds, Leicester and Manchester. However, the populations of Black and Minority Ethnic groups have also grown in wards outside these urban centres. Of the 8,850 wards of England and Wales in Figure 9.2, only 145 experienced a decrease in their percentage Black and Minority Ethnic, with only forty of these decreasing by more than one percentage point.

Catney (2015b) explores the changing geographies of ethnic-group populations further by considering the diversity of small areas across England and Wales and how these had changed between 1991 and 2011. The dominance of certain cities as sites of high ethnic diversity was apparent at all three census time points; higher levels of diversity were particularly notable in London and in the northern and midland cities of Bradford, Leeds, Manchester, Sheffield, Nottingham, Leicester and Birmingham. Over time, however, ethnic diversity has been spreading out into new locales. The suburban hinterland of these major cities has diversified, but so, too, have some rural areas with previously little history of ethnic diversity. As a result, ethnic diversity is now a feature of more neighbourhoods than ever before, and new spaces of diversity are emerging. This is mirrored in other countries, where minority presence has increased in previously 'White' spaces—for example, across Europe (Finney and Catney, 2012) and in the US (Lichter, 2012). One important mechanism for this geographical spread is internal migration from urban centres towards new locales (see next section). New immigration streams to less urban locales will also have contributed to these changes in the landscape of diversity—for example, asylum dispersal strategies that have favoured spaces outside traditional immigration settlement (Zetter et al., 2005) and economic migration from Eastern Europe following labour opportunities in rural areas (Robinson, 2010).

These striking new trends pose an obvious question: Are ethnic groups becoming more geographically mixed? Academic contributions to the British debate about neighbourhood integration in the early 2000s were fairly unanimous in demonstrating decreasing ethnic segregation over time

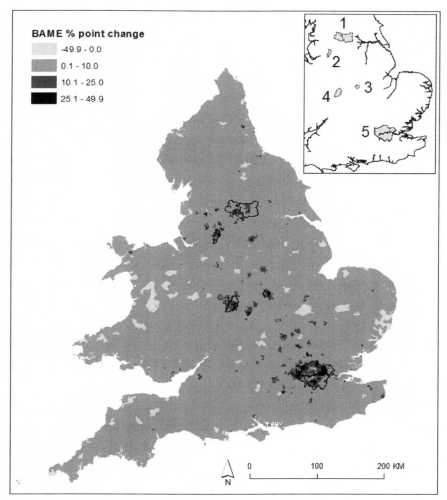

Figure 9.2 Change in the Minority Ethnic Population, 1991–2001, England and Wales.
Note: Selected place labels (with 2011 boundaries) are included for reference:
1 = Districts of Bradford and Leeds; 2 = Greater Manchester County; 3 = District of
Leicester; 4 = District of Birmingham; 5 = London.
Source: 2011 Census, Table KS201EW (Crown copyright), and complete population esti-
mates based on the 1991 and 2001 Censuses (Crown copyright); authors' own calculations.

(Simpson, 2007; Finney and Simpson, 2009) and urban deconcentration
(Rees and Butt, 2004). Revealing information about ethnic-group residential
patterns for small areas and for the whole population, the 2011 Census provides an exciting opportunity to observe change in the residential geographies
of ethnic-group populations for more recent years, as we now demonstrate.

Figure 9.3 uses the consistent wards of England and Wales shown in Figure 9.2 to consider change in segregation for the seven comparable ethnic groups between 1991 and 2011, plus the four combined Mixed groups between 2001 and 2011. Segregation is measured using the Index of Dissimilarity (D), a commonly applied measure of the spatial spread of ethnic groups that provides information on the evenness in the distribution of two groups, such as Indian and White British, or Indian and the rest of the population. In Figure 9.3, each ethnic group is compared to the rest of the population. For example, the proportion of the Indian ethnic group in England and Wales who live in a given ward is subtracted from the proportion of the rest of the population who live in that ward, the absolute value of the product is computed, and the results are summed for all wards; the end result is then multiplied by 50. If the two groups have the same proportions in all areas (e.g., 75 per cent Indian, 25 per cent rest of the population), then the two groups are identically distributed ($D = 0$), but if each zone comprises members of only the Indian ethnic group *or* all groups except Indian, they are unevenly distributed ($D = 100$).

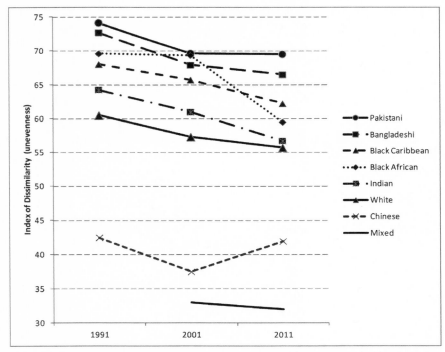

Figure 9.3 **Ethnic Group Segregation (Index of Dissimilarity) in England and Wales, 1991–2011.**
Source: 2011 Census, Table KS201EW (Crown copyright), and complete population estimates based on the 1991 and 2001 Censuses (Crown copyright); authors' own calculations.

Figure 9.3 shows the percentage point change in this value between the three censuses. It is clear that each ethnic group has become more spatially dispersed during the period. The Black African group experienced a decrease in unevenness of ten percentage points over the two decades, with a decrease of between five and eight percentage points for the South Asian groups— Indian, Pakistani and Bangladeshi. White segregation steadily decreased over time, from an already low level. As regards the Mixed category, segregation was already very low in 2001 and was lower still by 2011. The only exception to the trend of decreasing segregation is the Chinese ethnic group, albeit from a level much lower than that for the other six non-mixed groups. Its becoming more unevenly distributed since 2001 is very likely because of student immigration to specific university locales.

Changes in segregation for more detailed ethnic groups and specific places have been explored in several studies drawing on 2011 Census data. Catney (2016) examines change in neighbourhood segregation (measured for the smallest Census geography, Output Areas, which have an average of approximately three hundred people) for all sixteen comparable ethnic minority groups between 2001 and 2011. Using the Index of Dissimilarity, this work demonstrates decreasing minority group segregation in major urban areas, including by thirteen percentage points for the Indian group in Manchester; sixteen and thirteen percentage points for the Black African and Chinese groups, respectively, in Bradford; and twelve percentage points for the Bangladeshi group in outer London. Utilising their area classification scheme that categorises neighbourhoods according to their proportions of White and groups other than White (resulting in five area types with varying degrees of White and 'not-White' dominance), Johnston et al. (2013, 2015) used 2001 and 2011 Census data to demonstrate an increasingly multi-ethnic England and Wales—a trend that is particularly striking in London. They found increased ethnic mixing in areas of London where the White group was previously the dominant group, and no evidence of the development of 'enclaves' where one minority group dominated (Johnston et al., 2015). Exploring the ethnic mix of urban areas in England and Wales, they concluded that 'few cities, and certainly none in England and Wales, contain substantial blocks of territory in which one ethnic minority group comprises the great majority of the population. Instead, ethnic mix is the common characteristic in those parts of British towns and cities which are not predominantly White' (Johnston et al., 2016: 12–13).

These recent empirical observations have been accompanied by methodological developments in the measurement of segregation (for example, Harris, 2014, 2016; Catney, 2015c). The related international literature is long established and extensive (for a review of some of the key international contributions, see Wong, 2014), and UK scholars have been far from absent in these debates (see Peach, 2009). Small-area ethnic-group data available from the Census, accompanied by advances in computational power, have enabled researchers to address the challenges of how best to capture and understand the extent to which ethnic groups are mixed residentially at the very local level, thereby providing an ever-clearer picture of the considerable growth in diversity in Britain's neighbourhoods.

WITHIN-UK MIGRATION OF ETHNIC GROUPS

Whilst the uneven spatial impact of international migration and local differences in rates of natural change play a part in changing the distribution of ethnic-group populations, the primary drivers are local residential mobility and longer-distance internal migration. In the UK, studies of the ethnic dimension of internal migration have flourished over the last two decades, driven by broader social concerns about the extent to which ethnic groups are moving away from one another residentially and enabled by the availability of ethnic-group migration data from the 1991 Census onwards.

Some general points can be made about the internal migration of minority populations from a review of findings on thirteen European countries provided by Finney and Catney (2012). It is commonly found that minorities are more residentially mobile than the majority population, though evidence is mixed about inter-generational convergence in mobility towards a 'mainstream'. The characteristics of minority internal migrants are those well known to depict migrants generally—for example, renters and those with high levels of education are particularly mobile. In most of the countries considered, patterns of de-concentration, dispersal and suburbanisation are evident for minority groups.

For the UK, Finney et al. (2015: 41) identify three distinct features of studies of internal migration and ethnicity: they have been framed by assimilation theory and racialised political debates about ethnic residential segregation; they have predominantly used quantitative methods and secondary data analysis, particularly drawing on the Census; and they have been primarily concerned with questions of who migrates and where. Finney et al. (2015) suggest that, for UK studies to reveal more about the reasons for, and the experiences and consequences of, ethnic differences in internal migration, the development of three theoretical frameworks might be particularly fruitful: integration, inequalities and life course; links between international and internal migration and transnationalism; and neighbourhood change and policy. Certainly, more than one method of research is required to understand the drivers and impacts of ethnic differences in internal migration.

Recent research points to some illuminating approaches to these questions; we pick out three here (for a broader review, see Finney et al., 2015; Finney and Catney, 2012). One approach focusses on structural processes and inequalities. In the US and some European countries, attention has been paid to the relationship between residential mobility and housing markets. For example, Vidal and Windzio (2012) suggest that the high levels of immigrant mobility are related to housing adjustment, which is exacerbated by structural discrimination that prevents minorities satisfying their housing needs. Though rather little attention has been paid to the role of housing markets in shaping contemporary ethnic geographies in the UK (Ratcliffe, 2009; Markannen and Harrison, 2013), there is evidence of marked ethnic inequalities in housing (Finney and Harries, 2015), and socio-economic inequalities have been proposed as a factor in shaping ethnic-group migration patterns. Catney and Simpson (2010) examine whether migration from areas of immigrant settlement in the UK was socio-economically selective. They found clear evidence for a social gradient: for all ethnic groups, those in higher socio-economic groups were more likely than those in lower socio-economic groups to move away from areas of initial settlement.

Secondly, studies have begun to pay attention to how perceptions of places and populations affect mobility aspirations and decisions. Hedman et al. (2011) find that people are attracted to neighbourhoods where their population matches their own characteristics, particularly in relation to income but also in terms of ethnicity and other demographic and socio-economic characteristics. Perceptions of the racial character of neighbourhoods can also affect residential decision making (Bader and Krysan, 2015; van Ham and Fietjen, 2008). For minorities, the social support and security, as well as cultural and religious ties, of diverse neighbourhoods can be a reason not to move (Phillips, 2015). In political science, attitudes to immigration and diversity have been examined in relation to residential mobility. Kaufman and Harris (2015) examine whether attitudes to immigration underpin the direction of White internal migration with respect to diverse neighbourhoods. They investigate whether White British residents who are more hostile to immigration are more likely than others to leave diverse wards and more likely than others to move to less diverse wards. They find only weak evidence in support of these propositions.

Thirdly, studies have attempted to directly assess the impact of migration on segregation. This is difficult because, as mentioned at the start of this section, internal migration is only one component of neighbourhood population change. For ethnic groups with young population structures, an excess of births over deaths can contribute more to local population change than migration (Finney, 2010). International migration can also come into play; Stillwell and McNulty (2012), for example, find immigration to be replacing outward internal migration in some ethnic minority concentrations in London. Shuttleworth et al. (2013) provide one example of a UK study examining directly the impact on segregation of residential mobility, focussing on Northern Ireland. Although they find some evidence of differential mobility behaviour with regard to community affiliation (religion), they do not find evidence for resulting increases in segregation.

Given the geographical and temporal consistency of the broad findings that minorities are more mobile than the majority and also that minority internal migrants share characteristics of internal migrants generally and tend to disperse from (settlement) concentrations, it is plausible to expect such patterns to continue. However, it is possible that patterns may have shifted in recent years. In particular, the large-scale immigration from the European Union since 2004 and the re-emergence of 'the refugee crisis' in Europe in the current decade, along with the economic recession and the associated UK 'housing crisis', create a different terrain for internal migration from that in past decades (for more detail on this, see Chapter 8).

To test whether or not the earlier trends have continued, we examine patterns of internal migration by ethnic group using the 2011 Census question about place of residence one year ago. Table 9.3 presents rates of internal migration by ethnic group, ordered from the most mobile to the least mobile. The least mobile ethnic groups are the South Asian groups and the White group, for whom between 9 and 12 per cent moved house in the year prior to the Census. Black, Mixed and Other ethnic groups had above-average levels of internal migration, at around 15 per cent. The most mobile ethnic group was Chinese: a fifth of the Chinese population living in the UK in 2011 lived somewhere different from their UK address in 2010. In addition, 10 per cent

Table 9.3   Rates of Internal Migration by Ethnic Group, UK, 2010–2011

Ethnic Group	Non-Movers (%)	Internal Migrants (%)	Immigrants (%)
TOTAL	88.0	10.9	1.1
Chinese	68.7	20.6	10.7
Other	79.0	15.9	5.1
Other Asian	79.3	15.4	5.3
Mixed	82.7	15.6	1.7
Black	83.6	14.2	2.2
Gypsy/Traveller	84.4	14.4	1.2
Indian	84.6	11.9	3.6
White	88.7	10.5	0.8
Pakistani	89.0	9.0	1.9
Bangladeshi	89.1	9.7	1.2

Notes: Migration tables are published for the UK and therefore use UK harmonised ethnic group categories. This means that the 'White' group in this table contains all the 'White' categories listed in Figure 9.1, and the 'Black' group contains all the 'Black' categories from the Census question.
Source: Census 2011, Table MIG003; authors' own calculations.

of the Chinese population in 2011 had arrived from outside the UK since 2010. These results are generally consistent with results from the 2001 Census in terms of levels of mobility and ethnic-group rankings (see Finney and Simpson, 2008). The exception is the Chinese ethnic group, whose mobility in 2011 was higher than in 2001, very likely to be largely due to the increase in its student population.

Data from the 2011 Census suggest dispersal of ethnic minorities from areas of minority concentration, as was also the case in 2001 and 1991 (see Simpson and Finney, 2009). Table 9.4 shows net migration for Whites and Minorities from areas classified according to their level of minority concentration. The results are shown for Output Areas, wards and Local Authority districts. At all scales there is movement out, on balance, of Whites and minorities from ethnic minority concentrations. In all cases, the net movement of Whites is slightly higher than that of minorities. In general, there is net movement of both Whites and minorities towards less diverse neighbourhoods.

Previous studies have shown that there are important socio-economic distinctions to dispersal (Simpson and Finney, 2009; Catney and Simpson, 2010). Figure 9.4 demonstrates that this remains the case at the district level. The chart shows net internal migration from ethnic minority concentrations of ethnic minority groups and the White group by socio-economic class. Overall, there is movement out of minority concentrations by all ethnic groups and social classes. For concentrations of all the ethnic minority groups combined, the rate of net out-movement is higher for Whites than minorities. For areas with high concentrations of ethnic minorities, a shallow social gradient is found for minorities in that the rate of out-migration is highest for those in higher managerial and professional occupations. By contrast, a social gradient is not evident for Whites leaving ethnic minority concentration districts.

Table 9.4   Net Migration Rates (%) for Whites and Minorities, by Quintiles of Diversity, for UK Output Areas, Wards and Districts

	Output Area		Ward		District	
	White	*Minority*	*White*	*Minority*	*White*	*Minority*
1 Most diverse	−2.6%	−1.5%	−1.7%	−1.3%	−1.0%	−0.6%
2	−0.8%	+0.0%	−0.2%	−0.2%	−0.2%	−0.0%
3	+0.3%	+0.8%	+0.5%	+0.5%	−0.1%	+0.1%
4	+0.6%	+1.4%	+0.3%	+1.0%	+0.2%	+0.6%
5 Least Diverse	−0.1%	−0.6%	−0.1%	+0.0%	+0.0%	−0.1%

Notes: Sub-national areas have been grouped into quintiles of diversity by the ordering of all areas in descending order of the area's percentage of ethnic minorities, then allocating each area to one of five 'quintiles' each with one-fifth of the total UK ethnic minority population, from highest concentration to lowest concentration.
Source: Census 2011, Table MIG003; authors' own calculations.

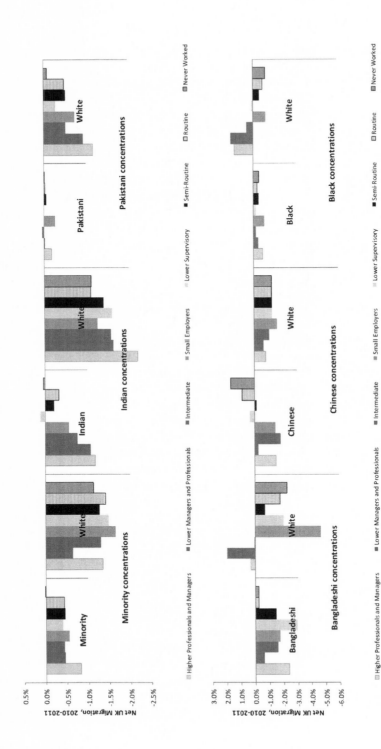

Figure 9.4   Net Migration Rates for Ethnic Minority Groups and the White Group for Districts of Highest Concentration for Selected Minority Groupings, UK, 2010–2011, by NS-SeC.

Note: Ethnic group concentrations are the quintile of most diverse districts for each ethnic group (see Table 9.2 note).

Source: 2011 Census, Table MIG003 (Crown copyright); authors' own calculations.

In terms of the individual ethnic groups, a much clearer social gradient is seen in the movement of Indians and Whites out of Indian concentrations. For areas of Pakistani concentration, managerial and professional Whites have the highest rate of out-migration, and there is a social gradient, but not so for Pakistanis. For Chinese concentrations, there is a social gradient for Chinese migration (i.e., out-migration of higher social classes and in-migration of lower social classes), but there is no clear gradient for White movement from these same districts.

Perhaps the most striking results are seen for the net migration from Bangladeshi and Black concentrations, which are all districts located in inner London. Although a social gradient in dispersal is not evident, ethnic and socio-economic distinctions are seen in the migration patterns: for Black and Bangladeshi concentrations, there is out-migration of all socio-economic categories apart from White managers and professionals who are, on balance, moving into these districts. This may reflect Fielding's (1992) 'escalator region' effect that brings well-qualified individuals into central and inner London and raises questions about how this may be operating differently across ethnic groups.

These 2011 Census findings on patterns of internal migration by ethnic group display considerable consistency with previous results, showing that ethnic differences in levels of mobility persist, as do general patterns of dispersal from ethnic minority concentrations. The analysis of Census data also adds weight to extant literature that demonstrates the importance of being attentive to the intersections of ethnicity and socio-economic position for understanding internal migration patterns and processes. These results suggest that, despite the changing international migration and political terrain, there are persistent underlying forces shaping residential mobility in Britain and its ethnic stratification.

CONCLUSIONS

The ethnic diversification of Britain's population over the last two decades has been a highly significant dimension of population change, both in its extent and pace and in its social and political resonance. Population researchers have responded to this by studying the nature of this diversity, with particular emphasis on the demographic characteristics of ethnic-group populations, their residential geographies and the internal migration patterns helping to shape these. They have also been central to the promotion of ethnic-group data that has resulted in the continuation of ethnic-group questions in censuses and surveys. In addition, the study of the changing ethnic-group populations of Britain has brought methodological innovations—for example, in how to measure their fertility, project their often small populations and most appropriately and accurately quantify their changing geographical patterns.

Population scholars have, thus, been part of the social change that has come to recognise ethnic diversity as a norm. Even in a political context of strong opposition to immigration, there is recognition of the benefits of diversity—for example, in the speeches given in 2015 by the prime minister and home secretary (Cameron, 2015; May, 2015). Of course, there is the pervasive danger of essentialising ethnic groups, and the challenge to researchers in this regard is in identifying when ethnicity is significant and when it is not—when ethnicity is the driver of difference and if, and how, this matters.

Two clear messages emerge from this chapter's review in relation to the significance of ethnicity. One is that ethnic differences are evident and persistent on a range of demographic markers, including age structure, fertility, mortality, household composition, partnership, urban location and residential mobility. Secondly, ethnic minority groups have experienced considerable change, demographically and geographically, since the early 1990s. This change can be interpreted as adaptation, or integration, and in general shows a gradual alteration of characteristics towards those of the population as a whole, along with clear trends of increased residential mixing. However, convergence would be too strong a claim, and particular practices and preferences that differentiate ethnic groups persist, including the higher number of adults in Asian households compared to other groups, the higher cohabitation and divorce rates for Caribbeans, the higher mortality rates for Bangladeshi and Pakistani populations, high residential mobility rates of the Chinese and Mixed groups and the persistence of residential clustering of ethnic minority groups alongside increasing mixing.

We suggested at the outset that ethnic differences can be thought of in terms of two processes of social change: immigrant integration, and racism and discrimination. In interpreting ethnic differences, the two are not easily disentangled. Both are important for understanding ethnic-group population change. Yet it could be argued that UK population research still has a long way to go to thoroughly engage with these issues and their intersection. On immigrant integration, UK work is somewhat special in prioritising concepts and measures of ethnicity over those of immigrant generation, which is the norm in continental Europe and more commonly sits alongside measures of race and ethnicity in North American and Australasian scholarship. To better enable comparisons and collaborations with other national contexts, UK studies would benefit from paying more attention to immigration history and immigrant generation. This is particularly pertinent given recent high levels of immigration, particularly from Europe, and rising interest in minority identities within the White population. Furthermore, political devolution is disaggregating the UK along lines of differing perspectives on immigration and, potentially, different immigration and integration policies.

In suggesting that greater attention be paid to immigration and immigration history in understanding population change, we are not proposing that less attention should be given to ethnicity. Ethnicity remains conceptually distinct and substantively relevant, particularly in the marked and persistent inequalities faced by minority groups observed for multiple social and economic factors, including employment, housing and health (Jivraj and Simpson, 2015). Understanding how these inequalities—and the discriminatory processes and behaviours that lie behind them—affect demographic patterns should be an academic and policy priority.

One of the most exciting challenges for UK research on ethnicity and ethnic diversity is to contribute to debates about life course and intergenerationality found in population studies more broadly. We have argued elsewhere (Finney and Catney, 2012) that these perspectives have much to offer in improving understandings of ethnic-group geographies, and this can be expanded to the other demographic dimensions considered in this chapter. For quantitative work, developments in this direction have been restricted by small samples, particularly for some age groups and cohorts, and by a lack of longitudinal data. However, we are reaching a stage at which the size of minority populations across the life course, including the older ages, will make quantitative research possible and where more longitudinal data are available, notably via the linked Census records in the UK's three Longitudinal Studies and panel studies such as *Understanding Society*. Furthermore, debates about national population data collection beyond the 2021 Census present an opportunity for considering how we measure ethnicity and how we address questions of population change through the integration and linking of a greater diversity of data and methods.

NOTES

1. Nissa Finney wishes to thank the Economic and Social Research Council for supporting this work via the Centre on Dynamics of Ethnicity (CoDE), as well as Ludi Simpson for collaboration in the analysis of 2011 Census data on internal migration.

2. Gemma Catney is sincerely grateful to the Leverhulme Trust, for funding an Early Career Fellowship, 'Geographies of Ethnic and Social Segregation in England and Wales, 1991–2011' (ECF-2011-065), under which some of this research was conducted. Thank you to Paul Norman for the provision of consistent ward boundaries. Thanks to Ludi Simpson and Albert Sabater for making available ethnic group population estimates for 1991 and 2011.

Chapter 10

Reproductive and Sexual Behaviour and Health

Ernestina Coast and Emily Freeman[1]

Changing population structure and composition, combined with dynamic social norms and behaviours, has implications for a population's sexual and reproductive health. Sexual relationships and sexual and reproductive behaviour and attitudes are key components of physical and mental well-being. Sexual and reproductive health (SRH) is not just the absence of ill health or disease but also 'a state of complete physical, mental and social wellbeing' (WHO, 2010). Good SRH implies a pleasurable and safe sex life, freedom in sexual expression and the ability to regulate fertility. This chapter considers key ways in which population change has shaped and has been shaped by SRH in the UK over the last twenty-five years.

The majority of the UK population are sexually active (Mercer, 2014). People have sex—volitional and non-volitional—for a wide range of reasons, and with a broad spectrum of positive and negative health outcomes that change over the life course. Strategies to improve SRH focus on both the public health outcomes of sexual behaviour, such as sexually transmitted diseases, and aspects of reproductive and sexual well-being that are important in their own right, such as sexual pleasure. SRH policies and interventions that address and support all aspects of positive sexual experiences are typically most effective in improving health.

SRH beliefs, behaviours and outcomes are shaped by demographic factors, including age, ethnicity, gender and socio-economic status. Recent demographic changes with salience for SRH discussed in previous chapters include population ageing, migration, rates and patterns of partnership formation and dissolution and later childbearing. Reflecting these and generational changes, major shifts in sexual behaviours in the UK since the 1980s include declining age at first intercourse (Hawes et al., 2010), increasing number of lifetime sexual partners and rates of partnership concurrency (Fenton and Hughes, 2003) and more same-sex sexual activity (Wellings and Johnson, 2013; Mercer, 2014).

Of these demographic trends, young people's SRH has arguably attracted the most research and policy attention. Of particular focus are rates of sexual initiation, partner change and conceptions amongst those aged under twenty-five and how these compare to other high-income countries (Hawes et al., 2010). Increased data availability and improved reporting allow better understanding of a broader range of sexual partnerships, behaviours and practices. For example, we know that people aged sixteen to twenty-five years in Britain are more likely to report oral than vaginal sex, and one in five report having anal sex (Hagell, 2014; Marston and Lewis, 2014). Such evidence is crucial if policies and services are to meet the SRH needs of the population, moving beyond a narrow focus on the risk of conception. The implications of non-sexual behaviours such as alcohol and drug misuse for SRH are also important (Tripp and Viner, 2005; Hawes et al., 2010; Aicken et al., 2011; Department of Health, 2013b).

There is also growing recognition of sexual health needs beyond the reproductive ages. Increasing longevity and years of healthy life, combined with older adults' changing expectations and attitudes to sex, increased frequency of divorce and new sexual partnering at older ages and the increasing 'medicalisation of sexuality', means that sexual health services for older adults will become increasingly important (Gott, 2006).

Changes in ethnic composition also have implications for SRH. In England and Wales, census data show that the non-White British population increased by 57 per cent between 1991 (seven million) and 2011 (eleven million), and that the population reporting African ethnicity has grown faster than any other minority in the last two decades (Jivraj, 2012; see also Chapter 9). Black and minority ethnic (BME) populations can be systematically disadvantaged by the design and delivery of SRH services and education, influencing outcomes at the individual and group level (Hennink et al., 1999; Weston, 2003; Saxena et al., 2006; Coleman and Testa, 2007).

Population change is accompanied, and in part driven, by changes in population-level attitudes. Attitudes towards sexuality and reproduction have become more socially inclusive over time (see Figure 10.1). In 2012 in Britain, nearly half (46 per cent) of the population born in the 1940s thought homosexuality was 'always or mostly wrong', compared with 18 per cent of those born in the 1980s. In 1983, 37 per cent of people felt that the law should allow abortion when a woman decides she does not wish to continue the pregnancy, compared to 62 per cent in 2012 (Park et al., 2013), and repeat polling has shown continued declines in support for an outright ban on abortion, down from 12 per cent in 2005 to 7 per cent in 2013 (YouGov, 2013).

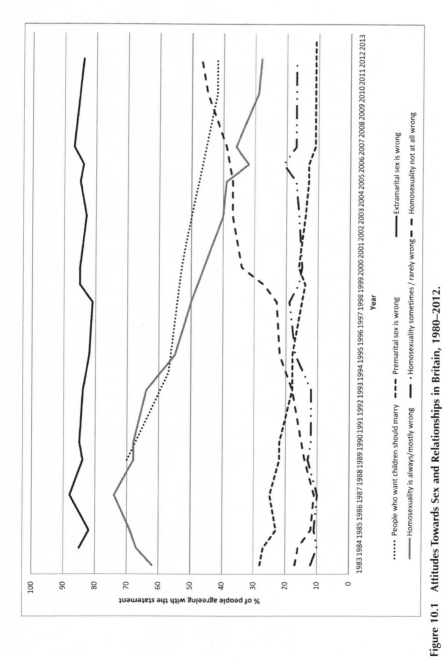

Figure 10.1 Attitudes Towards Sex and Relationships in Britain, 1980–2012.
Source: NatCen British Attitudes Survey data downloaded from http://www.bsa-data.natcen.ac.uk/?_ga=1.6275763.1068730213.1415366354, 5 October 2015.

SEXUAL HEALTH POLICIES

The UK's political system is relatively complex. To varying degrees, the four countries of the UK (Scotland, England, Wales and Northern Ireland) have different legislative powers, policies and responsibilities for collecting and disseminating data. SRH data are sometimes collected for the whole of the UK, sometimes just for Great Britain (Scotland, England and Wales combined) and, more recently, for each country separately.

Each of the four constituent countries of the UK produces their own SRH policies and strategies (Table 10.1). Both Scotland and Northern Ireland's policies describe a situation of 'poor' SRH. All prioritise reducing unintended pregnancies and sexually transmitted infections (STIs), and all but Scotland's policy identify young people as key focus populations for protecting and promoting SRH.

Given these priorities, all countries of the UK have sex-education policies targeted towards children and young people and delivered as part of school-based education programmes. Since around 2000, frameworks for sex

Table 10.1   **Sexual and Reproductive Health (SRH) Policy Priorities**

Country	Document	Date	Focus
England	*A Framework for Sexual Health Improvement in England*	2013– n/a	– Under-18 conceptions – Chlamydia diagnoses at 15–24 – Late diagnosis of HIV
Northern Ireland	*Sexual Health Promotion: Strategy and Action Plan 2008–2013* and *Progress and Priorities*, addendum to 2015	2008– 2015	– SRH of <25s, especially those in or leaving care – Men who have sex with men – Sex workers
Scotland	*Respect and Responsibility. A Strategy and Action Plan for Improving Sexual Health* and *Sexual Health and Blood Borne Virus Framework 2011* and *2015–2020 Update*	2005– 2020	– Accessibility of services – HIV incidence – Unintended pregnancies – Health inequalities in SRH – Outcomes for those with blood-borne viruses – Coercion and harm in sexual relationships – Attitudes to SRH
Wales	*Sexual Health and Wellbeing Action Plan for Wales 2010 to 2015*	2010– 2015	– Sexual health and relationships literacy – Accessibility of services – Unintended pregnancies, especially under 18 – STIs and HIV incidence – Outcomes for people with HIV – Surveillance and research

education have shifted from an emphasis on sex education that reflects moral and religious principles held by school management authorities and parents to emphases on positive sexual relationships and inclusion of topics such as contraception, abortion and sexually transmitted infections. However, provision of sex education is widely regarded to still be inadequate by those working to improve SRH (House of Commons Education Committee, 2015), as well as by young people themselves (Pound et al., 2015).

In England, relationships and sexuality education (RSE) is delivered as part of personal, social, health and economic education (PSHE) from age eleven onwards in most schools, but it does not, as of January 2016, have statutory status. This means that whilst it is compulsorily offered in state (state-funded and run) schools, independent (fee-paying 'private') and academy (state-funded but independently run) schools where curricula are not set by the government are not required to offer sex education. In 2013 the Office for Standards in Education, Children's Services and Skills reported that RSE required improvement in 40 per cent of state-run schools in England (Ofsted, 2013). In 2015 an all-party Government Education Committee reported that, without statutory status, schools were less committed to developing and delivering strong sex-education learning programmes (House of Commons Education Committee, 2015).

School-based sex education is undoubtedly a major source of information, and in surveys it is reported as a main source of information about sex (Wellings et al., 2001; Macdowall et al., 2006). However, school-based programmes are not the only source of information, with parents, peers and media also playing an important role (Yu, 2010; Currie et al., 2011). The impact of school-based sex education programmes on SRH outcomes is, however, mixed (DiCenso et al., 2002). A meta-analysis of school sex education programmes found a positive relationship with improved knowledge (Song et al., 2000), although impacts on outcomes such as conception or abortion are much less clear (Stephenson, 2004; Henderson et al., 2007; Vivancos et al., 2012).

CONTRACEPTION AND UNINTENDED PREGNANCY

The effective use of contraception is the major determinant of population fertility and contributes to reducing maternal morbidity and mortality; barrier methods are effective in preventing sexually transmitted infections. Since 1974, contraception has been available from the National Health Service (NHS) (Botting and Dunnell, 2000).

Most people do not use the same contraceptive method over their life course; they stop, start and switch methods according to their circumstances (partnership, health, age, fertility intentions). Before the 1960s, available fertility control included male and female condoms, intrauterine devices (IUDs), 'natural methods' involving abstinence or withdrawal and male and female sterilisation. In the 1960s female hormonal contraceptives became available as pills and have since dominated the population's 'method mix'—the proportion of people using different methods (Botting and Dunnell, 2000).

Although today there is a wide range of contraceptive options available in the UK, the majority are female controlled. Research to develop male hormonal methods over the last forty years has not been taken up by pharmaceutical companies (Wang and Swerdloff, 2010). Thus, the main male-controlled method remains the male condom.

To benchmark changes in availability of contraception (and abortion) and fertility in the 1960s and 1970s, the British Government commissioned a Survey of Family Planning Services (1975) and the Family Formation Survey (1976). Data on contraceptive use in Britain is available from surveys including the General Household Survey (until 2007), the National Statistics Omnibus Survey (until 2008/2009) and the National Survey of Sexual Attitudes and Lifestyles (NATSAL) (for 1990, 2000, 2010–2012 and 2013).

Data are, of course, political. For example, NATSAL was originally intended to include Northern Ireland, but interviewers there refused to ask sensitive questions, reflecting the prevailing social climate with regards to issues of sexual attitudes and lifestyles (Rolston et al., 2004). Responding to the shortage of Northern Irish data, the Family Planning Association commissioned a survey of young people in 2000 (Schubotz et al., 2002) and since 2010–2011 some data on contraception are available from the Health Survey Northern Ireland.

Trends in Contraceptive Use

Three-quarters of women in Britain aged fifteen to forty-nine used some form of contraception in 2008 and 2009. The majority of those who do not use any form were either already pregnant or trying to conceive or believed that they were not at risk of pregnancy due to lack of opposite-sex sexual activity or reckoned they are infecund (Lader and Hopkins, 2008). Although oral hormonal contraceptives (OCs) and male condoms are the most popular contraceptive methods in Britain, they have some of the highest failure rates, related to the need for their consistent and correct use (Wellings et al., 2007; Bury and Ngo, 2009). In a Scottish study of women undergoing abortion, almost half had been using these methods (Schünmann and Glasier, 2006).

Method mix changes by age. Levels of OC and male condom use amongst older (thirty-five to forty-four) women are much lower than younger (sixteen to twenty-four years) women (OC: 16.8 per cent versus 62.6 per cent; male condom: 26.3 per cent versus 63.3 per cent, respectively). By contrast, levels of IUD use rise with age, from 1.7 per cent at sixteen to twenty-four years to 7.9 per cent at thirty-five to forty-four years, as does female and male sterilisation (0.1 per cent aged sixteen to twenty-four versus 19.7 per cent and aged thirty-five to forty-four, 0 per cent aged sixteen to twenty-four versus 14.9 per cent aged thirty-five to forty-four, respectively) (National Centre for Social Research et al., 2005). A retrospective study of patient case files (1992–1999) for women (twenty to fifty-four years) and men (twenty to sixty-four years) showed a relative decline in female sterilisations over the period and constant levels of vasectomy (Rowlands and Hannaford, 2003).

A UK-wide review of trends in contraceptive use at first sex indicates that 70–80 per cent of people do use contraception, with higher rates reported by women than men (Hawes et al., 2010). Use is related to age of sexual debut, with those aged under sixteen less likely to use contraception at first sex than those aged sixteen to nineteen (Tripp and Viner, 2005). First partnerships involving relatively older or younger partners are less likely to involve contraception (Mercer et al., 2006). A review of contraceptive services for young people suggested that anonymity and confidentiality are their most significant concerns, representing a significant barrier to SRH service use (Baxter et al., 2011).

The male condom is the most frequently reported contraceptive used at first sex by younger people (Mercer et al., 2006), although survey data indicate that approximately 15 per cent of sixteen-to-twenty-four-year-olds had sex with at least two partners in the past year without one (Hagell, 2014). Use of condoms over other methods at younger ages may reflect easier access to condoms (unlike most other contraceptives that are available without a prescription and from a wider range of outlets), or increased acceptability for users (and prescribers) over hormonal methods, or a reluctance to use longer-term methods to protect against pregnancy when sexual activity is sporadic. Levels of OC use at first sex are low, although this varies by age at first sex. In Scotland, over 20 per cent of eighteen-year-old women reported using OC at first sex (West, 1993, cited in Hawes et al., 2010), compared to less than 3 per cent amongst fourteen-year-olds (Henderson, 2002, cited in Hawes et al., 2010). A study of the association between contraceptive method at first sex and subsequent pregnancy amongst sixteen-year-olds in England and Scotland suggests that, even though OC are more effective at pregnancy prevention than condoms, young teenagers may use OC less effectively than condoms (Parkes et al., 2009).

Long-acting reversible contraceptives (LARCs)—contraceptive injections, implants, intrauterine systems (IUS) and IUDs—are more effective at preventing pregnancy than user-controlled quick-acting hormonal methods and condoms. They are currently a policy and service priority in England,

Scotland and Wales, reflecting new NICE guidance (Department of Health, 2013b). A multi-year (2004–2010) study of the use of LARCs in the UK using the general practice (GP) database found overall increases in use, whilst remaining low at younger ages (Cea Soriano et al., 2014). Data from England suggest that LARC usage is associated with decreased abortion and unintended pregnancy rates amongst women aged less than twenty years, but not with those aged twenty years and older (Connolly et al., 2014).

Despite increases in their use, an attitudes study of general-practice clinicians in England found that, whilst a substantial proportion (80.2 per cent) were supportive of LARCs for preventing adolescent pregnancies, less than half (47.1 per cent) thought young women would want to use them. The study identified the need for substantial professional and public education and training to increase the provision of LARCs, especially for younger women amongst whom LARC knowledge was low (Wellings et al., 2007).

Trends in contraceptive use by ethnicity suggest that women from all ethnic minority groups are less likely to report using hormonal or permanent contraception than White women, but there are significant differences by partnership status. In Britain, cohabiting or never-married women of Indian and Pakistani ethnicity are less likely to use contraception (78 per cent and 74 per cent, respectively) than other cohabiting or never-married women. However, never-married and non-cohabiting Black Caribbean and Black African women (88 per cent and 82 per cent, respectively) are less likely to use contraception than similar Indian and White women (100 per cent and 95 per cent, respectively). These differences persist after taking parity and educational achievement into account (Saxena et al., 2006). The reason for differences between ethnicities has not been fully explored but may reflect differing access to contraceptive services or fertility preferences. Migrants' use of contraception may reflect culture and services in their place of origin. For example, qualitative interviews with Chinese asylum applicants to the UK show how their experience of (very) different contraceptive service and policy in China continued to influence their decisions about contraception once in the UK (Verran et al., 2015). The limited evidence suggests a need for contraceptive service provision to respond more effectively to the needs of the UK's changing population composition.

Emergency Hormonal Contraception

Emergency hormonal contraception (EHC), launched in the UK in the 1960s, has been widely available without prescription since 2001 (Anderson and Blenkinsopp, 2006). Analyses of data for women aged sixteen to forty-nine years from the 2000–2002 Omnibus Survey, however, showed no significant change in the proportion of women using EHC or of having unprotected sex:

8.4 per cent in 2000, 7.9 per cent in 2001 and 7.2 per cent in 2002 (Marston et al., 2005). Whilst knowledge levels about EHC in the UK are high (Dawe and Rainford, 2004), rates of use remain relatively low, possibly reflecting low levels of knowledge about how to access EHC, or barriers to access. Research amongst women presenting for an abortion in Scotland in 2004–2005 found that 11.8 per cent had used EHC to try to prevent the pregnancy. We conclude that, with such low levels of EHC use even amongst women who were not planning a pregnancy, EHC is unlikely to significantly reduce unintended pregnancy rates (Lakha and Glasier, 2006). Use of EHC is highest amongst women aged below twenty years, possibly reflecting greater levels of knowledge and awareness amongst younger cohorts. A study of factors associated with the use of EHC amongst British women aged sixteen to forty-four showed use was more common amongst young, single women, women using male condoms for contraception and women with more than one sexual partner in the preceding year (Black et al., 2006).

Unintended Pregnancy

Understanding patterns of sexual behaviour and contraceptive use, including EHC, is critical for the reduction of unintended pregnancy. Unintended pregnancy—particularly amongst younger women—remains a priority focus for health policy and services (Baxter et al., 2011). It is estimated in Britain that one in six pregnancies in Britain is unplanned (Wellings et al., 2013). A study of women attending antenatal care in Scotland found only 65.6 per cent describing their pregnancy as intended, whilst nearly a third were 'ambivalent' (Lakha and Glasier, 2006). Evidence from NATSAL-3 suggests that unplanned pregnancy is associated with receiving sex education mainly from a non-school-based source, highlighting the linkages between sex education and reproductive outcomes (Wellings et al., 2013). Nevertheless, conceptions amongst the under-eighteens are decreasing. In 2012–2013, the overall conception rate fell and the number of under-eighteen conceptions was the lowest since 1969 (ONS, 2015s).

Whilst some pregnancies result from the failure of a contraceptive method, most pregnancies occur either because no contraception was used or because the method was used inconsistently or incorrectly (Price et al., 1997; Schünmann and Glasier, 2006; Rowlands, 2007a; Bury and Ngo, 2009). It is estimated in the UK that up to 25 per cent of unwanted pregnancies that end in induced abortion are due to these reasons (Lakha and Glasier, 2006). These data point to the need for improved education and services to reduce inconsistent, incorrect or non-use of contraception amongst those wishing to limit their fertility, and to increase awareness and use of EHC services. A prospective cohort study of women in England found that women who stopped or switched their contraceptive method were younger, better educated and more likely to be single compared to women who continuously used the same method for a year (Wellings et al., 2015).

ABORTION

Whilst some women will proceed with their pregnancies, many of which will become wanted, some women will end them. In England and Wales in 2013 (ONS, 2015s), around one in five pregnancies were aborted, a proportion that has remained relatively stable over the past two decades (19.2 per cent in 1993; 22.5 per cent in 2003). Governments in England (Department of Health, 2013b), Wales (NAW, 2000; WAG, 2010) and Scotland (Scottish Executive, 2005; NHSQIS, 2008) have all published policy documents that include recommendations for improving abortion services, including promoting equitable access to high-quality services. However, access to abortion in the UK is unequal, with different legal frameworks for Britain and Northern Ireland.

Abortion Law in the UK

In Britain the law regarding abortion is set out in the Abortion Act of 1967. This permits abortions up to twenty-four weeks of gestation if the pregnancy would involve a greater risk than termination to the life or physical or mental health of the pregnant woman or her family, taking account of her foreseeable environment. Abortions at any gestation are permitted to prevent death or grave permanent injury to the pregnant woman's mental or physical health or in cases where there is a substantial risk that if a child were born, it would suffer from 'such physical or mental abnormalities as to be seriously handicapped' (UK Abortion Act, 1967).

There are fewer circumstances under which abortion is permitted in Northern Ireland. A judicial review there in 2003 clarified the legal grounds for abortion to be where continuation of the pregnancy threatens the life of the pregnant woman, or where it presents serious 'permanent or long-term' harm to her physical or mental health. Whilst possibility of death is sufficient for abortion to be legal, harm to physical or mental health is required to be probable. It has, however, been argued that the abortion provision remains inconsistent in Northern Ireland (FPA, 2014). The majority of women travel to England to access abortion services. In 2011–2012, thirty-five women received a legal abortion in Northern Ireland, compared with a conservative estimate of 1,007 Northern Ireland residents who received a legal abortion in England in 2011 and 905 in 2012 (FPA, 2014).

Access to Abortion for Residents of Northern Ireland

Women from Northern Ireland who travel to Britain are not entitled to use NHS abortion services. Further, whilst early gestation abortions do not normally involve an overnight stay, appointments may mean that women travelling from Northern Ireland typically have to travel the day before their procedure. It is estimated that this travel to and accommodation in England, along with medical fees, costs women around £600 for terminations under fourteen weeks' gestation and up to £2,000 for later terminations (more if someone accompanies them) (FPA, 2014). Women who are either unable to pay or unable to travel risk unsafe abortion within Northern Ireland or continue with their unwanted pregnancies.

Trends over Time

The incidence of abortion in Britain increased after the 1967 Abortion Act came into effect but has declined recently. In Scotland, the rate of abortion peaked in 2008 at 13.1 per 1,000 women aged fifteen to forty-four (ISD, 2015). Figure 10.2 shows the rate of abortion in England and Wales over time. In England and Wales, there were 184,571 abortions to residents in 2014, a slight decrease (0.4 per cent and 0.6 per cent) for the previous two years. This equates to 15.9 abortions per 1,000 women resident in England and Wales aged fifteen to forty-four (Department of Health, 2015). Although this is the lowest rate since 1997, it is double the rate (7.8 per 1,000) recorded in 1970 (Department of Health, 2015).

Abortion rates in Scotland have been consistently lower than those in England and Wales, although they have also been decreasing recently. There were 11,475 abortions in 2014, equivalent to 11.0 abortions per 1,000 women aged fifteen to forty-four, a 17.5 per cent decrease on the peak number of abortions recorded in 2008 (ISD, 2015).

Age

Rates of abortion are higher amongst younger people than older people (Table 10.2). British data for 2014 indicate that the rate is highest for women aged twenty to twenty-four (Department of Health, 2015; ISD, 2015). In England and Wales, the rate amongst women aged twenty-two—the highest rate—was 28 per 1,000 women in 2014 and 30 per 1,000 in 2013 (Department of Health, 2015).

The under-sixteen and under-eighteen abortion rates have decreased over the last decade. In Scotland, rates of abortion amongst under-sixteens and six-teen-to-nineteen-year-olds dropped from 3.8 per 1,000 in 2008 to 2.0 per 1,000

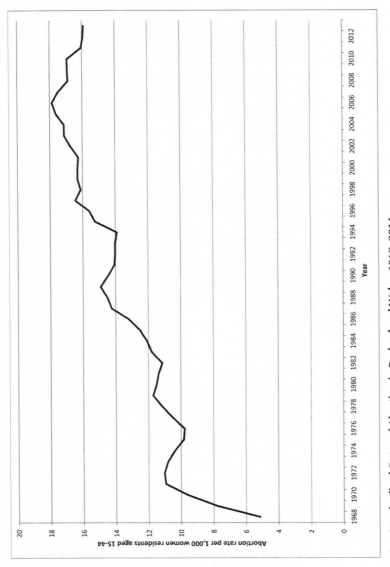

Figure 10.2 Age-Standardised Rates of Abortion in England and Wales, 1968–2014.
Notes: 1968 figures contain only eight months of data as the legislation came into effect on 27 April 1968. Graph shows NHS-funded and privately funded abortions from 1981, when the collection of information on the independent sector commenced. Rates for all women residents are age-standardised using the 2013 European Standard Population for ages fifteen to forty-four.
Source: Department of Health (2015).

Table 10.2 Abortion Incidence and Rate for Residents, Britain, 2012–2014

England and Wales, 2014			Scotland, 2012		
Age	Total	Age Standardised Rate Per 1,000 Women	Age	Total	Age Standardised Rate Per 1,000 Women
<15	698	1	<16	249	3
15–19	26,757	16	16–19	2,248	18
20–24	52,722	28	20–24	3,809	21
25–29	44,157	23	25–29	2,730	16
30–34	32,108	17	30–34	1,786	11
35–39	19,771	11	35–39	1,128	7
40–44	7,639	4	40≤	497	3
45–49	695	0			
50≤	24	-			

Source: ISD (2013); Department of Health (2015).

in 2014, a 46 per cent decrease, and from 24.0 per 1,000 in 2008 to 14.3 in 2014, a 40 per cent reduction (ISD, 2015). In England and Wales, the abortion rate amongst under-eighteens in 2014 was 11.1 per 1,000 women, down from 17.8 per 1,000 women in 2004 (Department of Health, 2015). Similarly, abortion amongst under-sixteens reduced to 2.5 per 1,000 from 3.7 in 2004.

Whilst the abortion rate is lower amongst those aged under twenty than those in their twenties, of those women who do conceive in this age group, the proportion of pregnancies that are terminated is much higher than at older ages, and the proportion is increasing. In 2013 in England and Wales, 61.6 per cent of conceptions to women aged under sixteen ended in abortion, compared to 49.8 per cent in 1993. The gradual increase in proportion of conceptions ending in abortion is similar amongst women aged under eighteen (50.7 per cent in 2013) and those under twenty (44.2 per cent) (ONS, 2015s).

Although the conception rate for women aged forty and over has more than doubled since 1990 from 6.6 to 14.2 conceptions per thousand women in 2013, the percentage of conceptions leading to abortion fell from 43 per cent in 1990–28 per cent in 2010, and it has since remained constant (ONS, 2015s). Women aged thirty to thirty-nine have typically had the lowest rates of abortion across Britain (Department of Health, 2015). In England and Wales in 2013 only 13 per cent of conceptions to women aged thirty to thirty-four in England and Wales ended in abortion, a proportion that has remained relatively constant (ONS, 2015s).

Ethnicity

Since 2002, information on the ethnicity of women accessing abortion services has been recorded in England and Wales (Department of Health, 2014). These data indicate that women of Black or Asian ethnicities are overrepresented. In 2014, 77 per cent of women receiving abortion were reported as White, 9 per cent as having Asian ethnicity and 8 per cent as having Black ethnicity. In the 2011 Census, 86 per cent of the population identified as White and only 7.5 per cent and 3.3 per cent identified as having Asian and Black ethnicities (Department of Health, 2015).

The age of women seeking abortion services appears to be similar, irrespective of ethnicity (Department of Health, 2015). Nevertheless, amongst the youngest women, who have the highest likelihood of abortion following conception, qualitative research suggests that different social and cultural dynamics influence abortion decision making. In some minority ethnic communities, particularly Muslim ones, teenage pregnancy within marriage is unlikely to end in abortion, whilst teenage pregnancy outside marriage is heavily socially sanctioned against (Higginbottom et al., 2006). Young women who had not been pregnant in Bangladeshi and Indian communities in London, Manchester and Birmingham expected that they would be required to marry if they became pregnant and reported that they would seek abortion to avoid such an outcome. In contrast, young women living in communities of Jamaican origin expect support from family and friends should they become pregnant and report a lower likelihood of seeking abortion (French et al., 2005).

Previous Abortions

The proportion of women accessing abortion services who have previously had an abortion is increasing. In England and Wales in 2014, 37 per cent of women receiving an abortion had one or more previous abortions, up from 32 per cent in 2004. However, increases in the proportion of all abortions that are repeat abortions could be a reflection of the decrease in the number of all abortions in recent years. The rate of repeat abortions expressed as a proportion of all women of reproductive age—an indicator of the overall frequency of repeat abortions—has in fact been fairly static over the last decade. In Scotland, the 31.7 per cent of abortions amongst women who had a previous abortion equates to a rate of 3.5 per 1,000 women aged fifteen to forty-four. This rate has remained stable at around 3.0 to 3.5 per 1,000 women aged fifteen to forty-four since 2005 (ONS, 2015s).

The likelihood of having had more than one abortion increases with age (7 per cent for the under-eighteens versus 45 per cent for those aged thirty-five and over), as women spend longer periods at risk of having an unwanted pregnancy (Department of Health, 2013a). There is little evidence to suggest that women presenting for an abortion more than once over their lifetimes differ from those who present only once (Rowlands, 2007b). Public health concerns, therefore, focus on women for whom multiple abortions are more likely to indicate vulnerability.

For example, the higher rates of multiple abortions observed amongst women experiencing domestic violence (Aston and Bewley, 2009) are likely to reflect lack of choice in sexual and reproductive behaviour, as well as the persistency of abuse. Multiple abortions amongst very young women are more likely to reflect the presence of barriers to using contraception, a failing of post-abortion contraceptive advice and/or limited power in negotiating sexual activity. In England and Wales in 2014, 7 per cent of women aged sixteen or seventeen and 2 per cent of women aged fifteen or younger receiving an abortion had undergone a previous abortion (Department of Health, 2013a). In 2014, 48 per cent of women of Black ethnicity having an abortion in England and Wales had had one before, compared to 34 per cent of Asian women and 36.6 per cent of White women (Department of Health, 2013a). Whilst this ethnic differential is noted as a SRH priority in England by the Department of Health (Department of Health, 2013b), there has been very little research into the reasons for these differences.

Sex-Selective Abortion

The last twenty-five years have seen an increase in sex-selective abortion amongst some Indian ethnic communities in England and Wales, reflecting a cultural preference for sons. The sex ratio of births to mothers born in India was relatively stable in the 1970s and 1980s, but it increased after the 1980s, deviating from sex ratio of births to women of all ethnicities. Between 1969 and 1989, the average sex ratio at birth was 104.1, rising to 107.9 between 1990 and 2005, and averaging 108.3 between 1995 and 2005. Higher-order births to women of Indian origin, particularly third or later, are now more likely to be male. The scale and sudden timing of this shift in gender balance is likely to indicate the abortion of female foetuses (Dubuc and Coleman, 2007). As a result, in 2014 the Department of Health clarified that the law, drafted before prenatal sex diagnosis was available, did not permit abortion based on gender preference. In 2015 MPs voted to review the extent of sex-selective abortion in England, Wales and Northern Ireland.

SEXUALLY TRANSMITTED INFECTIONS

Sexually transmitted infections (STIs) affect mortality and fertility. Left untreated, they can cause death from a range of cancers and further illnesses, infertility, ectopic pregnancy, spontaneous abortion and stillbirth. In addition, STIs are often associated with social stigma and psychological distress (Fenton and Hughes, 2003). Early diagnosis and treatment of STIs can reduce the likelihood of all these complications, reflected in the inclusion of STIs in more recent sex-education curricula. STIs are a significant, preventable and increasing public health concern: rates of new diagnoses have been rising steadily since the mid-1990s across the UK's four countries. In England, rates of new STI diagnoses rose by 11 per cent and 52 per cent amongst men and women between 2005 and 2014 (PHE, 2015c), whilst in Northern Ireland the annual number of new STI diagnoses increased by 37 per cent between 2001 and 2010 (PHA, 2014).

Data Sources

Data on STIs in the UK are primarily sourced from genito-urinary medicine (GUM) clinics and integrated GUM and sexual and reproductive health (SRH) clinics that offer free, open-access STI and HIV testing, diagnosis and management services. However, since some STIs, including chlamydial and gonococcal infections in women, are usually asymptomatic, GUM/SRH clinic data are likely to under-represent their prevalence at the population level. In Britain, chlamydia test and diagnosis data are therefore additionally sourced from community-based settings. The English National Chlamydia Screening Programme (NCSP) began in 2003 and provides opportunistic screening of sexually active young people aged fifteen to twenty-four at primary-care settings (general practices and pharmacies), community SRH services and abortion clinics as well as GUM clinics, whilst Scottish and Welsh strategies similarly encouraged community-based testing in this age group, but with no formal programme. In Northern Ireland, however, chlamydia data come from symptomatic testing in primary-care and GUM clinics, and there is no chlamydia testing programme (PHA, 2014).

Whilst only GUM clinics have a statutory duty to report HIV data to the four public health bodies of the UK (Public Health England, Public Health Wales, Public Health Agency and Health Protection Scotland), information about new diagnoses of HIV infections, AIDS cases and deaths is also collected through voluntary reporting systems, including the Survey of Prevalent HIV Infections Diagnosed (SOPHID) (from 1995) and the Unlinked Anonymous HIV Surveillance Program. Unlike other STIs, therefore, HIV data are available UK-wide.

Overall Trends in Diagnoses

There are over twenty types of STIs, caused by bacteria, parasites and viruses. Increases in the rates of new STIs in the UK are accounted for by the human papillomavirus (HPV), HIV, chlamydia and genital warts, as well as outbreaks of previously rare gonorrhoea and syphilis (Department of Health, 2013b). Rates of syphilis diagnoses in England increased by 27 per cent over the ten-year period from 2005 to 2014, and gonorrhoea almost doubled (PHE, 2015d).

Although more widespread screening (Sonnenberg et al., 2013) and more sensitive diagnostic tests partly explain increasing rates of STI diagnoses, changes in sexual behaviour are also important (Fenton and Hughes, 2003; PHE, 2015b). Not only do STIs influence demographic outcomes, but their prevalence also reflects demographic trends, including younger ages at sexual debut and increasing migration. Whilst the sub-populations most at risk of infection varies between different STIs, the majority of all reported STI cases in the UK are amongst people aged under twenty-five, men who have sex with men (MSM) and people of Black ethnicity (Department of Health, 2013b).

Sex at Younger Ages

The percentage of men and women aged sixteen to twenty-four who had opposite-sex sexual intercourse before age sixteen in Britain increased between 1990–1992 and 2010–2012, rising from 27 per cent and 18 per cent, respectively, to 30 per cent and 29 per cent (NATSAL, 2013). Young people have the highest rates of concurrent sexual partners and partner change (Mercer et al., 2013) and are at a disproportionate risk of acquiring STIs. Figure 10.3 shows rates of new STI diagnoses by age group and gender for England in 2014. The higher rates of STIs amongst older men are accounted for by diagnoses of STIs amongst MSM (PHE, 2015b).

Same-Sex Sex

More men and women are reporting same-sex sexual experiences now than twenty-five years ago (Mercer et al., 2013). Men with same-sex partners are at higher risk of STIs in the UK. In Northern Ireland, MSM make up less than 5 per cent of the male population but accounted for 83 per cent of male syphilis, 46 per cent of male gonorrhoea and 12 per cent of male chlamydia infections in 2014 (PHA, 2014). In England in 2014, they accounted for 81 per cent of syphilis, 52 per cent of gonorrhoea and 21 per cent of chlamydia diagnoses amongst men attending GUM clinics. Whilst diagnoses of genital warts, genital herpes and chlamydia are concentrated amongst men and women with exclusively opposite-sex sexual partners (92 per cent, 92 per cent and 86 per cent of diagnoses, respectively), rates of these STIs amongst MSM are increasing. Genital warts diagnoses amongst MSM attending GUM clinics increased by 10 per cent in 2013–2014, genital herpes by 10 per cent and chlamydia by 26 per cent. Recently, acute bacterial STIs have risen sharply amongst MSM with HIV, with rates now four times higher for these than amongst other MSM (PHE, 2015b). Prevalence of STIs amongst young MSM is particularly high. In 2011, 34 per cent of genital warts,

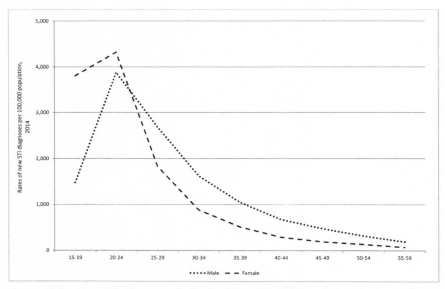

Figure 10.3   New STI Diagnoses in England Per 100,000 Population, by Sex and Age, 2014.
Source: Data provided by Public Health England. Data are from routine GUM service returns (GUMCADv2) and chlamydia data from community services. Rates are calculated using ONS population estimates based upon the 2011 Census. Rates for 2014 have been calculated using 2013 population estimates. Data includes patients accessing services located in England—data may include people who are resident in England, Wales, Scotland, Northern Ireland or abroad.

24 per cent of gonorrhoea, 22 per cent of genital herpes and chlamydia and 13 per cent of syphilis cases diagnosed amongst MSM were in those aged fifteen to twenty-four (Department of Health, 2013b).

Higher risks of STIs amongst MSM can be explained by the high per-act transmission probability of STIs' transmission in receptive anal sex and role versatility, as well as decreasing use of condoms amongst men adopting HIV seroadaptive behaviours—for example, HIV-negative men only choosing HIV-negative partners (serosorting) and HIV-positive men only having receptive anal sex (seropositioning) (Beyrer et al., 2012). Reflecting more sexually inclusive social norms, there are now more opportunities for men to meet prospective partners, including an increase in traditional venues in British cities (e.g., saunas) and targeted social media (e.g., smartphone applications and matching websites).

Partnership Concurrency and Number of Lifetime Partners

Concurrent partnerships—having more than one partnership at the same time—increase the probability of onward transmission of STIs. Concurrency has become more common since 1990 (Fenton and Hughes, 2003). Between 1990 and 1991 and 2010 and 2012, the number of people reporting opposite- and same-sex sexual experience has increased, as has the number of lifetime partners from 3.7 to 7.7 opposite-sex partners for women and from 8.6 to 11.7 opposite-sex partners for men (Mercer et al., 2013).

Geographic Variation

There is spatial variation in the distribution of STIs reflecting the distribu- tion of population sub-groups most at risk of infection, clustering of sexual networks and access to diagnosis and treatment services. Outbreaks of syphilis in England in the early and mid-2000s were predominantly amongst MSM and concentrated in Manchester, Brighton and London, cities with homosexual communities (Fenton, 2002). Urban areas are typically more ethnically diverse, so they are where the majority of STI diagnoses amongst people of Black ethnicity are made (Fenton et al., 2005). Geographical clus- tering around sexual networks is particularly clear in gonorrhoea: in 2014 in Lambeth the rate of gonorrhoea diagnosis was 634 per 100,000 population, compared to 0 per 100,000 in the Isles of Scilly (PHE, 2015c).

Chlamydia

Genital chlamydia is the most commonly diagnosed STI in the UK (PHA, 2014; PHE, 2015c). In England, 206,774 new diagnoses were made in 2014, accounting for 47 per cent of all STI diagnoses (PHE, 2015b). Chlamydia is frequently asymptomatic, increasing the risk of onwards transmission and longer-term health outcomes such as pelvic inflammatory disease, ectopic pregnancy and infertility in women and urethritis, epididymitis and reactive arthritis in men. Chlamydia infection facilitates the transmission of HIV infection in both men and women (Baeten and Overbaugh, 2003).

Rates of chlamydia diagnoses are consistently and significantly higher amongst younger people, particularly women. According to Sonnenberg et al. (2013), weighted age-specific prevalence data from NATSAL indicates that chlamydia is highest for women aged eighteen to nineteen (4.7 per cent) and men aged twenty to twenty-four years (3.4 per cent). In Northern Ireland, peak diagnostic rates amongst women are slightly later: between 2000 and 2013, prevalence was highest amongst both men and women aged twenty to twenty-four. Prevalence of chlamydia in the sixteen-to-twenty-four age group targeted by England's NCSP and Scotland and Wales' strategies to increase testing is 3.1 per cent in women and 2.3 per cent in men.

Spatial variation in chlamydia detection rates amongst younger people (e.g., from 4,270 per 100,000 in Hackney to 530 per 100,000 in Isles of Scilly) could be due to differences in sexual behaviours, data quality or testing coverage (PHE, 2015c). Rates of chlamydia diagnoses have increased amongst young adults following the 2003 launch of the NCSP in England (Department of Health, 2013b). Testing amongst young women and men in Scotland and Wales, where strategies to increase testing were not embedded within formal programmes, is significantly lower—32.4 per cent and 45.6 per cent, respectively, compared to 57.1 per cent in England (Sonnenberg et al., 2013). As well as increasing testing and access to treatment amongst those offered the service, in England the programme is credited with raising general awareness of chlamydia and other STIs amongst young adults, suggesting that their Scottish and Welsh counterparts may be at higher risk of undiagnosed and untreated STIs as well as of infection via onward transmission.

Sex without using a condom significantly increases the risk of chlamydia transmission. Across all age groups, data suggest 5.3 per cent of people having condomless sex with two or more sexual partners in the past year may have chlamydia, compared to 1.1 per cent of those who do not (Sonnenberg et al., 2013).

Gonorrhoea

Since 2009 the UK has seen large increases in gonorrhoea diagnoses amongst at-risk populations; it is now the second most commonly reported bacterial STI in the UK (Department of Health, 2013b). In England, 34,958 new diagnoses in 2014 represented a 98 per cent increase from 2013 (PHE, 2015d). In Northern Ireland, new diagnoses more than doubled between 2010 and 2013 (PHA, 2014). Although the rise in diagnoses coincides with the introduction of a more sensitive dual test for chlamydia and gonorrhoea and an increase in the number of people tested, the continued increase is also likely to represent increased transmission. In Wales, the number of people who were tested for gonorrhoea increased by 61 per cent between 2010 and 2012, whereas the number of people testing positive for gonorrhoea increased by 219 per cent (PHW, 2013).

Recent increases in diagnoses were initially focussed amongst females, reflecting more women accessing the dual chlamydia/gonorrhoea test. Since 2013, all UK countries have documented increasing prevalence amongst males. In Scotland and England, males accounted for 74.9 per cent and 76 per cent of episodes in 2014, respectively, larger than in the previous four years (PHE, 2015b).

Increases in male prevalence hide regional differences in risk groups. In Northern Ireland and Wales, there has been a recent decline in gonorrhoea amongst MSM and an increase in new diagnoses amongst men having exclusively opposite-sex sexual activity (PHW, 2013; PHA, 2014). In London, whilst the number of new diagnoses amongst men having exclusively oppo-site-sex sex has also increased, it is infection amongst MSM that has been driving increases in male diagnoses, accounting for 54 per cent of the 5,139 men newly diagnosed in 2010 and 80 per cent of the 14,449 diagnosed in 2014 (PHE, 2015e).

The highest rates of gonorrhoea diagnoses are amongst young men aged twenty to twenty-four (151 per 100,000 in 2009) and women aged sixteen to nineteen (123.4 per 100,000 in 2009), although gonorrhoea diagnoses are increasing at all ages (PHW, 2013). Diagnoses at older ages (adults aged forty-five years and older) increased by 8 per cent between 2000 and 2009, from 4.7 to 4.8 per 100,000 (FPA, 2010).

Untreated gonorrhoea can enter the bloodstream and joints, and in women it can lead to pelvic inflammatory disease, infertility and ectopic pregnancy. Some strains are now less susceptible to antibiotic treatments (PHE, 2014a), increasing the likelihood of onward transmission and more serious clinical outcomes amongst infected individuals.

Human Immunodeficiency Virus (HIV)

HIV is a progressive illness that suppresses the body's immune system, making an infected individual vulnerable to other infections and to chronic diseases. It is associated with significant mortality and morbidity. In 2013 around 107,800 people had diagnosed or undiagnosed HIV in the UK. This equates to an overall prevalence of 2.8 per 1,000 population aged fifteen to fifty-nine years (1.9 per 1,000 women and 3.7 per 1,000 men) (PHE, 2014b). Arguably more than any other STI, HIV is still frequently understood to be a stigmatising condition, contributing to late diagnoses and HIV transmission.

The advent and availability of anti-retroviral therapy (ART) has reduced rates of acquired immunodeficiency syndrome (AIDS) and HIV-related death in the UK, as well as onwards transmission. ART is most effec-tive when HIV diagnosis and treatment commences early. Those treated promptly can now expect a near-normal life expectancy. However, there are high rates of late HIV diagnoses, 42 per cent of diagnoses in 2013 (Yin et al., 2014). This is poorly understood, as are new infections at all ages and an increasing population of people living with HIV into older ages at which the interaction between HIV-related and age-related morbidity (High et al., 2012) means that HIV remains a SRH priority in the UK (Department of Health, 2013b).

In 2013, there were an estimated 5,740 new (probably) sexually acquired HIV diagnoses in the UK, a decline from peak levels in 2003–2005. However, declines have only been seen amongst people with exclusively opposite-sex partners. Numbers of new HIV diagnoses amongst MSM have increased over this period, from 33 per cent in 2004 to 58 per cent in 2013 (PHE, 2014c).

Women and, to a lesser extent, men of African ethnicity disproportionately account for new HIV diagnoses amongst those with exclusively opposite-sex partners. In 2013, people of Black African ethnicity accounted for two-thirds (65 per cent) of HIV prevalence in this population group.

The majority of new HIV diagnoses are amongst adults aged twenty-five to forty-nine, but newly diagnosed infection amongst older adults is a growing concern. The numbers of adults aged above forty-nine being diagnosed with HIV has increased since 1998: in 2013, two-thirds more older adults were diagnosed than in 2004. Following increased transmission at older ages and improved survival following treatment, Public Health England estimates that one in four people living with a diagnosed HIV infection in the UK is now aged fifty or older (Yin et al., 2014).

Prevalence of HIV in the UK is increasing, in part because of new infections, but also because of increased survival of people diagnosed and initiating treatment in previous years. However, a quarter of those estimated to be infected with HIV do not know their HIV status (PHE, 2014b). This rate is expected to be even higher amongst adults aged fifty and over (HPA, 2012) and men and women of Black African ethnicity, of whom nearly two in five men and almost one in three women are unaware of their infection (PHE, 2014b). As well as being at risk of HIV-related morbidity and mortality, those who are unaware they have HIV increase the risk of onwards transmission of the virus, especially if they are also infected with an STI such as chlamydia or syphilis.

HUMAN PAPILLOMAVIRUS (HPV)

HPV is the most common viral infection of the reproductive tract; most sexually active people will be infected at some period over their lifetime. Cervical cancer is the most common HPV-related disease. HPV is mainly transmitted through sexual contact, although penetration is not required for infection. The majority of infections with HPV occur soon after the onset of sexual activity, highlighting the need for comprehensive sex education to incorporate this topic. Risk factors for cervical cancer include early age at sexual debut, multiple partners and immune suppression. Cervical cancer, developing five to twenty years later, remains primarily a disease of the young: in England 62 per cent of diagnoses are made before age fifty, with the highest diagnosis rates being at twenty-five to twenty-nine (ONS, 2013d; PHE, 2015a).

Table 10.3 Annual HPV Vaccine Coverage: UK 2008/2009 to 2013/2014, and England, Scotland, Wales and Northern Ireland 2013/2014

	% With 1 Dose ≤	% With 2 Doses ≤	% With 3 Doses ≤
UK Coverage			
2008/2009	88.4	86.6	80.9
2009/2010	85.0	83.1	77.5
2010/2011	89.0	87.6	83.8
2011/2012	90.8	89.7	87.0
2012/2013	91.0	89.7	85.8
2013/2014	91.3	89.9	85.9
Coverage in 2013/2014			
England	91.1	89.8	86.7
Scotland	93.6	91.7	81.4
Northern Ireland	91.5	90.8	87.2
Wales	89.6	87.6	77.2

Source: PHE (2015a).

In the UK in 2012, around 920 women died from cervical cancer (CRUK, 2014), although survival rates are increasing. In England, the cervical cancer mortality rate declined significantly between 1971 and 2011 from 8 to 2 deaths per 100,000 women, and for 2007–2011 the survival rate was 67 per cent (ONS, 2013d). Survival is higher at younger ages—almost 90 per cent for women aged under forty (CRUK, 2014).

HPV Vaccination

HPV vaccines are highly effective at preventing the infection of specific HPV types and aim to reduce the incidence of cervical cancer. In 2008, HPV vaccination was introduced routinely for girls aged twelve to fourteen (NHS, 2015). HPV in sexually active sixteen-to-eighteen-year-old females undergoing chlamydia screening was 66 per cent lower in post-immunisation in 2010–2013 than in 2008 pre-immunisation (PHE, 2015a). Coverage of vaccination programmes in the UK has increased (see Table 10.3).

However, there are inequalities in vaccination uptake by ethnicity (Kumar and Whynes, 2011). In 2011, 72 per cent of White but only 56 per cent of Asian and 55 per cent of Black females aged thirteen to nineteen years attending sexual health services in England had the recommended three (Sacks et al., 2014). Similarly, White females aged sixteen to seventeen offered vaccinations as part of a 'catch-up' cohort were more likely to receive the vaccine than their BME counterparts (Bowyer et al., 2014), with a significant relationship between vaccination coverage and level of deprivation (Hughes et al., 2014). The evidence suggests that HPV vaccine services need to make special efforts in order to reduce inequalities in uptake.

CONCLUSION

The sexual and reproductive health of the UK's population over the last twenty-five years has been shaped by its changing demography. SRH differences exist along age, ethnic and gender axes. There are clear and compelling health and well-being implications of improved SRH. Beyond individuals' health, the population benefits of improving SRH are wide. For example, the annual direct medical cost of unintended pregnancy to the UK National Health Service (NHS) is estimated to be £382 million. The majority (67 per cent) of these pregnancies result from poor contraceptive adherence. The cost of both unintended pregnancies and contraception to the NHS could be reduced if more people were to use long-acting reversible contraceptives (Hassan et al., 2012).

Understanding SRH across the four countries of the UK involves a complex and changing set of policy, service and data systems that deal with one, two or three and less frequently, all four. Some aspects of SRH, such as contraception and STIs, are well established, with substantial evidence and policy support. Other aspects of SRH are less well understood, reflecting their more recent emergence in the UK as a result of its changing demographic composition. For example, whilst the growth of the population aged over sixty-five is well established, how the SRH needs of changing cohorts of older people will manifest is rather less well understood. Similarly, changing migration and linked sexual attitudes have meant that in the UK, female genital mutilation (FGM) has relatively recently necessitated data, policy and service interventions, despite being illegal in the UK since 1985. In October 2015, it became mandatory for all regulated healthcare professionals in England and Wales to record FGM patient data (HSCIC, 2015); there are no equivalent datasets for Scotland or Northern Ireland.

Changing sexual behaviours, combined with changing population structure and composition in the UK, have implications for SRH policies and the funding and evidence to support them. The spatial distribution of incidence and prevalence of SRH issues in the UK are sometimes the outcome of unrelated policies. For example, policies relating to the dispersal of asylum seekers in the UK might explain changing geographic distribution of populations potentially affected by FGM. The UK National Asylum Support System has a principle of dispersal to cities outside of the southeast of England of destitute asylum seekers whilst a decision about their asylum claim is pending. This policy is likely to explain why Glasgow has the highest number of potentially-affected-by-FGM population in Scotland (Baillot et al., 2014).

Changes in population behaviours and attitudes mean that responding to these changes is a constantly moving target. For example, evidence suggests that young people are reporting that they get much of their sex and relationship information from web-based pornography (Marston and Lewis, 2014), which is likely to influence sexual attitudes, expectations and relationships in ways that are not yet well understood (Wellings and Johnson, 2013). Understanding and supporting SRH across the life course is integral to understanding population change in the UK.

NOTE

1. Thanks to Alexis Palfreyman for research assistance in identifying data sources.

Chapter 11

The Changing Geography of Deprivation in Britain, 1971–2011 and Beyond

Paul Norman[1]

Following a period of austerity after World War II, by the end of the 1950s Britain was entering a time of economic growth and associated improvements in standards of living. There was, however, a need to reconstruct bomb-damaged town centres and residential areas, as well as an increasing awareness of problems of inequality and deprivation, as some places benefited from the improvements much faster than others (Rydin, 1993). Concurrently, population was growing through family formation and the baby boom of the late 1950s and early 1960s, and near-full employment encouraged immigration from Commonwealth countries (see Chapters 1 and 4). As a result, there was increasing pressure on the existing housing stock in what were already dense urban areas (Ward, 1994). Improved housing quality was also needed, and the slum clearance approaches of the 1930s were resumed to address problems of unfit dwellings and urban decay (Cullingworth and Nadin, 1994). Redevelopment programmes involved a reduction in previous densities since new homes tended to be larger so as to eliminate overcrowding problems and provide bathrooms and better kitchens as well as car parking spaces (Rydin, 1993; see also Chapter 7). Then, from the 1960s onwards, a succession of government initiatives intervened in order to raise educational and other standards, with attempts at targeting the worst-performing (or 'priority') areas—what became known as the 'inner city problem' (Champion, 1989: 125–29).

To be implemented efficiently as well as have their effectiveness monitored, these sorts of measures required much greater intelligence than had been available before then, needing data both on a wider range of indicators of deprivation and well-being and at a much finer geographical scale than the whole local authority districts for which most Census output had previously been released. As the main source of sociodemographic data in Britain, the scope of the Census has responded to this challenge, with the number of questions increasing. In addition to basic questions about each individual, the 1951 Census included questions on household amenities for the first time. These questions were repeated in 1961 with additional enquiries about country of birth and housing tenure, but a 'long form' questionnaire with these questions was only collected from 10 per cent of households (Denham and Rhind, 1983). It was not until 1971 that this detailed information, plus the inclusion of car ownership, was available at a small-area level for the population rather than for a sample. Moreover, during this period, geography as a discipline went through a 'quantitative revolution', with many practitioners starting to use a wide array of analytical tools for which the multivariate nature of Census data was an ideal source (Robinson, 1998).

The combination of policy and practical needs, improved Census data availability and enhanced practitioner skillsets has led to a variety of Census-based schemes being developed in the UK for measuring small-area deprivation as a composite of sets of indicator variables, following pioneering work using the 1971 Census on urban deprivation (Holtermann, 1975). These deprivation measures have many uses, including the targeting of resources for regeneration and as explanatory variables in studies of health and education. They help us to identify whether small areas have changed their level of deprivation over time and thereby assess, for example, whether declining populations are associated with poorer economic circumstances, the impact of area-based planning initiatives and whether a change in the level of deprivation leads to a change in health.

Even decades later, however, there are several facets that make the measurement of changing deprivation challenging. First, the variables used as inputs to a composite deprivation measure may not be available in successive censuses. Second, the geographies for which data are released at small-area level change at each Census so that, over time, comparisons are not necessarily for the same place and areal extent, even if the location has the same name (Norman and Riva, 2012). Third, the deprivation index score for an area is cross-sectional, calculated relative to the year in question, so that a score cannot be directly compared with the score for another time point to identify absolute change in deprivation. If a measure can be derived that is comparable over time, then practitioners can use that information to assess whether places are becoming more or less deprived in parallel with economic cycles and other changes such as housing development schemes.

This chapter begins with an overview of previously devised deprivation schemes and then goes on to outline the method used to develop a time-series of area deprivation for 1971–2011, using data from all five censuses harmonised to contemporary small-area geographies in Great Britain. Areas that are persistently deprived or advantaged over time are highlighted and trajectories of change used to reveal locations that are improving socioeconomically or becoming more deprived. Changes in population size and age structure are then analysed against this backdrop of changing deprivation. Given the view expressed by the National Statistician that data sources other than the Census should be exploited as much as possible (ONS, 2014i), the chapter concludes with some thoughts on future approaches that might be adopted to identify deprivation if the 2021 Census proves to be the last.

DEPRIVATION MEASURES

There is no clear-cut definition of the concept of deprivation (Carstairs and Morris, 1989), but deprivation is often taken to be a state of disadvantage relative to the local community, wider society or the nation to which an individual, family or group belongs (Townsend, 1987). People can be deprived of adequate education, housing of good quality, rewarding employment, sufficient income, good health and opportunities for enjoyment (Dorling, 1999). Multiple deprivation reflects concentrations of people in areas of 'slums, unemployment and health risks but also in their resources in terms of rateable value, the quality of their hospitals and schools and their numbers of doctors and teachers' (Holman, 1978: 37).

A major use of Census data has been to determine the sociodemographic characteristics of small areas by combining a set of variables into a single, summary measure. A motivation has been to produce a deprivation index that can then be used in policy and research applications to identify and address social and economic inequalities. Despite repeated calls from academics and others, the UK Census has not included an income question (Dorling, 1999; Boyle and Dorling, 2004). For this reason, deprivation indices use proxy indicators of income and other dimensions of deprivation. Following Holtermann's (1975) identification of urban deprivation using the small-area statistics of the 1971 Census, various schemes have been developed, including the Jarman Underprivileged Area index (UPA) (1983), the Townsend index (1987) and the Carstairs index (Carstairs and Morris, 1989). Official schemes include the Index of Local Conditions (DoE, 1983 and 1994). These deprivation measures have been highly influential for the allocation of public resources (Simpson, 1996; Brennan et al., 1999; Blackman, 2006) and regularly provide explanatory variables in models of various outcomes including health (Law and Morris, 1998; Senior et al., 2000; Boyle et al., 2002; Boyle et al., 2004; Norman et al., 2005) and educational achievement (Higgs et al., 1998). Underpinned by Census data but using other sources where appropriate, deprivation indices have also been developed in Australia, Canada, France, New Zealand, South Africa, the US and elsewhere (Broadway and

Jesty, 1998; Eroğlu, 2007; Bell et al., 2007; Havard, 2008; Noble et al., 2010; Pornet et al., 2012; Fu et al., 2015; Norman et al., 2016).

These types of schemes use a set of variables, each of which is believed to represent a dimension of deprivation, that are then combined into a single index score. The input variables to the different schemes vary, but a deprivation indicator that is ubiquitous is unemployment (Haynes et al., 1996), with non–car access, non–home ownership, low social class and household overcrowding also commonly used (Senior, 2002). The choices of which input variables to use at which geographical scale and of which method to use to combine them into a single number have all been subject to wide debate (e.g., Senior, 1991; Carr-Hill and Rice, 1995; Coombes et al., 1995; Bradford et al., 1995; Simpson, 1996; Senior, 2002). Whilst there is a lack of consensus on technical aspects, Census-based index construction is generally well understood and transparent to practitioners. Despite differences in the detail of schemes, strong correlations between indices have consistently been found (Morris and Carstairs, 1991; Mackenzie et al., 1998; Hoare, 2003).

A need for deprivation measures outside of Census years, the potential for the use of administrative data sources as deprivation indicators (on the same and further dimensions than those available in the Census) and the recognition that small-area Census geographies may not be appropriate for technical and applied reasons has led to alternatives being explored. In the late 1990s, the then Department of the Environment, Transport and the Regions (DETR) commissioned Indices of Deprivation for England (Noble et al., 2000; Noble et al., 2006). Several innovations in this work are of value: a national set of small-area population estimates were produced for a post-censal year; the small-area geography used was contemporary and accounted for post-censal boundary change; and various 'domains' of deprivation were indicated by administrative data for a post-censal year, consistently across space and contained indicators not available in the Census (e.g., income, crime, skills and training; access to services). During the 2000s, a series of updates were released, referred to as Indices of Multiple Deprivation (IMD) in England and the UK's other constituent countries. Much of the innovation of the pre-2001 version was retained, and the IMDs have become the official measures of deprivation in the UK (Norman, 2010a).

The following features of these alternative approaches are notable:

• Input variables are derived from post-2001 administrative records, so the schemes are regularly updated.
• There are different IMDs in each of the UK countries with the different indicator variables used seen as the most relevant to each country.
• The small-area geographies used are the 'statistical' geographies of Lower-Layer Super Output Areas (LSOAs) in England, LSOAs in Wales,

Datazones (DZs) in Scotland and Super Output Areas (SOAs) in Northern Ireland.
- A sophisticated methodology is used to produce domains of deprivation.
- Much of the usage by practitioners is based on an area's rank, so it has a straightforward interpretation.

However, the methodology is not as well understood as the methods used for the Census-based measures, such as the Townsend and Carstairs schemes, and there is a risk that the IMDs are used inappropriately (Adams and White, 2006). A change in rank over time does not mean that an area necessarily has different characteristics since the changing ranks depend on change in other areas.

As noted above, a drawback with the regularly used schemes, whether based on Census or administrative data sources, is that they are cross-sectional, devised for one point in time. This means that the impact of a policy or a changing deprivation/outcome relationship cannot be judged if the 'before' and 'after' situations are based on deprivation measures that use time-point-specific variables, methods and geographies.

The updatability of the IMDs and range of indicators used are advantages over a purely Census-based scheme, but due to different variables being used at different times and because of the methodology used, the IMDs are not comparable over time. Although the range of indicator variables is more restricted than the administrative sources used in the IMDs and the time increments are once every ten years rather than more frequent, the Census-based schemes can be developed as long-term measures of deprivation change.

In terms of geographical coverage, the development of different IMDs for each of the UK's constituent countries helps ensure their policy relevance. However, combining the separate IMDs to a UK coverage is inappropriate, and the lack of an official UK scheme is something of a weakness (Morelli and Seaman, 2007; Whynes, 2008)—a situation that has been explicitly recognised by the ONS (2010b). Schemes such as the Townsend and Carstairs indices have been produced for Great Britain with data from the 1971, 1981, 1991, 2001 and 2011 censuses and for the UK (i.e., including Northern Ireland) from the 1991, 2001 and 2011 censuses.

The geography of the Census-based deprivation indices has most commonly been the electoral wards used for the dissemination of Census data, though other geographies such as 'Enumeration Districts' (EDs) and 'Output Areas' (OAs) have also been used. The statistical geographies used for the IMDs (LSOAs, DZs and SOAs; see above), having a much more even population size than wards that can vary from five hundred to twenty thousand (Norman et al., 2007), are designed to allow the safe release of population-related data and are more numerous than electoral wards, allowing a very detailed geographic focus.

A barrier to time-series analysis of sociodemographic data is that geographical boundaries are revised regularly. Unless a consistent geographical approach is taken with a data time-series, it cannot be known whether changes in sociodemographic data collected for areas at different time points are genuine social change or an artefact of boundary changes (Norman et al., 2003). Dolan et al. (1995) and Freeman et al. (2015) look at change in small-area characteristics between 1981–1991 and 2001–2011, respectively, but are not necessarily comparing like with like geographically due to boundary changes in the intervening periods. The geographies of Census data release change over time (Norman and Riva, 2012), but conversions between geographies can be carried out to yield a harmonised set of zones (Norman et al., 2003). The small-area geographies used for the IMDs are frozen between 2001 and 2011, allowing short-term time-series analysis unaffected by boundary change. However, due to demographic change in the inter-censal period, these statistical geographies were revised for outputs from the 2011 Census to maintain evenness of population size across zones. Direct comparisons of 2001 and 2011 data cannot necessarily be readily achieved.

Previous work has developed UK-coverage deprivation measures that were comparable over time from 1991–2001 by harmonising Census small-area geographies (wards in England, Wales and Northern Ireland and postal sectors in Scotland). The method is detailed in Norman (2010a), used in Norman (2010b) and Norman et al. (2011), applied for alternative geographies in Scotland by Exeter et al. (2011) and subsequently for small areas in Australia (Norman et al., 2016). The same approach was extended back in time to devise a set of comparable deprivation measures for each Census from 1971 to 2001 for small areas across Great Britain. These 1971–2001 deprivation scores have been used to analyse changes in cancer registrations and survival (see, for example, Basta et al., 2014; Blakey et al., 2014; McNally et al., 2012, 2014a and b, 2015). Changes in deprivation have also been related to environmental equity in England (Mitchell and Norman, 2012) and levels of air pollution in Great Britain (Mitchell et al., 2015). A UK coverage deprivation scheme prior to 1991 is, however, difficult due to differences in data availability in Northern Ireland (Norman, 2010a).

DEVELOPING A 1971–2011 MEASURE OF CHANGING SMALL-AREA DEPRIVATION

The aim here is to produce a deprivation index for each Census from 1971 to 2011 for the same set of small-area zones, so that if a score is different at each time point, this can readily be seen whether an area's deprivation reduced or increased over time. The approach is based on the Townsend index because the input variables are available in similar enough definitions at each Census across Great Britain, though not for Northern Ireland (Norman, 2010a). The small areas selected for use here are the LSOAs in England and Wales and the DZs in Scotland, using 2011 boundary definitions so as to have contemporary relevance. This section describes the methods of data processing, starting with obtaining the raw input variables, then converting the data from the original Census to the LSOA/DZ geographies and calculating comparable deprivation scores.

Input Deprivation Indicators

The Townsend index uses four input variables that identify levels of unemployment (as a percentage of those who are economically active) and non–car ownership, non–home ownership and household overcrowding (each as a percentage of all households) (Senior, 2002; Norman, 2010a). Household overcrowding is defined as more than one person per room. The appropriate numerators and denominators have been obtained from the UK Data Service for the 1971, 1981, 1991 and 2001 Censuses and from Nomis for the 2011 Census, all for the smallest geographical areas for which data are available by year and country (EDs and OAs as appropriate).

Converting Between Geographies

The small-area geographies used for the dissemination of Census data alter between censuses despite the recognition that redefining boundaries hampers time-series analysis (Norman et al., 2003). Data can be converted between zonal systems by apportioning data using the area of population overlap between different boundary systems. The weights to apportion the data can be calculated by counting unit postcodes (a proxy for population distribution) that fall in both the source area (the zone in which the data exist) and the target area (the zone the data are needed for). This geographical data conversion approach is stepped through and illustrated in both Norman et al. (2008) and Norman (2010a) for converting 1991 data to 2001 geography, whilst variations relating to the older censuses are detailed in Norman and Riva (2012). This method of geographical data conversion is reliable as relationships between variables are retained (Norman et al., 2003). Reliability is ensured when converting from smaller (ED/OA) to larger areas (LSOA/DZ) since, even if there is not a perfect fit, aggregating up geographical scales is less prone to the uncertainties involved in estimating from larger to smaller areas (Norman and Riva, 2012).

Conversion tables have been developed for the work reported here, which link the smallest areas relevant to each Census 1971–2001 to the 2011 boundary definitions of the LSOAs/DZs. These tables have been used to convert the numerators and denominators of the deprivation indicator variables along with population age structure from the geography of each earlier Census into the 2011 LSOAs/DZs.

Calculating Comparable Deprivation Scores

The steps involved in calculating Townsend scores on a cross-sectional basis are as follows: obtain the raw input numerators and denominators; calculate percentages of all four variables; log transform the unemployment and over-crowding variables to be (near) normal distributions; standardise all the variables so that they are all on the same scale; and sum the standardised variables (equally here; some schemes weight the inputs at this stage based on perceived importance) to derive the final deprivation score. A final step categorises the scores into quantiles based on an equal number of areas in each category or equal numbers of people, the latter having current support as a choice.

The method used for standardisation in a cross-sectional scheme such as Townsend is to calculate z-scores. This involves, for each area: subtracting the mean of observations of all areas from the observation for the area and then dividing by the standard deviation across all areas. In effect, a variable's value for an area is placed relative to the national level. For individual variable z-scores and when summed to single deprivation scores, a positive value represents greater deprivation in relation to the national level, and negative values mean lesser deprivation.

To calculate changing deprivation over time, the method previously adopted (within the UK by Norman, 2010a; Exeter et al., 2011; and for Australia by Norman et al., 2016) has been to calculate the z-scores for each area in every year relative to the average national level over the whole time period. For example, if non–home ownership across all areas was 10 per cent at one time point and 5 per cent at the next, the average rate for all areas in both years was 7.5 per cent and the standard deviation 3.5. An area's non–home ownership rate in both years is then compared with 7.5 per cent to determine whether its level of non–home ownership has improved or worsened during the time interval. For the deprivation indicators for the five censuses from 1971 to 2011, observations in each area and year are placed relative to the average across all areas and years. Population-weighted quintiles are calculated by ranking all areas across all years and then by dividing the result into five categories of equal population size.

Once the z-scores have been summed in each year to a deprivation score, an increase or reduction of an area's score over time can be interpreted as worsening or improving deprivation. Similarly, if an area changes deprivation quintile, this has a ready interpretation. It should be noted that the categorisation of the continuous scores imposes boundary effects whereby for one area a small change in deprivation might result in a change of quintile whilst for another location a large change may find the area remaining in the same quintile. The results of adopting this approach are described in the next section.

CHANGING DEPRIVATION: 1971–2011

National-Level Changes

Figure 11.1a illustrates the changing level of mean deprivation for Great Britain from 1971 to 2011. Since zero is the level with which deprivation is compared for both areas and over time, deprivation was higher in 1971 and 1981 but decreased to 1991 and then to 2001. There is a slight increase in the mean level of deprivation to 2011, but this still indicates that Great Britain is substantially less deprived in 2011 than in earlier years. There are differences between Great Britain's constituent countries (Figure 11.1b), with Scotland experiencing a much higher level of deprivation in 1971 but with the level reducing rapidly to 2001 and then with a further slight improvement by 2011. Both England and Wales follow a path similar to that of Great Britain as a whole, though England appears to worsen more between 2001 and 2011.

Figure 11.1a Changing National-Level Deprivation, 1971–2011: Mean Townsend Score: Great Britain.
Source: Author's calculations.

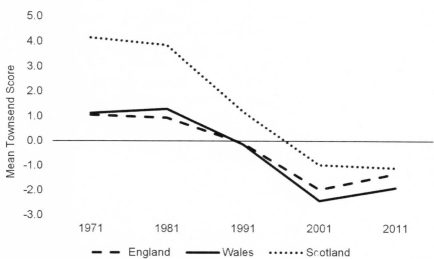

Figure 11.1b Changing National-Level Deprivation, 1971–2011: Mean Townsend Score: England, Wales and Scotland.
Source: Author's calculations.

Subnational Deprivation Changes

Table 11.1a reports correlations between Census years of the time comparable deprivation scores for the LSOAs/DZs in Great Britain. The correlations between adjacent censuses are stronger than between censuses further apart in time. The correlation between deprivation in 1971 and in 2011 is 0.68, which indicates that, whilst there will be some differences in areas, the distribution of deprivation is broadly similar over time. Given that correlations between adjacent censuses become stronger over time, this implies that there was more change in the distribution of deprivation in the 1970s and 1980s than in the 1990s and 2000s.

Table 11.1b has the cross-tabulation between quintiles of deprivation in 1971 and in 2011. The highlighted diagonal in the table contains counts of areas that stayed in the same quintile over time, the cells below the diagonal are those areas that became less deprived over time and the cells above the line are the areas that become more deprived. Of the 41,729 LSOAs/DZs, 21 per cent stayed in the same quintile with 76 per cent becoming less deprived and 3 per cent more deprived. It is telling that 3,569 areas were in the most deprived quintile 5 at both the beginning and the end of the study period. Comparing the frequency distributions of quintiles at each Census time point (Table 11.1c) shows that the percentage of most deprived areas increased marginally between 1971 and 1981, decreased rapidly to 2001 and then increased a little again. The middle ground (quintiles 2–4) saw

Table 11.1 Relationships Between Area Deprivation in Great Britain Over Time

(a) Correlations between deprivation scores at each census time point

	1981	1991	2001	2011
1971	0.86	0.79	0.74	0.68
1981		0.91	0.85	0.80
1991			0.92	0.90
2001				0.94

(b) Cross-tabulations between 1971 and 2011 deprivation quintiles

		2011					
		Q1	Q2	Q3	Q4	Q5	Total
1971	Q1	670	75	12	3	3	763
	Q2	4,050	951	229	74	13	5,317
	Q3	5,562	3,294	1,321	505	53	10,735
	Q4	2,659	3,501	3,298	2,104	498	12,060
	Q5	849	1,412	2,674	4,350	3,569	12,854
	Total	13,790	9,233	7,534	7,036	4,136	41,729
Between 1971		Least	Less	Same	More	Most	
and 2011		deprived	deprived	deprived	deprived	Deprived	

(c) Frequencies of areas within each quintile at each census

	1971	1981	1991	2001	2011
Q1	2%	6%	15%	39%	33%
Q2	13%	18%	25%	23%	22%
Q3	26%	22%	20%	17%	18%
Q4	29%	22%	19%	14%	17%
Q5	31%	33%	21%	7%	10%
Total	100%	100%	100%	100%	100%

Note: Numbers here may not add up exactly to 100 per cent because of rounding. Q1 = least deprived quintile; Q5 = most deprived quintile.
Source: Author's calculations.

progressive changes towards less deprived distributions by 2001 paralleled by large rises in the percentages of areas that are least deprived. Between 2001 and 2011, there are shifts downwards. In terms of capturing areas' changing quintile, it should be noted that there are floor and ceiling constraints since areas in quintile 5 cannot become more deprived and areas in quintile 1 cannot become less deprived.

Continuing with the combinations of 1971 and 2011 levels of deprivation, Figure 11.2 illustrates those areas that are in the least deprived areas (Q1) in both 1971 and 2011, those areas that became more deprived and those that were in the most deprived areas (Q5) in both of these years. In the main, these differently classified areas are located in urban areas. The most striking pattern is in London and surrounding areas (Figure 11.2d), with the least

Figure 11.2a Persistent and Changing Levels of Deprivation, 1971 and 2011: Areas Staying Least Deprived.
Note: The boundaries shown are the Government Office Regions in England and the countries of Wales and Scotland.
Source: Author's calculations.

Figure 11.2b Persistent and Changing Levels of Deprivation, 1971 and 2011: Areas Becoming More Deprived.
Note: The boundaries shown are the Government Office Regions in England and the countries of Wales and Scotland.
Source: Author's calculations.

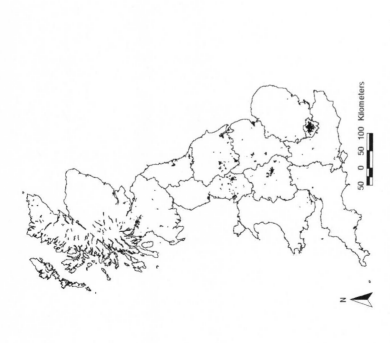

Least deprived

More deprived

Most deprived

Figure 11.2c Persistent and Changing Levels of Deprivation, 1971 and 2011: Areas Staying Most Deprived.
Note: The boundaries shown are the Government Office Regions in England and the countries of Wales and Scotland.
Source: Author's calculations.

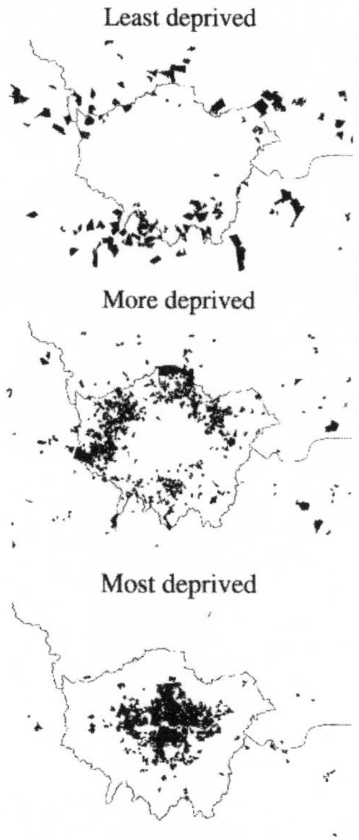

Figure 11.2d Persistent and Changing Levels of Deprivation, 1971 and 2011: London and Surrounding Areas.
Note: The boundaries shown are the Government Office Regions in England and the countries of Wales and Scotland.
Source: Author's calculations.

50 0 50 100 Kilometers

deprived areas in 1971 and 2011 forming northern and southern crescents in the 'metropolitan green belt'. The areas becoming more deprived over time form a ring around the outer London 'suburban' boroughs, and the areas most deprived at both time points are concentrated in inner London. It is interesting that Hanna and Bosetti (2015) also find outer London becoming more deprived, albeit only looking at 2001–2011 and for London Boroughs. Across Great Britain, the (white coloured) areas other than those mapped in Figures 11.2a, b and c have all become less deprived (i.e., these are the 76 per cent of LSOAs/DZs below the diagonal in Table 11.1b), at least on the basis of switches between quintiles.

In terms of which local government areas (LGAs) have small areas in these different categories, those with the highest proportions of least deprived areas (with around 20 per cent of their LSOAs/DZs classified as least deprived in both 1971 and 2011) include Epsom and Ewell, Oadby and Wigston, Brentwood, Solihull and Mole Valley. LGAs in which high percentages (up to 100 per cent) of their LSOAs/DZs became less deprived include Rutland, Bolsover and Newark and Sherwood in England, Moray and Aberdeenshire in Scotland and Gwynedd in Wales. London boroughs dominate those locations in which high proportions of areas become more deprived over time, headed by Enfield, Harrow and Redbridge, in which over 40 per cent of LSOAs were more deprived in 2011 than was the case in 1971. Away from London, Milton Keynes, Peterborough and Crawley had over 25 per cent of their LSOAs more deprived by 2011, suggesting that these new and expanded towns have experienced social decline. Although founded in 1967, in 1971 Milton Keynes was still predominately a rural, non-deprived area characterised by country villages, so the development of the urban area since then has been paralleled by increasing deprivation. For those LGAs with areas most deprived in both 1971 and 2011, the list is headed by London boroughs (Hackney, Tower Hamlets and Newham, for example). Elsewhere, over 35 per cent of the DZs in Glasgow City have been persistently deprived over time (consistent with Norman et al., 2011; Exeter et al., 2011).

Population Change and Deprivation Change

For small-area planning purposes, information is needed on whether the population is growing or declining because areas with shrinking populations are often found to be in economic decline and more deprived over time (Reher, 2007; Hollander et al., 2009; Norman, 2010b; Johansson, 2014). Since people move to different types of places at different ages (Norman and Boyle, 2014), for service planning it is also useful for know whether the population is youthful or ageing. Between 1971 and 2011 the Great Britain population grew from fifty-four million to over sixty-one million mainly due to increased longevity and net international migration gain, but to a small extent from natural increase including a resurgence in births after 2001 (Tromans et al., 2008; see also Chapter 1).

Figure 11.3a illustrates population change in this period for areas classified by their deprivation quintile in 2011. This shows that the most deprived quintile 5 has a loss of population between 1971 and 2011, but with decreasing deprivation there is a progressive increase in population gain, reflecting that the growth has been in less deprived areas. This growth has been shown in other studies to be the result of net sub-national migration gain (Norman, 2010b; Norman et al., 2016) rather than natural change gain, but disaggregation by demographic component is not possible here.

Figure 11.3b classifies the population change by the persistent and changing deprivation categories used above and including those areas whose level of deprivation does not change in the middle deprived quintiles 2–4. There is a net loss of population in the areas that are most deprived in both 1971 and 2011 and small net population gains in areas becoming more deprived and those that are middle deprived. The areas becoming less deprived are where there is the majority of the population growth. This will reflect both the demographic and deprivation change process. People are more likely to move

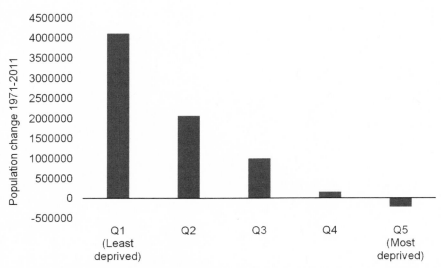

Figure 11.3a   Changing Population and Deprivation, 1971–2011: Population Change by the 2011 Deprivation Quintiles.
Source: Author's calculations.

to less deprived circumstances when they are able to (Norman et al., 2005) and, given the relationship between mortality and deprivation, may then live longer than people in more deprived circumstances.

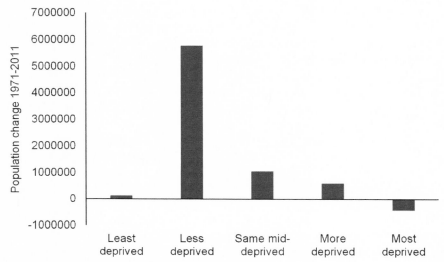

Figure 11.3b Changing Population and Deprivation, 1971–2011: Population Change by Persistent and Changing Deprivation.
Source: Author's calculations.

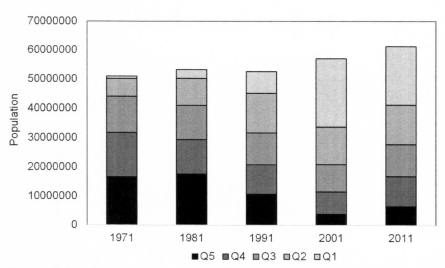

Figure 11.3c Changing Population and Deprivation, 1971–2011: Population Distribution by Deprivation Quintile.
Source: Author's calculations.

Figure 11.3c illustrates both change in total population at each Census and the distribution of the population across the deprivation quintiles. This shows the increase in national population, particularly since 1991. At the same time, there is a change in the distribution across deprivation quintiles between 1971 and 1991, with fewer people living in the most deprived areas and more people living in less deprived areas. Between 1991 and 2001, this continues with a marked reduction of population in the more deprived areas mirrored by increases in the less, and particularly the least, deprived quintile. Whilst overall there is a slight increase in deprivation between 2001 and 2011 (as noted in Figure 11.1), more people are living in less deprived than more deprived locations compared with the pre-2001 era.

Figure 11.4 illustrates dependency ratios using the same two sets of geographies as in Figures 11.3a and 11.3b. Dependency ratios reveal differences in population structures by expressing the ratio of the young and the elderly to the working-age population. Youth dependency ratios take the size of the zero-to-nineteen age group relative to those aged twenty to sixty-four, and elderly dependency ratios, those persons aged sixty-five and over relative to those aged twenty to sixty-four, with both expressed per 100 (Holdsworth et al., 2013). Changes in dependencies show whether populations are becoming more youthful or are ageing. Figure 11.4a shows dependency ratios calculated for 1971 and 2011, classified by their deprivation quintile in 2011. In both years, youth dependencies increase with level of deprivation, showing that more deprived areas have more youthful populations. There is a large decrease in these youth dependencies between 1971 and 2011 and a flattening of the deprivation gradient. The opposite is true for elderly dependencies, with less deprived areas having larger proportions of elderly relative to the working-age population. These dependencies have increased between 1971 and 2011, reflecting that the ageing population and the negative gradient with deprivation has also increased.

Figure 11.4b illustrates dependency ratios by persistent and changing deprivation categories. The youth dependencies show little relationship with these categories in 1971, except for the areas classified in quintile 5 in both years, and even less so in 2011. This suggests that population change of youth ages (relative to the working ages) is evenly spread across types of areas. Conversely, the elderly (relative to the working ages) are distributing away from the more and most deprived areas, which will be through both migration and premature mortality (Norman et al., 2011). The increased elderly dependencies in less and least deprived areas may be accounted for by this migration from more to less deprived areas (Norman et al., 2005) and by increasing longevity in less deprived locations (Rees et al., 2009).

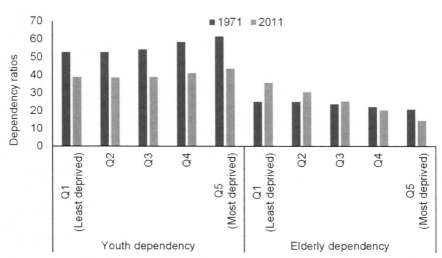

Figure 11.4a   Changing Dependency Ratios and Deprivation, 1971–2011: Dependency Ratios by the 2011 Deprivation Quintiles.
Source: Author's calculations.

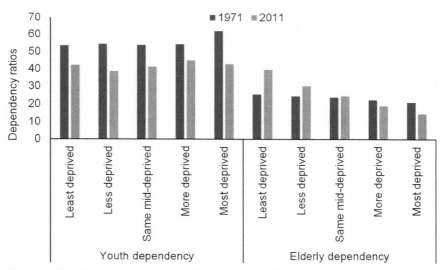

Figure 11.4b   Changing Dependency Ratios and Deprivation, 1971–2011: Dependency Ratios by Persistent and Changing Deprivation.
Source: Author's calculations.

THE FUTURE OF DEPRIVATION MEASURES

The UK's decennial Census is the most comprehensive source of sociodemographic information at a range of geographical scales (especially the small-area level), but the future of the Census as a source is uncertain (Norman,

2013). Rapid population change and the need for more timely statistics increasingly drive the need for alternative methods for the collection and dissemination of population-related data in the UK. In recent decades, Census taking has become more costly, whilst the concept of a snapshot of the population at one time point has become less relevant (Dugmore et al., 2011; Yacyshyn and Swanson, 2011). In May 2010, Sir Michael Scholar, chair of the UK Statistics Authority (UKSA), wrote to the Minister for the Cabinet Office, 'As a Board we have been concerned about the increasing costs and difficulties of traditional Census-taking. We have therefore already instructed the ONS to work urgently on the alternatives, with the intention that the 2011 Census will be the last of its kind' (ONS, 2011c). As a result, following the 2011 Census, ONS established the 'Beyond 2011' programme to assess the feasibility of using administrative statistics as an alternative to the Census. Informed by Beyond 2011, the National Statistician recommended that there *will* be a 2021 Census, but that the country's statistical system should be *enhanced* by greater use of administrative data (ONS, 2014i). Since it can be anticipated that the variables used here to measure 1971–2011 deprivation change will also be available in the 2021 Census, extending the time-series will be possible to that point, but not beyond it.

Looking further ahead in terms of measuring deprivation, the IMD has already paved the way, given that this scheme is underpinned by administrative sources. Government departments and other organisations collect so-called administrative data for various purposes, but not necessarily to count or characterise the population or for others to use in their research. There are various advantages to the use of administrative data, including cost savings, relieving the burden on survey respondents and even providing data on individuals who may not normally respond to the Census (such as the use of benefits data). Notwithstanding some drawbacks with the IMD already noted (specificity to each of the UK's constituent countries and lack of comparability over time), there *is* a future for deprivation measures using administrative data.

The complex IMD methodology is, however, beyond the skills of many practitioners and so is hard to emulate. It is possible, though, to construct a deprivation measure from many fewer administrative variables than used in the IMD (since the IMD comprises seven domains of deprivation, each one informed by multiple variables) and calculate a deprivation score using the same approach as the Townsend or Carstairs schemes. A local scheme for Doncaster's LSOAs in 2007 has just three variables, but even so a correlation of 0.96 with the IMD 2007 (D'Silva and Norman, 2015), whilst one for England's LSOAs for 2001, 2006 and 2010 with only five input variables (Ajebon and Norman, 2015) also correlates highly. These less sophisticated schemes would lead to very similar conclusions being drawn about the geography of deprivation, and their production is within the skill set of most practitioners.

So, can a scheme based on administrative data measure deprivation change over time? Ajebon and Norman (2015) calculate three cross-sections using equivalent data inputs, although without producing time-comparable scores and quintiles as used in this chapter for 1971–2011, but the potential is there. There are, however, some risks with using administrative data. If data have been collected by an organisation for their purposes, then there is little control by researchers regarding data collection and dissemination, whereas for Census data there are extensive consultations on the topics, questions, variable definitions and the table content for data release. The nature of the administrative data released will affect what can subsequently be achieved with the source in terms of data type, variable definition and the geography for which data are available (D'Silva and Norman, 2015). There is less risk when the scheme assessing the character of areas has few variables and a simple methodology. Indeed, a scheme with just one input variable—namely, the ratio of claimants of means-tested benefits to the number of households in each small area in Great Britain—has successfully been used to measure neighbourhood change annually (Gambaro et al., 2015). However, if the qualification criteria for access to the benefit were to change, there would be a lack of comparability from one year to the next.

CONCLUSION

There is a long track record of using the decennial Census to characterise small areas by their level of deprivation, relative to the national situation. Through extensive academic debate, the pros and cons are well known about variable input applicability, methods of normalisation and standardisation and the weighting of variable combinations into single deprivation scores. As alternatives, from the late 1990s onwards, the construction of the various Indices of Multiple Deprivation (IMD) has moved away from the reliance on Census data towards greater use of administrative data, with the result that more timely measures can be generated. Recently, simpler schemes than the IMD have been developed that use fewer input variables and have methodologies emulating the more traditional Census-based schemes. Whilst there are differences in the detail of outputs, generally the various deprivation schemes correlate very closely such that similar conclusions would be drawn about whether or not particular locations are relatively deprived and about relationships with other phenomena such as health (Ajebon and Norman, 2015).

A drawback with both Census-based and administrative-data-based schemes is that they are cross-sectional and only applicable close to the point in time for which they were devised. Since equivalent variables are available at the small-area level for all censuses since 1971, the input variables for the

Townsend scheme can be used to calculate changing deprivation over time, once the geography of data dissemination has been harmonised, as shown in this chapter. So that the measures have contemporary relevance, the older Census data have been adjusted to the 2011 Lower Super Output Areas in England and Wales and the Datazones in Scotland. The resulting deprivation scores for these small areas in Great Britain are then comparable for the 1971, 1981, 1991, 2001 and 2011 censuses such that, if a score increases or decreases for a particular area, this can be interpreted as worsening or improving deprivation over time. The results show that, in the main, areas become less deprived over time, but some areas remain persistently deprived whilst others retain their advantaged position. Few areas become more deprived, but there are locations where this occurs, including new and expanded towns. There are distinct patterns of change in the London area, with inner London persistently deprived, and the suburban areas towards the edge of Greater London becoming more deprived, but these are surrounded by areas remaining non-deprived. In Glasgow, there are concentrations of some of the most deprived areas in Great Britain that persist over time.

There are caveats that should be noted about the time-series of Census-based deprivation measures reported here. In terms of the input variables used in the Townsend scheme, whilst unemployment represents the same kind of personal and community-level stress over time, perhaps household overcrowding is less applicable as a deprivation indicator given very low levels for the last few censuses. Car ownership, too, is less of an indicator of material circumstances and more about accessibility now. This may have different meanings in rural and urban areas for which the latter will have better public transport availability than the former. Non–home ownership, too, may not be as diagnostic a deprivation indicator as it once was, with the separation of 'social housing' from 'private rental' tenure being an alternative to be explored. A simple fix with the available data is to weight the indicators, though their relative importance would largely be subjective. The categorisation of the deprivation index into population-weighted quintiles shows clearer patterns, which the continuous scores are unable to provide. However, as noted above, areas may change their level of deprivation substantially but not cross a quintile boundary or vice versa. It is both a strength and a drawback that the comparable deprivation presented here has ten-year intervals: on the one hand, this gives long-run patterns less affected by annual fluctuations, but alternatively there is merit in adopting Hincks's (2015) approach to identify typologies of neighbourhood change on an annual basis using administrative sources that capture short-term changes as well as medium-term trends.

In sum, with the future of Census taking after 2021 in doubt, the use of administrative data is becoming essential. Alternative schemes to the IMD show that simpler approaches result in similar geographies of deprivation and advantage. Simpler methods have the merit of less skilled practitioners being able to produce their own schemes and have the potential for using measures that are comparable over time and are available for smaller time increments than the decennial Census. Since the IMD itself is used to formulate local policy, devising a scheme to measure change based on time-robust administrative variables is becoming essential, as also is a measure that is applicable across all four of the UK's constituent countries.

NOTE

1. The research reported in this chapter used Census data, the National Statistics Postcode Directory and GIS boundary data obtained via MIMAS CASWEB and EDINA UKBORDERS, which are academic services supported by ESRC and JISC. The Census, official Mid-Year Estimates and National Statistics Postcode Directory for England, Wales and Scotland have been provided by the Office for National Statistics and National Records of Scotland and the digital boundary data by Ordnance Survey. These data are copyright of the Crown and are reproduced with permission of the Controller of HMSO.

Bibliography

Adams, J. and White, M. (2006) Removing the health domain from the Index of Multiple Deprivation 2004—effect on measured inequalities in census measure of health. *Journal of Public Health* 28 (4): 379–83.

Aicken, C. R. H., Nardone, A. and Mercer, C. H. (2011) Alcohol misuse, sexual risk behaviour and adverse sexual health outcomes: Evidence from Britain's national probability sexual behaviour surveys. *Journal of Public Health* 33 (2): 262–71.

Ajebon, M. and Norman, P. (2015) Beyond the census: A spatial analysis of health and deprivation in England. *GeoJournal* doi:10.1007/s10708-015-9624-8.

Alders, M. (2000) Cohort fertility of migrant women in the Netherlands. Developments in fertility of women born in Turkey, Morocco, Suriname and the Netherlands Antilles and Aruba. Paper for the BSPS-NVD-URU Conference, 31 August–01 Sept. Utrecht: Statistics Netherlands.

Amato, P. R. (2010) Research on divorce: Continuing trends and new developments. *Journal of Marriage and Family* 72: 650–66.

Anderson, C. and Blenkinsopp, A. (2006) Community pharmacy supply of emergency hormonal contraception: A structured literature review of international evidence. *Human Reproduction* 21 (1): 272–84.

Andersson, G. (2004) Childbearing after migration: Fertility patterns of foreign-born women in Sweden. *International Migration Review* 38 (2): 747–75.

Arango, J. (2000) Explaining migration: A critical view. *International Social Science Journal* 52 (165): 283–96.

Aston, G. and Bewley, S. (2009) Abortion and domestic violence. *Obstetrician and Gynaecologist* 11 (3): 163–68.

Bader, M. D. M. and Krysan, M. (2015) Community attraction and avoidance in Chicago: What's race got to do with it? *Annals of the American Academy of Political and Social Science* 660: 261–81.

Baeten, J. M. and Overbaugh, J. (2003) Measuring the infectiousness of persons with HIV-1: Opportunities for preventing sexual HIV-1 transmission. *Current HIV Research* 1 (1): 69–86.

Baillot, H., Murray, N., Connelly, E. and Howard, N. (2014) *Tackling Female Genital Mutilation in Scotland: A Scottish Model of Intervention*. Technical Report. Glasgow. Scottish Refugee Council. December 2014.

Bajekal, M., Harries, T., Breman, R. and Woodfield, K. (2004) *Review of Disability Estimates and Definitions*. DWP In-house Report 128. London: Department for Work and Pensions.

Ballard, R. (1990) Migration and kinship: the differential effect of marriage rules on the processes of Punjabi migration to Britain. In Clarke, C., Peach, C. and Vertovek, S. (Eds.) *South Asians Overseas: Contexts and Communities*. Cambridge: Cambridge University Press, 219–49.

Banks, J., Karlsen, S. and Oldfield, Z. (2004) Socio-economic position. In Marmot, M., Banks, J., Blundell, R., Lessof, C. and Nazroo, J. (Eds.) *Health, Wealth and Lifestyles of the Older Population in England. The 2002 English Longitudinal Study of Ageing*. London: The Institute for Fiscal Studies.

Banks, J. and Smith, S. (2006) Retirement in the UK. *Oxford Review of Economic Policy* 2 (1): 40–56.

Bartley, M. (2004) *Health Inequality: An Introduction to Theories, Concepts and Methods*. Cambridge: Polity Press.

Basta, N. O., James, P. W., Gomez-Pozo, B., Craft, A. W., Norman, P. D. and McNally, R. J. Q. (2014) Survival from teenage and young adult cancer in northern England, 1968–2008. *Pediatric Blood and Cancer* 61 (5): 901–6.

Bate, R. (1999) Household projections: A sheep in wolf's clothing. In Dorling, D. and Simpson, S. (Eds.) *Statistics in Society: The Arithmetic of Politics*. London: Arnold, 369–75.

Baxter, S., Blank, L., Guillaume, L., Squires, H. and Payne, N. (2011) Views of contraceptive service delivery to young people in the UK: A systematic review and thematic synthesis. *Journal of Family Planning and Reproductive Health Care* 37 (2): 71–84.

Beard, J. R., Blaney, S., Cerda, M., Frye, V., Lovasi, G., Ompad, D., Rundle, A. and Vlahov, D. (2009) Neighborhood characteristics and disability in older adults. *Journals of Gerontology. Series B, Psychological Sciences and Social Sciences* 64 (2): 252–57.

Beatty, C. and Fothergill, S. (2005) The diversion from 'unemployment' to 'sickness' across British regions and districts. *Regional Studies* 39 (7): 837–54.

Beekman, A., Deeg, D., Van Tilburg, T., Smit, J., Hooijer, C. and Tilburg, W. (1995) Major and minor depression in later life: A study of prevalence and risk factors. *Journal of Affective Disorders* 36: 65–75.

Bell, M. and Charles-Edwards, E. (2013) *Cross-National Comparisons of Internal Migration: An Update on Global Patterns and Trends*. Technical Paper No. 2013/1. New York: United Nations Department of Economic and Social Affairs.

Bell, M., Charles-Edwards, E., Ueffing, P., Stillwell, J., Kupiszewski, M. and Kupiszewska, D. (2015) Internal migration and development: Comparing migration intensities around the world. *Population and Development Review* 41: 33–58.

Bell, N., Schuurman, N. and Hayes, M. V. (2007) Using GIS-based methods of multicriteria analysis to construct socioeconomic deprivation indices. *International Journal of Health Geographics* 6: 17.

Bennet, J., Li, G., Foreman, K., Best, N., Kontis, V., Pearson, C., Hambly, P. and Ezzati, M. (2015) The future of life expectancy and life expectancy inequalities in England and Wales: Bayesian spatiotemporal forecasting. *The Lancet* 386: 163–70.

Bentham. G., Eimermann, J., Haynes, R., Lovett, A. and Brainard, J. (1995) Limiting long-term illness and its associations with mortality and indicators of social deprivation. *Journal of Epidemiology and Community Health* 49: S57–S64.

Berrington, A. (1996) Marriage patterns and inter-ethnic unions. In Coleman, D. and Salt, J. (Eds.) *Ethnicity in the 1991 Census: Demographic Characteristics of the Ethnic Minority Populations.* London: HMSO, 178–212.

Berrington, A. (2014) *The Changing Demography of Lone Parenthood in the UK.* CPC Working Paper 48. Southampton: ESRC Centre for Population Change. http:// www.cpc.ac.uk/publications/cpc_working_papers/pdf/2014_WP48_The_chang- ing_demography_of_lone_parenthood_Berrington.pdf.

Berrington, A. and Pattaro, S. (2014) Educational differences in fertility desires, intentions and behaviour: A life course perspective. *Advances in Life Course Research* doi:10.1016/j.alcr.2013.12.003.

Berrington, A. and Stone, J. (2014) Young adults' transitions to residential independence in the UK: The role of social and housing policy. *Young People and Social Policy in Europe: Dealing with Risk, Inequality and Precarity in Times of Crisis.* New York: Palgrave Macmillan, 210–25.

Berrington, A., Stone, J. and Beaujouan, E. (2015) Educational differences in timing and quantum of childbearing in Britain: a study of cohorts born 1940–1969. *Demographic Research* (in press).

Beyrer, C., Baral, S. D., van Griensven, F., Goodreau, S. M., Chariyalertsak, M., Wirtz, A. L. and Brookmeyer, R. (2012) Global epidemiology of HIV infection in men who have sex with men. *The Lancet* 380 (9839): 367–77.

Bhachu, P. (1985) *Twice Migrants: East African Sikh Settlers in Britain.* London: Tavistock. http://www.cpc.ac.uk/publications/cpc_briefing_papers/pdf/BP28_How %20to%20forecast%20international%20migration.pdf.

Bijak, J. (2010) *Forecasting International Migration in Europe: A Bayesian View.* Springer Series on Demographic Methods and Population Analysis, vol. 24. Dordrecht: Springer.

Bijak, J., Disney, G., Lubman, S. and Wiśniowski, A. (2013) *Towards Reliable Migration Statistics for the United Kingdom.* Response to the House of Commons Public Administration Select Committee Call for Evidence on Migration Statistics. http://www.parliament.uk/business/committees/committees-a-z/commons-select/ public-administration-select-committee/inquiries/parliament-2010/statistics/ migration-statistics.

Bijak, J., Disney, G. and Wisniowski, A. (2015) *How to Forecast International Migration.* CPC Briefing Paper 28. Southampton: ESRC Centre for Population Change.

Black, K. I., Mercer, C. H., Johnson, A. M. and Wellings, K. (2006) Sociodemographic and sexual health profile of users of emergency hormonal contraception: Data from a British probability sample survey. *Contraception* 74 (4): 309–12.

Blackman, T. (2006) *Placing Health. Neighbourhood Renewal, Health Improvement and Complexity.* Bristol: Policy Press.

Blakey, K., Feltbower, R. G., Parslow, R. C. et al. (2014) Is fluoride a risk factor for bone cancer? Small area analysis of osteosarcoma and Ewing sarcoma diagnosed among 0–49 year olds in Great Britain, 1980–2005. *International Journal of Epidemiology* 43 (1): 224–34.

Blazer, D. G. (2003) Depression in late life: Review and commentary. *Journals of Gerontology. Series A, Biological Sciences and Medical Sciences* 58 (3): 249–65.

Blinder, S. (2014) *Briefing: Migration to the UK, Non-European Student Migration to the UK*. Oxford: Migration Observatory, University of Oxford. http://www.migrationobservatory.ox.ac.uk/briefings/non-european-student-migration-uk.

Botting, B. and Dunnell, K. (2000) Trends in fertility and contraception in the last quarter of the 20th century. *Population Trends* 100: 32–39.

Bowling, A. and Stafford, M. (2007) How do objective and subjective assessments of neighbourhood influence social and physical functioning in older age? Findings from a British survey of ageing. *Social Science & Medicine* 64 (12): 2533–49.

Bowyer, H. L., Forster, A. S., Marlow, L. A. and Waller, J. (2014) Predicting human papillomavirus vaccination behaviour among adolescent girls in England: Results from a prospective survey. *Journal of Family Planning and Reproductive Health Care* 40 (1): 14–22.

Boyle, P. and Dorling, D. (2004) The 2001 UK census: Remarkable resource or bygone legacy of the 'pencil and paper era'? *Area* 36 (2): 101–10.

Boyle, P., Norman, P. and Rees, P. (2002) Does migration exaggerate the relationship between deprivation and limiting long-term illness? A Scottish analysis. *Social Science and Medicine* 55: 21–31.

Boyle, P., Norman, P. and Rees, P. (2004) Changing places: do changes in the relative deprivation of areas influence limiting long-term illness and mortality among non-migrant people living in non-deprived households? *Social Science and Medicine* 58: 2459–71.

Bradford, M. G., Robson, B. T. and Tye, R. (1995) Constructing an urban deprivation index: A way of meeting the need for flexibility. *Environment and Planning A* 27: 519–33.

Bramley, G. (1994) An affordability crisis in British housing: dimensions, causes and policy impact. *Housing Studies* 9 (1): 103–24.

Bramley, G., Pawson, H., White, M. and Watkins, D. (2010) *Estimating Housing Need*. London: Department of Communities and Local Government.

Brennan, A., Rhodes, J. and Tyler, P. (1999) The distribution of SRB challenge fund expenditure in relation to local-area need in England. *Urban Studies* 36 (12): 2069–84.

Broadway, M. J. and Jesty, G. (1998) Are Canadian inner cities becoming more dissimilar? An analysis of urban deprivation indicators. *Urban Studies* 35 (9): 1423–38.

Brown, J. M. (2006) *Global South Asians. Introducing the Modern Diaspora*. Cambridge: Cambridge University Press.

Burstrom, B., Whitehead, M., Lindholm, C. and Diderichsen, F. (2000) Inequality in the social consequences of illness: How well do people with long-term illness fare in the British and Swedish labor markets? *International Journal of Health Services* 30 (3): 435–51.

Bury, L. and Ngo, T. D. (2009) *The Condom Broke! Why Do Women in the UK Have Unintended Pregnancies?* London: Marie Stopes International.

Byron, M. (1994) *Post-War Caribbean Migration to Britain: The Unfinished Cycle.* Aldershot: Avebury.

Byron, M. (1998) Migration, work and gender: The case of post-war labour migration from the Caribbean to Britain. In Chamberlain, M. (Ed.) *Caribbean Migration: Globalised Identities.* London: Routledge.

Cameron, D. (2015) Conservative Party Conference Speech, Manchester. Available at: http://www.independent.co.uk/news/uk/politics/tory-party-conference-2015-david-camerons-speech-in-full-a6684656.html.

Carers UK (2011) *Valuing Carers 2011: Calculating the Value of Carers' Support.* London: Carers UK.

Carmichael, F. and Charles, S. (2003) The opportunity costs of informal care: Does gender matter? *Journal of Health Economics* 22 (5): 781–803.

Carr-Hill, R., and Rice, N. (1995) Is enumeration district level an improvement on ward level analysis in studies of deprivation and health? *Journal of Epidemiology and Community Health* 49 (2): S28–S29.

Carstairs, V. and Morris, R. (1989) Deprivation: Explaining differences in mortality between Scotland, England and Wales. *British Medical Journal* 299: 886–89.

Castles, S. and Miller, M. J. (2009) *The Age of Migration: International Population Movements in the Modern World*, 4th edition. Basingstoke: Palgrave Macmillan.

Catney, G. (2015a) Has neighbourhood ethnic residential segregation decreased? In Jivraj, S. and Simpson, L. (Eds.) *Ethnic Identity and Inequalities in Britain: The Dynamics of Diversity.* Bristol: Policy Press, 109–21.

Catney, G. (2015b) The changing geographies of ethnic diversity in England and Wales, 1991–2011. *Population, Space and Place.* In press. doi:10.1002/psp.1954.

Catney, G. (2015c) Towards an enhanced understanding of ethnic group geographies using measures of clustering and unevenness. *The Geographical Journal.* In press. doi:10.1111/geoj.12162.

Catney, G. (2016) Exploring a decade of small area ethnic (de-)segregation in England and Wales. *Urban Studies* 53 (8): 1691–709. doi:10.1177/0042098015576855.

Catney, G. and Simpson, L. (2010) Settlement area migration in England and Wales: Assessing evidence for a social gradient. *Transactions of the Institute of British Geographers* 35: 571–84.

Catney, G. and Simpson, L. (2014) How persistent is demographic variation between ethnic groups? The case of household size in England and Wales. *Population Space and Place* 20 (3): 201–21.

Cea Soriano, L., Wallander, M.-A., Andersson, S., Filonenko, A. and García Rodríguez, L. A. (2014) Use of long-acting reversible contraceptives in the UK from 2004 to 2010: Analysis using the Health Improvement Network Database. *European Journal of Contraception and Reproductive Health Care* 19 (6): 439–47.

Centre for Cities (2015) *Cities Outlook 2015.* London: Centre for Cities.

Champion, T. (1989) Internal migration and the spatial distribution of population. In Joshi, H. (Ed.) *The Changing Population of Britain.* Oxford: Blackwell, 110–32.

Champion, T. (2012) Testing the return migration element of the 'escalator region' model: An analysis of migration into and out of south-east England, 1966–2001. *Cambridge Journal of Regions, Economy and Society* 5: 255–70.

Champion, T. (2014) *People in Cities: The Numbers*. Foresight Future of Cities Working Paper 3. London: Government Office for Science.

Champion, T. (2015) Urban population—can recovery last? *Town and Country Planning* 84: 338–43.

Champion, T., Coombes, M. and Gordon, I. (2014) How far do England's second-order cities emulate London as human-capital 'escalators'? *Population Space and Place* 20: 421–33.

Champion, T., Coombes, M., Raybould, S. and Wymer, C. (2007) *Migration and Socio-Economic Change: A 2001 Census Analysis of Britain's Larger Cities*. Bristol: Policy Press.

Champion, T. and Shuttleworth, I. (2016a) Is longer-distance migration slowing? An analysis of the annual record for England and Wales since the 1970s. *Population Space and Place*. doi:10.1002/psp.2024.

Champion, T. and Shuttleworth, I. (2016b) Are people changing address less? An analysis of migration within England and Wales, 1971–2011. *Population Space and Place*. doi:10.1002/psp.2026.

Champion, T. and Townsend, A. (2013) Great Britain's second-order city regions in recessions. *Environment and Planning A* 45 (2): 362–82.

Chandler, D. and Tetlow, G. (2014) *Retirement in the 21st Century*. IFS Report R98. London: The Institute for Fiscal Studies.

Charlton, J., Wallace, M. and White, I. (1994) Long-term illness: Results from the 1991 census. *Population Trends* 75: 18–25.

Cheung, S. Y. and Phillimore, J. (2013) *Social Networks, Social Capital and Refugee Integration*. Research Report for Nuffield Foundation. University of Cardiff and University of Birmingham.

Chu, B. (2014) Britain is suffering from a housing crisis. Who is to blame and how can we fix it? *The Independent*. http://www.independent.co.uk/property/house-and-home/property/britain-is-suffering-from-a-housing-crisis-who-is-to-blame-and-how-can-we-fix-it-9113329.html (last accessed 17 October 2015).

Clarke, B. (2015) *The Challenge Facing First-Time Buyers*. Council of Mortgage Lenders. http://www.cml.org.uk/news/news-and-views/723/ (last accessed 23 December 2015).

Clarke, L. (1992) Children's family circumstances: Recent trends in Great Britain. *European Journal of Population* 8 (4): 309–40.

Clarke, L. (1996) Demographic change and the family situation of children. In Brannen, J. and O'Brien, M. (Eds.) *Children in Families: Research and Policy*. London: Falmer Press, 66–83.

Clarke, L. and Jensen, A.-M. (2004) Children's risk of parental break-up—Norway and England/Wales compared. *Acta Sociologica* 47 (1): 51–69.

Clarke, L. and Joshi, H. (2003) Children's changing families and family resources. In Jensen, A.-M. and McKee, L. (Eds.) *Children and the Changing Family: Between Transformation and Negotiation*. London: Routledge, 15–26.

Cohen, G., Forbes, J. and Garraway, M. (1995). Interpreting self-reported limiting long-term illness. *British Medical Journal* 311: 722–24.

Coleman, D. (2013) *Immigration, Population and Ethnicity: The UK in International Perspective*. Briefing paper. Oxford: Migration Observatory. http://www. migrationobservatory.ox.ac.uk/briefings/immigration-population-and-ethnicity-uk-international-perspective.

Coleman, D. and Dubuc, S. (2010) The fertility of ethnic minority populations in the United Kingdom, 1960s–2006. *Population Studies* 64 (1): 19–41.

Coleman, D. and Salt, J. (Eds.) (1996) *Ethnicity in the 1991 Census: Demographic Characteristics of the Ethnic Minority Populations*. London: The Stationery Office.

Coleman, L. and Testa, A. (2007) Sexual health knowledge, attitudes and behaviours among an ethnically diverse sample of young people in the UK. *Health Education Journal* 66 (1): 68–81.

Commission of the European Communities (2007) *Green Paper on the Future Common European Asylum System in Europe*. COM (2007) 301 final. Brussels: European Commission.

Commons Library (2015) *Controlling Immigration Targets: Key Issues for the 2015 Parliament*. Commons Library briefing paper. London: House of Commons. http:// www.parliament.uk/business/publications/research/key-issues-parliament-2015/ social-change/controlling-immigration/. *Acta Sociologica* 47 (1): 51–69.

COMPAS/DCLG (2015) Migration and Integration Policy Roundtable Meetings. Briefings available at: http://www.compas.ox.ac.uk/event/integration-and-integration-policy-roundtable-meetings/.

Conley, D. and Glauber, R. (2008) All in the family? Family composition, resources, and sibling similarity in socioeconomic status. *Research in Social Stratification and Mobility* 26 (4): 297–306.

Connolly, A., Pietri, G., Yu, J. and Humphreys, S. (2014) Association between long-acting reversible contraceptive use, teenage pregnancy, and abortion rates in England. *International Journal of Women's Health* 6: 961.

Cooke, T. J. (2011) It is not just the economy: Declining migration and the rise of secular rootedness. *Population Space and Place* 17: 193–203.

Coombes, M., Raybould, S., Wong, C. and Openshaw, S. (1995) Towards an index of deprivation: a review of alternative approaches. *1991 Deprivation Index: A Review of Approaches and a Matrix of Results*, 1–67.

Craig, N. (2005) Exploring the generalisability of the association between income inequality and self-assessed health. *Social Science and Medicine* 60 (11): 2477–88.

CRUK (2014) *Cancer Statistics Key Statistics: Cervical Cancer*. London: Cancer Research UK.

CSDH (2008). *Closing the Gap in a Generation: Health Equity Through Action on the Social Determinants of Health*. Final Report of the Commission on Social Determinants of Health. Geneva: World Health Organization.

Cullingworth, J. B. and Nadin, V. (1994) *Town and Country Planning in the UK*. London: Routledge.

Cummins, S., Stafford, M., Macintyre, S., Marmot, M. and Ellaway, A. (2005) Neighbourhood environment and its association with self rated health: Evidence from Scotland and England. *Journal of Epidemiology and Community Health* 59 (3): 207–13.

Currie, C., Levin, K. A., Kirby, J. L. M., Currie, D. B., van der Sluijs, W. and Inchley, J. C. (2011) Health behaviour in school-aged children: World Health Organization collaborative cross-national study. Findings from the 2010 HBSC survey in Scotland. HBSC Scotland National Report. Edinburgh: Child and Adolescent Health Research Unit (CAHRU), University of Edinburgh.

Daley, P. (1996) Black-Africans: Students who stayed. In Peach, C. (Ed.) *Ethnicity in the 1991 Census. Volume 2: The Ethnic Minority Populations of Great Britain.* London: HMSO, 44–65.

Daly, L., Ashbourne L. and Hawkins, L. (2008) Work-life issues for fathers. In Korabik, K., Lero, D. S. and Whitehead, D. L. (Eds.) *Handbook of Work-Family Integration. Research, Theory, and Best Practice.* Amsterdam and Boston: Elsevier, 249–64.

Dannefer, D. (2003) Cumulative advantage/disadvantage and the life course: Cross-fertilizing age and social science theory. *Journals of Gerontology. Series B, Psychological Sciences and Social Sciences* 58B (6): 327–37.

Dawe, F. and Rainford, L. (2004) *Contraception and Sexual Health 2003.* A report on research using the ONS Omnibus Survey London. Produced by the Office for National Statistics on behalf of the Department of Health.

DCLG (2006) *The State of the English Cities.* London: Department of Communities and Local Government.

DCLG (2010a) *Updating the Department for Communities and Local Government's Household Projections to a 2008 Base: Methodology.* London: Department of Communities and Local Government.

DCLG (2010b) *Testing Methodological Changes to the Household Projections Model: Research Report.* London: Department for Communities and Local Government.

DCLG (2015a) *2012-Based Household Projections in England, 2012 to 2037.* London: Department of Communities and Local Government.

DCLG (2015b) *Planning Practice Guidance: Housing and Economic Development Needs Assessments.* http://planningguidance.planningportal.gov.uk, 26 March 2015. London: Department of Communities and Local Government.

DCLG (2015c) *2012-Based Household Projections—England: Household Types (Stage 2) and National Variants.* London: Department of Communities and Local Government.

DCLG (2015d) *2012-Based Household Projections: Detailed Data for Modelling and Analytical Purposes.* https://www.gov.uk/government/collections/household-projections#2012-based-projections (last accessed 17 October 2015).

de Oliveira, C., Shankar, A., Kumari, M., Nunn, S. and Steptoe, A. (2010) Health risk and health protective biological measures in later life. In Banks, J., Lessof, C., Nazroo, J., Rogers, N., Stafford, M. and Steptoe, A. (Eds.) *Financial Circumstances, Health and Well-Being of the Older Population in England: The 2008 English Longitudinal Study of Ageing.* London: The Institute for Fiscal Studies, 275–347.

Demey, D., Berrington, A., Evandrou, M. and Falkingham, J. (2011) The changing demography of mid-life, from the 1980s to the 2000s. *Population Trends* 145: 16–34.

Demey, D., Berrington, A., Evandrou, M. and Falkingham, J. (2013) Pathways into living alone in mid-life: Diversity and policy implications. *Advances in Life Course Research* 18 (3): 161–74.

Denham, C. J. and Rhind, D. W. (1983) The 1981 Census and its results. In Rhind, D. (Ed.) *A Census Users Handbook.* London: Methuen, 17–88.

Department of Health (2011) *Fairer Care Funding: The Report of the Commission on Funding of Care and Support.* London: The Stationery Office.

Department of Health (2013a) *Abortion Statistics, England and Wales: 2013.* London, Department of Health.

Department of Health (2013b) *A Framework for Sexual Health Improvement in England.* London: Department of Health.

Department of Health (2014) *Abortion Notification Forms for England and Wales.* Retrieved 6 October 2015 from https://www.gov.uk/government/publications/abortion-notification-forms-for-england-and-wales.

Department of Health (2015) *Abortion Statistics, England and Wales: 2014.* London: Department of Health.

Devlin, C., Bolt, O., Patel, D., Harding, D., and Hussain, I. (2014) *Impacts of Migration on UK Native Employment: An Analytical Review of the Evidence.* Home Office Occasional Paper 109. London: Home Office. https://www.gov.uk/government/uploads/system/uploads/attachment_data/file/287287/occ109.pdf.

Diamond, I. and Clarke, S. (1989) Demographic patterns among Britain's ethnic groups. In Joshi, H. (Ed.) *The Changing Population of Britain.* Oxford: Blackwell, 177–98.

DiCenso, A., Guyatt, G., Willan, A. and Griffith, A. (2002) Interventions to reduce unintended pregnancies among adolescents: systematic review of randomised controlled trials. *British Medical Journal* 324 (7351): 1426.

Diez Roux, A. V. and Mair, C. (2010) Neighborhoods and health. *Annals of the New York Academy of Sciences* 1186: 125–45.

Disney, G. (2015) Model-based estimates of UK immigration. PhD Thesis. University of Southampton.

Disney, G., Wiśniowski, A., Forster, J. J., Smith, P. W. F. and Bijak, J. (2015) *Evaluation of Existing Migration Forecasting Methods and Models.* Report to the Migration Advisory Committee. Southampton: Centre for Population Change. https://www.gov.uk/government/publications/evaluation-of-existing-migration-forecasting-methods-and-models.

DoE (1983) *Urban Deprivation: Information Note 2, Inner Cities Directorate.* London: Department of the Environment.

DoE (1994) *A 1991 Index of Local Conditions.* London: Department of the Environment.

Dolan, S. A., Jarman, B., Bajekal, M., Davies, P. M. and Hart, D. (1995) Measuring disadvantage: Changes in the underprivileged area, Townsend and Carstairs scores 1981–91. *Journal of Epidemiology and Community Health* 49 (Suppl 2): S30–S33.

Doran, T., Drever, F. and Whitehead, M. (2003) Health of young and elderly informal carers: Analysis of UK census data. *British Medical Journal* 327 (7428): 1388.

Dorling, D. (1999) Who's afraid of income inequality? *Environment and Planning A* 31: 571–74.

Dorling, D. (2014) *All That Is Solid: How the Great Housing Disaster Defines Our Times, and What We Can Do About It*. London: Penguin.

Dorling, D. and Thomas, B. (2004) *People and Place: A 2001 Census Atlas of the UK*. Bristol: Policy Press.

Downey, D. B. (1995) When bigger is not better: Family size, parental resources, and children's educational performance. *American Sociological Review* 60 (5): 746–61.

D'Silva, S. and Norman, P. (2015) Impacts of mine closure in Doncaster: An index of social stress. *Radical Statistics* 112: 23–33.

Dubuc, S. (2009) Application of the Own-Children method for estimating fertility of women by ethnic groups in the UK. *Journal of Population Research* 26 (3): 207–25.

Dubuc, S. (2012) Immigration to the UK from high-fertility countries: Intergenerational adaptation and fertility convergence. *Population and Development Review* 38 (2): 353–68.

Dubuc, S. (2015) Fertility and education of the British Indian and Chinese women: A success story of social mobility? Paper presented at the Vienna Institute of Demography International Conference: Education and Reproduction in Low-Fertility Settings. Vienna, 3–5 December.

Dubuc, S. (2016, in press) Fertility of immigrants. In Bean, F. and Brown, S. (Eds.) *Encyclopedia of Migration*. Springer Science editions.

Dubuc, S. and Coleman, D. (2007) An increase in the sex ratio of births to India-born mothers in England and Wales: Evidence for sex-selective abortion. *Population and Development Review* 33 (2): 383–400.

Dubuc, S. and Haskey, J. (2010) Ethnicity and fertility in the UK. In Stillwell, J. and van Ham, M. (Eds.) *Understanding Population Trends and Processes, Volume 3: Ethnicity and Integration*. Dordrecht: Springer, 63–82.

Dubuc, S. and Waller, L. (2011) Fertility and education: Ethnic differentials and second generation groups in the UK. Paper presented at the Royal Geographical Society-with-IBG Conference, London, 1–3 September.

Dubuc, S. and Waller, L. (2014) Reproductive choices and education of immigrant and second generation women in the UK. Paper presented at the Annual Meeting of the Population Association of America conference, Boston, 1–3 May 2014.

Dugmore, K., Furness, P., Leventhal, B. and Moy, C. (2011) Beyond the 2011 Census in the United Kingdom. *International Journal of Market Research* 53 (5): 619–50.

Duncan, C., Jones, K. and Moon, G. (1995) Psychiatric morbidity: A multilevel approach to regional variations in the UK. *Journal of Epidemiology and Community Health* 49 (3): 290–95.

Dustmann, C., Casanova, M., Fertig, M., Preston, I. and Schmidt, C. M. (2003) *The Impact of EU Enlargement on Migration Flows*. Home Office Online Report 25/03. London: Home Office.

Dustmann, C. and Frattini, T. (2013) *The Fiscal Effects of Immigration to the UK*. Discussion Paper Series No. 22/13. London: Centre for Research and Analysis of Migration. http://www.cream-migration.org/publ_uploads/CDP_22_13.pdf.

Dustmann, C., Frattini, T., and Preston, I. (2008) *The Effect of Immigration on the Distribution of Wages*. Discussion Paper Series No. 03/08. London: Centre for Research and Analysis of Migration. http://www.cream-migration.org/publ_uploads/CDP_03_08.pdf.

Dustmann, C. and Theodoropoulos, N. (2010) Ethnic minority immigrants and their children in Britain. *Oxford Economic Papers.* Oxford University Press. doi:10.1093/oep/gpq004.

Eade, J., Vamplew, T. and Peach, C. (1996) The Bangladeshis: The encapsulated community. In Peach, C. (Ed.) *Ethnicity in the 1991 Census Volume Two. The Ethnic Minority Populations of Great Britain.* London: Office for National Statistics, 150–60.

Emerson, C. and Muriel, A. (2008) Financial resources and wellbeing. In Banks, J., Breeze, E., Lessof, C. and Nazroo, J. (Eds.) *Living in the 21st Century: Older People in England. The 2006 English Longitudinal Study of Ageing.* London: The Institute for Fiscal Studies.

Engels, F. (1845; reprinted in 1987) *The Condition of the Working Class in England.* London: Penguin.

Ermish, J. and Francesconi, M. (2001) *The Effects of Parents' Employment on Outcomes for Children.* London: Family Policy Studies Centre for Joseph Rowntree Foundation.

Eroğlu, S. (2007) Developing an index of deprivation which integrates objective and subjective dimensions: Extending the work of Townsend, Mack and Lansley, and Halleröd. *Social Indicators Research* 80 (3): 493–510.

Eurostat (2015) *People in the EU: Who are we and how do we live?* Brussels: European Commission.

Evandrou, M. (2005) Health and social care. In Soule, A., Baab, P., Evandrou, M., Balchin, S. and Zealey, L. (Eds.) *Focus on Older People.* ONS/DWP Focus On Series. Basingstoke: Palgrave Macmillan, 51–66.

Evandrou, M., Falkingham, J., Robards, J. and Vlachantoni, A. (2015) *Who Cares? Continuity and Change in the Prevalence of Caring and Characteristics of Informal Carers in England and Wales, 2001–2011.* CPC Working Paper 68. Southampton: ESRC Centre for Population Change.

Evandrou, M., Falkingham, J., Robards, J. and Vlachantoni, A. (2016) The prevalence of informal care and its association with health: Longitudinal research using census data for England and Wales. In Stillwell, J. and Duke-Williams, O. (Eds.) *A Handbook of Census Resources, Methods and Applications: Unlocking the UK 2011 Census.* Farnham: Ashgate.

Exeter, D. J., Boyle, P. J. and Norman, P. (2011) Deprivation (im)mobility and cause-specific premature mortality in Scotland. *Social Science and Medicine* 72: 389–97.

Falkingham, J. (2016) *The Changing Meaning of Old Age.* CPC Briefing Paper 32. Southampton: ESRC Centre for Population Change.

Falkingham, J., Evandrou, M. and Vlachantoni, A. (2014) *Exploring the Link Between Demographic Change and Poverty in the UK.* CPC Working Paper 54. Southampton: ESRC Centre for Population Change.

Fenton, K. A. (2002) Sexual health and HIV positive individuals: Emerging lessons from the recent outbreaks of infectious syphilis in England. *Communicable Disease and Public Health* 5 (1): 4–6.

Fenton, K. A. and Hughes, G. (2003) Sexual behaviour in Britain: Why sexually transmitted infections are common. *Clinical Medicine* 3 (3): 199–202.

Fenton, K. A., Mercer, C. H., McManus, S., Erens, B., Wellings, K., Macdowall, W., Byron, C. L., Copas, A. J., Nanchahal, K. and Field, J. (2005) Ethnic variations in sexual behaviour in Great Britain and risk of sexually transmitted infections: A probability survey. *The Lancet* 365 (9466): 1246–55.

Fielding, A. J. (1989) Inter-regional migration and social change: A study of South East England based upon data from the Longitudinal Study. *Transactions of the Institute of British Geographers New Series* 14 (1): 24–36.

Fielding, A. J. (1992) Migration and social mobility: South East England as an escalator region. *Regional Studies* 26 (1): 1–15.

Fielding, A. J. (2012) *Migration in Britain: Paradoxes of the Past, Prospects for the Future.* Cheltenham: Edward Elgar.

Finney, N. (2010) Ethnic group population change and integration: A demographic approach to small area ethnic geographies. In Stillwell, J. and van Ham, M. (Eds.) *Understanding Population Trends and Processes Volume 3: Ethnicity and Integration.* Dordrecht: Springer, chapter 2.

Finney, N. and Catney, G. (2012) Minority internal migration in Europe: Research progress, challenges and prospects. In Finney, N. and Catney, G. (Eds.) *Minority Internal Migration in Europe.* Farnham: Ashgate, 313–27.

Finney, N., Catney, G. and Phillips, D. (2015) Ethnicity and internal migration. In Smith, D., Finney, N., Halfacree, K. and Walford, N. (Eds.) Internal Migration: Geographical Perspectives and Processes. Farnham: Ashgate, 31–45.

Finney, N. and Harries, B. (2015) Which ethnic groups are hardest hit by the housing crisis? In Jivraj, S. and Simpson, L. (Eds.) *Ethnic Identity and Inequalities in Britain: The Dynamics of Diversity.* Bristol: Policy Press, 141–60.

Finney, N. and Simpson, L. (2008) Internal migration and ethnic group: Evidence for Britain from the 2001 Census. *Population, Space and Place* 14: 63–83.

Finney, N. and Simpson, L. (2009) *Sleepwalking to Segregation? Challenging Myths about Race and Migration.* Bristol: Policy Press.

Foner, N. (2009) Gender and migration: West Indians in comparative perspective. *International Migration Review* 47 (1): 3–29.

FPA (2010) *Sexually Transmitted Infections.* Factsheet. London: The Family Planning Association.

FPA (2014) *Abortion in Northern Ireland.* Factsheet. Belfast: The Family Planning Association.

Freeman, L., Cassola, A. and Cai, T. (2015) Displacement and gentrification in England and Wales: A quasi-experimental approach. *Urban Studies*, 1–18 doi:10.1177/0042098015598120.

Frejka, T. and Sardon, J.-P. (2007) Cohort birth order, parity progression ratio and parity distribution trends in developed countries. *Demographic Research* 16: 315–74.

French, R. S., Joyce, L., Fenton, K. et al. (2005) *Indian and Jamaican Young People in Relation to Reproductive and Sexual Health.* A report for the Teenage Pregnancy Unit. London: Department for Education and Skills.

Fu, M., Exeter, D. J., and Anderson, A. (2015) 'So, is that your "relative" or mine?' A political-ecological critique of census-based area deprivation indices. *Social Science and Medicine* 142: 27–36.

Gambaro, L., Joshi, H., Lupton, R., Fenton, A., and Lennon, M. C. (2015) Developing better measures of neighbourhood characteristics and change for use in studies of residential mobility: A case study of Britain in the early 2000s. *Applied Spatial Analysis and Policy*, doi:10.1007/s12061-015-9164-0.

Gambaro, L., Stewart, K. and Waldfogel, J. (2013) *A question of quality: Do children from disadvantaged backgrounds receive lower quality early years education and care in England?* CASE Paper 171. London: Centre for Analysis of Social Exclusion, London School of Economics. Accessed on February 18, 2016, under http://sticerd.lse.ac.uk/dps/case/cp/CASEpaper171.pdf.

Garssen, J. and Nicolaas, H. (2008) Fertility of Turkish and Moroccan women in the Netherlands: Adjustment to native level within one generation. *Demographic Research* 19: 1249–80.

George, A., Meadows, P., Metcalf, H., and Rolfe, H. (2011) *Impact of Migration on the Consumption of Education and Children's Services and the Consumption of Health Services, Social Care and Social Services*. London: National Institute of Economic and Social Research.

Goldscheider, C. and Uhlenberg, P. R. (1969) Minority group status and fertility. *American Journal of Sociology* 74 (4): 361–73.

Goodhart, D. (2013) *The British Dream: Successes and Failures of Post-War Immigration*. London: Atlantic Books.

Gordon, I. R. (2013) Ambition, human capital acquisition and the metropolitan escalator. *Regional Studies* 49 (6): 1042–55.

Gordon, I., Champion, T. and Coombes, M. (2015) Urban escalators and interregional elevators: The difference that location, mobility, and sectoral specialisation make to occupational progression. *Environment and Planning A* 47 (3): 588–606.

Gott, M. (2006) Sexual health and the new ageing. *Age and Ageing* 35 (2): 106–7.

Gregg, P., Harkness, S. and Smith, S. (2009) Welfare reform and lone parents in the UK. *Economic Journal* 119: F38–F65.

Hagell, A. (2014) *Sexual Health and Under-18 Conceptions*. AYPH Research Update No 17. London: Association for Young People's Health.

Han, W. J., Waldfogel, J. and Brooks-Gunn, J. (2001) The effects of early maternal employment on children's later cognitive and behavioural outcomes. *Journal of Marriage and Family* 63 (2): 336–54.

Hanna, K. and Bosetti, N. (2015) Inside out: The new geography of wealth and poverty in London. Centre for London. [Accessed January 2016]. Available from http://centreforlondon.org/publication/inside-out-the-new-geography-of-wealth-and-poverty-in-london-2/.

Hannemann, T. and Kulu, H. (2015) Union formation and dissolution among immigrants and their descendants in the United Kingdom. *Demographic Research* 33 (10): 273–312.

Hansen, K., Joshi, H. and Verropoulou, G. (2006) Childcare and mothers' employment: Approaching the millennium. *National Institute Economic Review* 195: 84–102.

Hansen, R. (1999) The politics of citizenship in 1940s Britain: The British Nationality Act. *Twentieth Century British History* 10 (1): 67–95.

Harding, T. (2014) *A Summary of the Key Findings from the New Dynamics of Ageing Research Programme.* http://newdynamics.group.shef.ac.uk/assets/files/NDA-Handbook-(2nd-Ed).pdf.

Harkness, S., Gregg, P. and MacMillan, L. (2012) *Poverty: The Role of Institutions, Behaviours and Culture.* York: Joseph Rowntree Foundation.

Härkönen, J. (2014) Divorce: Trends, patterns, causes, and consequences. In Treas, J., Scott, J. and Richards, M. (Eds.) *The Wiley Blackwell Companion to the Sociology of Families.* Chichester: Wiley Blackwell, 303–32.

Harper, S., Howse, K. and Baxter, S. (2011) *Living Longer and Prospering: Designing an Adequate, Sustainable and Equitable UK State Pension System.* Oxford: Oxford Institute of Ageing and Club Vita.

Harris, R. (2014) Measuring changing ethnic separations in England: A spatial discontinuity approach. *Environment and Planning A* 46 (9): 2243–61.

Harris, R. (2016) Measuring segregation as a spatial optimisation problem, revisited: A case study of London, 1991–2011. *International Journal of Geographical Information Science* 30 (3).

Haskey, J. (1998) One-parent families and their dependent children in Great Britain. *Population Trends* 91: 5–14.

Haskey, J. (2002) One-parent families—and the dependent children living in them—in Great Britain. *Population Trends* 109: 46–57.

Hassan, F., Henry, N., Wichmann, K., Priaulx, J. and Filonenko, A. (2012) Cost of unintended pregnancy in the UK: A role for increased use of long-acting reversible contraceptive methods. *Value in Health* 15 (7): A538.

Hatton, T. (2003) *Emigration from the UK, 1870–1913 and 1950–1998.* IZA Discussion Paper 830. Bonn: Institute for the Study of Labor.

Hatton, T. (2005) Explaining trends in UK immigration. *Journal of Population Economics* 18 (4): 719–40.

Hatton, T. and Price, S. (1999) *Migration, Migrants and Policy in the United Kingdom.* CEPR Discussion Paper 1960. London: Centre for Economic Policy Research.

Hatton, T. and Tani, M. (2005) Immigration and inter-regional mobility in the UK 1982–2000. *Economic Journal* 115 (507): 342–58.

Hatton, T. and Williamson, J. (1998) *The Age of Mass Migration: Causes and Economic Impact.* Oxford: Oxford University Press.

Havard, S., Deguen, S., Bodin, J., Louis, K., Laurent, O. and Bard, D. (2008) A small-area index of socioeconomic deprivation to capture health inequalities in France. *Social Science & Medicine* 67 (12): 2007–16.

Hawes, Z. C., Wellings, K. and Stephenson, J. (2010) First heterosexual intercourse in the United Kingdom: A review of the literature. *Journal of Sex Research* 47 (2–3): 137–52.

Haynes, R., Gale, S., Lovett, A. and Bentham, G. (1996) Unemployment rate as an updatable health needs indicator for small areas. *Journal of Public Health Medicine* 18 (1): 27–32.

Heath, A., Rothon, C. and Kilpi, E. (2008) The second generation in Western Europe: education, unemployment and occupational attainment. *Annual Review of Sociology* 34: 211–35.

Heath, S. (2014) *Housing Demand and Need (England)*. London: House of Commons Library.

Heaven, B., Brown, L., White, M., Errington, L., Mathers, J. C. and Moffatt, S. (2013) Supporting well-being in retirement through meaningful social roles: Systematic review of intervention studies. *Milbank Quarterly* 91 (2): 222–87. 30 (3): 474–93.

Hedman, L., van Ham, M. and Manley, D. (2011) Neighbourhood choice and neighbourhood reproduction. *Environment and Planning A,* 43: 1381–99.

Heinrich, C. J. (2014) Parents' employment and children's wellbeing. *The Future of Children* 24 (1): 121–46.

Henderson, M., Wight, D., Raab, G. M., Abraham, C., Parkes, A., Scott, S. and Hart, G. (2007) Impact of a theoretically based sex education programme (SHARE) delivered by teachers on NHS registered conceptions and terminations: Final results of cluster randomised trial. *British Medical Journal* 334 (7585): 133.

Hennink, M., Diamond, I. and Cooper, P. (1999) Young Asian women and relationships: Traditional or transitional? *Ethnic and Racial Studies* 22 (5): 867–91.

HESA (2010) *Non-UK Domiciled Students*. Cheltenham: Higher Education Statistics Authority. https://www.hesa.ac.uk/pr184.

Higginbottom, G. M. A., Mathers, N., Marsh, P., Kirkham, M., Owen, J. M. and Serrant-Green, L. (2006) Young people of minority ethnic origin in England and early parenthood: Views from young parents and service providers. *Social Science and Medicine* 63 (4): 858–70.

Higgs, G., Senior, M. L. and Williams, H. C. W. L. (1998) Spatial and temporal variation of mortality and deprivation 1: Widening health inequalities. *Environment and Planning A* 30 (9): 1661–82.

High, K. P., Brennan-Ing, M., Clifford, D. B. et al. (2012) HIV and aging: State of knowledge and areas of critical need for research. *Journal of Acquired Immune Deficiency Syndromes* 60 Suppl 1: S1–18.

Hincks, S. (2015) Deprived neighbourhoods in transition: Divergent pathways of change in the Greater Manchester city-region. *Urban Studies*, doi:10.1177/0042098015619142.

Hoare, J. (2003) Comparison of area-based inequality measures and disease morbidity in England, 1994–1998. *Health Statistics Quarterly* 18: 18–24.

Holdsworth, C., Finney, N., Marshall, A. and Norman, P. (2013) *Population and Society*. London: Sage Publications Ltd.

Hollander, J. B., Pallagst, K., Schwarz, T. and Popper, F. J. (2009) Planning shrinking cities. *Progress in Planning* 72 (4): 223–32.

Holman, R. (1978) *Poverty: Explanations of Social Deprivation*. London: Martin Robertson.

Holmans, A. E. (2005) *Historical Statistics of Housing in Britain*. Cambridge: Cambridge Centre for Housing and Planning Research.

Holmans, A. (2013) *New Estimates of Housing Demand and Need in England, 2011 to 2031*. Tomorrow Series Paper 16. London: Town and Country Planning Association.

Holmans, A. (2014) *Housing Need and Effective Demand in England: A Look at the 'Big Picture'*. Cambridge: University of Cambridge Centre for Housing and Planning Research.

Holtermann, S. (1975) Areas of urban deprivation in Great Britain: An analysis of 1971 Census data. *Social Trends* 6: 33–45.

Home Office (2002) *Secure Borders, Safe Haven: Integration with Diversity in Modern Britain.* White Paper. London: The Stationery Office.

Home Office (2010) *Summary of the Survey of New Refugees, December 2005–March 2009.* Research Report 35. London: Home Office. https://www.gov.uk/government/uploads/system/uploads/attachment_data/file/116070/horr35.pdf.

Home Office (2014) *The Reason for Migration and Labour Market Characteristics of UK Residents Born Abroad.* Occasional Paper 110. London: Home Office.

Home Office (August 2015) *Asylum Data Tables, Immigration Statistics April to June 2015, Volume 1.* Part of Immigration Statistics, April–June 2015: data tables.

House of Commons Education Committee (2015) *Life Lessons: PSHE and SRE in Schools.* Fifth Report of Session 2014–15. House of Commons. London: The Stationery Office.

House of Lords (2013) *Select Committee on Public Service and Demographic Change Report of Session 2012–13, Ready for Ageing?* HL Paper 140. London: The Stationery Office.

House of Lords (2016) *The Select Committee on Economic Affairs Inquiry into the Economics of the Housing Market,* Evidence Session No. 5, 19 January.

HPA (2012) *HIV in the United Kingdom: 2012 Report.* London: Health Protection Agency.

HSCIC (2014) *Personal Social Services: Expenditure and Unit Costs, England, 2013–14.* London: Health and Social Care Information Centre.

HSCIC (2015) *FGM Prevention Programme: Understanding the FGM Enhanced Dataset—Updated Guidance and Clarification to Support Implementation.* London: Health and Social Care Information Centre, Department of Health.

Hughes, A., Mesher, D., White, J. and Soldan, K. (2014) Coverage of the English national human papillomavirus (HPV) immunisation programme among 12 to 17 year old females by area-level deprivation score, England, 2008 to 2011. *Eurosurveillance* 19 (2): 1–6.

Hughes, G. and McCormick, B. (1987) Does migration reduce differential in regional unemployment rates? Paper presented at the International Conference on Migration and Labour Market Efficiency, October, mimeo.

Humphries, R., Forder, J. and Fernandez, J.-L. (2010) *Securing Good Care for More People.* London: The Kings Fund.

Idler, E. and Benyamini, Y. (1997) Self-rated health and mortality: a review of twenty-seven community studies. *Journal of Health and Social Behavior* 38: 21–37.

ISD (2013) *Abortion Statistics.* Edinburgh. National Statistics Publication for Scotland, Information Services Division Scotland.

ISD (2015) *Termination of Pregnancy Statistics. Year ending 31 December 2014.* Edinburgh. National Statistics Publication for Scotland, Information Services Division Scotland.

Jagger, C. (2015) Trends in life expectancy and healthy life expectancy. In *Future of an Ageing Population: Evidence Review.* London: Government Office for Science, Foresight.

Jamieson, L. and Simpson, R. (2013) *Living Alone: Globalization, Identity and Belonging*. Basingstoke: Palgrave Macmillan.

Jarman, B. (1983) Identification of underprivileged areas. *British Medical Journal* 286: 1705–9.

Jefferies, J. (2005) The UK population: Past, present and future. In Jefferies, J. (Ed.) *Focus on People and Migration*. Basingstoke: Palgrave Macmillan, 1–17.

Jennissen, R. (2004) *Macro-Economic Determinants of International Migration in Europe*. Amsterdam: Dutch University Press.

Jivraj, S. (2012) *How Has Ethnic Diversity Grown 1991–2001–2011? The Dynamics of Diversity: Evidence from the 2011 Census*. Manchester: Centre on Dynamics of Ethnicity (CoDE), University of Manchester.

Jivraj, S., Goodman, A. and Ploubidis, G. (2015) Health inequalities in British post-war cohorts: Are later born generations less healthy than earlier generations? Paper presented at the British Society for Population Studies Annual Conference, Leeds, September.

Jivraj, S., Nazroo, J. and Barnes, M. (2015) Short- and long-term determinants of social detachment in later life. *Ageing and Society*. doi:10.1017/S0144686X14001561.

Jivraj, S., Nazroo, J., Vanhoutte, B. and Chandola, T. (2014). Aging and subjective well-being in later life. *Journals of Gerontology, Series B: Psychological Sciences and Social Sciences*. doi:10.1093/ geronb/gbu006.

Jivraj, S. and Simpson, L. (Eds.) (2015) *Ethnic Identity and Inequalities in Britain: The Dynamics of Diversity*. Bristol: Policy Press.

Johansson, M. (2014) Demographic trends in rural Europe. In Copus, A. K. and de Lima, P. (Eds.) *Territorial Cohesion in Rural Europe: The Relational Turn in Rural Development*. Abingdon: Routledge, 99–125.

Johnston, R., Poulsen, M. and Forrest, J. (2013) Commentary: Multiethnic residential areas in a multi-ethnic country? A decade of major change in England and Wales. *Environment and Planning A* 45 (4): 753–59.

Johnston, R., Poulsen, M. and Forrest, J. (2015) Increasing diversity within increasing diversity: The changing ethnic composition of London's neighbourhoods, 2001–2011. *Population, Space and Place* 21 (1): 38–53.

Johnston, R., Poulsen, M. & Forrest, J. (2016) Ethnic residential patterns in urban England and Wales, 2001–2011: A system-wide analysis. *Tijdschrift voor Economische en Sociale Geografie* 107 (1): 1–15.

Jones, T. (1993) *Britain's Ethnic Minorities: An Analysis of the Labour Force Survey*. PSI Research Report. London: Policy Studies Institute.

Joshi, H. (Ed.) (1989a) *The Changing Population of Britain*. Oxford: Blackwell.

Joshi, H. (1989b) The changing form of women's economic dependency. In Joshi, H. (Ed.) *The Changing Population of Britain*. Oxford: Blackwell, 157–76.

Kaufmann, E. and Harris, G. (2015) 'White flight' or positive contact? Local diversity and attitudes to immigration in Britain. *Comparative Political Studies* 48 (12): 1563–90.

Kemp, P. A. (2011) Low-income tenants in the private rental housing market. *Housing Studies* 26 (7–8): 1019–34.

Kemp, P. A. (2015) Private renting after the global financial crisis. *Housing Studies* published online: 7 April 2015.

Kennett, P., Forrest, R. and Marsh, A. (2013) The global economic crisis and the reshaping of housing opportunities. *Housing, Theory and Society* 30 (1): 10–28.

Kiernan, K. (1989) The family: Formation and fission. In Joshi, H. (Ed.) *The Changing Population of Britain*. Oxford: Blackwell, 27–41.

Kiernan, K. (1996) Lone motherhood, employment and outcomes for children. *International Journal of Law, Policy and the Family* 10: 233–49.

Kiernan, K., McLanahan, S., Holmes, J. and Wright, M. (2011) Fragile families in the US and UK. Working Paper WP 11-04-FF. Center for Research on Child Well-Being, Princeton University.

King, R., Findlay, A. and Ahrens, J. (2010) *International student mobility literature review*. Report to HEFCE, co-funded by the British Council and UK National Agency for Erasmus. London: Higher Education Funding Council for England.

Kitching, B. (1990) Migration behaviour among the unemployed and low skilled. In Johnson, J. H. and Salt, J. (Eds.) *Labour Migration: The Internal Geographical Mobility of Labour in the Developed World*. London: David Fulton, 72–90.

Klett-Davies, M. (2016) *Under Pressure? Single Parents in the UK*. Gütersloh: Bertelsmann Foundation.

Knauth, B. (2011) Migration Statistics Mainstreaming. Paper presented at the 58th ISI Congress, 21–26 August 2011, Dublin. http://2011.isiproceedings.org/papers/650162.pdf.

Kumar, V. and Whynes, D. K. (2011) Explaining variation in the uptake of HPV vaccination in England. *BMC Public Health* 11: 172. Epub. http://www.biomed-central.com/1471-2458/11/172.

Lader, D. and Hopkins, G. (2008) *Contraception and Sexual Health 2007/08*. Omnibus survey report. London: Office for National Statistics.

Lakha, F. and Glasier, A. (2006) Unintended pregnancy and use of emergency contraception among a large cohort of women attending for antenatal care or abortion in Scotland. *The Lancet* 368 (9549): 1782–87.

Large, P., Gosh, K. and Fry, R. (2006) *Population Estimates by Ethnic Group*. Methodology Paper. London: Office for National Statistics (revised 2008).

Laslett, P. (1996) *A Fresh Map of Life*. London: Palgrave Macmillan, 2nd edition.

Law, M. R. and Morris, J. K. (1998) Why is mortality higher in poorer areas of England and Wales? *Journal of Epidemiology and Community Health* 52: 344–52.

Layton-Henry, Z. (2002) *Transnational Communities, Citizenship and African-Caribbeans in Birmingham*. Transnational Communities Programme Working Paper, WPTC-02-07. Institute of Social and Cultural Anthropology (ISCA), University of Oxford. http://www.transcomm.ox.ac.uk/working%20papers/WPTC-02-07%20LaytonHenry.pdf.

Lesthaeghe, R. (1995) The second demographic transition in Western Countries: an interpretation. In Mason, K. O. and Jensen, A.-M. (Eds.) *Gender and Family Change in Industrialized Countries*. Oxford: Clarendon Press, 17–62.

Lichter, D. T. (2012) Immigration and the new racial diversity in rural America. *Rural Sociology* 77 (1): 3–35.

Lomax, N., Stillwell, J., Norman, P. and Rees, P. (2014) Internal migration in the United Kingdom: Analysis of an estimated inter-district time series, 2001–2011. *Applied Spatial Analysis and Policy* 7 (1): 25–45.

London Housing Commission (2016) *Building a New Deal for London*. Final Report of the London Housing Commission. London: IPPR.

Lucchino, P., Rosazza-Bondibene, C. and Portes, J. (2012) *Examining the Relationship between Immigration and Unemployment Using National Insurance Number Registration Data*. NIESR Discussion Paper 286. London: National Institute of Economic and Social Research. http://www.niesr.ac.uk/sites/default/files/publications/090112_163827.pdf.

Macdowall, W., Wellings, K., Mercer, C. et al. (2006) Learning about sex: Results from NATSAL 2000. *Health Education and Behavior* 33 (6): 802–11.

Mackenzie, I. F., Nelder, R., Maconachie, M. and Radford, G. (1998) My ward is more deprived than yours. *Journal of Public Health Medicine* 20: 186–90.

Malpass, P. (1986) *The Housing Crisis*. London: Routledge and Kegan Paul.

Manor, O., Matthews, S. and Power, C. (2001) Self-rated health and limiting longstanding illness: Inter-relationships with morbidity in early adulthood. *International Journal of Epidemiology* 30: 600–607.

Markannen, S. and Harrison, M. (2013) 'Race', deprivation and the research agenda: Revising housing, ethnicity and neighbourhoods. *Housing Studies* 28 (3): 409–28.

Marshall, A., Jivraj, S., Nazroo, J., Tampubolon, G., and Vanhoutte, B. (2014) Does the level of wealth inequality within an area influence the prevalence of depression among older people? *Health & Place* 27: 194–204.

Marshall, A. and Nazroo, J. (2015) Trajectories in the prevalence of self-reported illness at retirement. *Journal of Population Ageing*. doi:10.1007/s12062-015-9130-2.

Marshall, A., Nazroo, J., Tampubolon, G. and Vanhoutte, B. (2015) Socio-economic and gender inequalities in frailty: Findings from a growth modelling approach. *Journal of Epidemiology and Community Health* 69: 316–21.

Marshall, A. and Norman, P. (2013) Geographies of the impact of retirement on health in the United Kingdom. *Health and Place* 20: 1–12.

Marston, C. and Lewis, R. (2014) Anal heterosex among young people and implications for health promotion: A qualitative study in the UK. *British Medical Journal Open* 4 (8): e004996.

Marston, C., Meltzer, H. and Majeed, H. (2005) Impact on contraceptive practice of making emergency hormonal contraception available over the counter in Great Britain: Repeated cross sectional surveys. *British Medical Journal (Clinical Research Edition)* 331 (7511): 271. Epub. http://www.bmj.com/content/331/7511/271.

Massey, D. (1981) Dimensions of the new immigration to the United States and the prospects for assimilation. *Annual Review of Sociology* 7: 57–85.

Massey, D., Arango, J., Hugo, G., Kouaouci, A., Pellegrino, A. and Taylor, E. (1993) Theories of international migration: A review and appraisal. *Population and Development Review* 19 (3): 431–66.

Matthews, K., Demakakos, P., Nazroo, J. and Shankar, A. (2014) The evolution of lifestyles in older age in England. In Banks, J., Nazroo, J. and Steptoe, A. (Eds.) *The Dynamics of Ageing: Evidence from the English Longitudinal Study of Ageing (2002–2012)*. London: The Institute for Fiscal Studies.

May, T. (2015) Conservative Party Conference Speech, Manchester. Available at: http://www.independent.co.uk/news/uk/politics/theresa-may-s-speech-to-the-conservative-party-conference-in-full-a6681901.html.

Mayer, J. and Riphaln, R. T. (2000) Fertility assimilation of immigrants: Evidence from count data models. *Journal of Population Economics* 13: 241–61.

McDonald, N. and Whitehead, C. (2015) *New Estimates of Housing Requirements in England*. Tomorrow Series Paper 17. London: Town and Country Planning Association.

McGovern, P. and Nazroo, J. (2015) Patterns and causes of health inequalities in later life: A Bourdieusian approach. *Sociology of Health and Illness* 37 (1): 143–60.

McKee, K. (2012) Young people, homeownership and future welfare. *Housing Studies* 27 (6): 853–62.

McKinsey (2013) *Understanding Patients' Needs and Risk: A Key to a Better NHS*. London: McKinsey & Company.

McNally, R. J. Q., Basta, N. O., Errington, S., James, P. W., Norman, P. D. and Craft, A. W. (2014a) Socio-economic patterning in the incidence and survival of children and young people diagnosed with malignant melanoma in northern England. *Journal of Investigative Dermatology* 134 (11): 2703–8.

McNally, R. J. Q., Basta, N. O., Errington, S., James, P. W., Norman, P. D., Hale, J. P. and Pearce, M. S. (2015) Socio-economic patterning in the incidence and survival of boys and young men diagnosed with testicular cancer in northern England. *Urologic Oncology: Seminars and Original Investigations*. http://dx.doi.org/10.1016/j.urolonc.2015.07.014.

McNally, R. J. Q., Blakey, K., Parslow, R. C. et al. (2012) Small area analyses of bone cancer diagnosed in Great Britain provide clues to aetiology. *BMC Cancer* 12: 270. doi:10.1186/1471-2407-12-270.

McNally, R. J. Q., James, P. W., Ducker, S., Norman, P. D. and James, O. F. W. (2014b) No rise in incidence but geographical heterogeneity in the occurrence of Primary Biliary Cirrhosis in northeast England. *American Journal of Epidemiology* 179 (4): 492–98.

Mercer, C. H. (2014) Sexual behaviour. *Medicine* 42 (6): 291–93.

Mercer, C. H., Tanton, C., Prah, P., Erens, P. et al. (2013) Changes in sexual attitudes and lifestyles in Britain through the life course and over time: Findings from the National Surveys of Sexual Attitudes and Lifestyles (Natsal). *The Lancet* 382 (9907): 1781–94.

Mercer, C. H., Wellings, K., Macdowall, W. et al. (2006) First sexual partnerships—age differences and their significance: Empirical evidence from the 2000 British National Survey of Sexual Attitudes and Lifestyles ('NATSAL 2000'). *Journal of Adolescent Health* 39 (1): 87–95.

Migration Advisory Committee (2012) *Analysis of the Impacts of Migration*. London: MAC. https://www.gov.uk/government/uploads/system/uploads/attachment_data/file/257235/analysis-of-the-impacts.pdf.

Migration Watch (2015) *International Migration, Population Growth and Households in the UK*. Migration Watch Briefing Paper. http://www.migrationwatchuk.org/briefing-paper/7.18.

Milewski, N. (2010) *Fertility of Immigrants. A Two-Generational Approach in Germany.* Berlin/Heidelberg: Springer.

Millar, J. (2010) Lone mothers, poverty and paid work in the UK. In Chant, S. (Ed.) *The International Handbook of Gender and Poverty: Concepts, Research and Policy.* Cheltenham: Edward Elgar, 147–52.

Mindell, S., Knott, C. S., Ng Fat, C. S., Roth, M. A., Manor, O., Soskolne, V. and Daoud, N. (2014) Explanatory factors for health inequalities across ethnic and gender groups: Data from a national survey in England. *Journal of Epidemiology and Community Health* 68: 1133–44.

Mitchell, G. and Norman, P. (2012) Longitudinal environmental justice analysis: Co-evolution of environmental quality and deprivation in England, 1960–2007. *Geoforum* 43: 44–57.

Mitchell, G., Norman, P. and Mullin, K. (2015) Who benefits from environmental policy? An environmental justice analysis of air quality change in Britain, 2001–2011. *Environmental Research Letters* doi:10.1088/1748-9326/10/10/105009.

Mitchell, R. (2005). Commentary: The decline of death—how do we measure and interpret changes in self-reported health across cultures and time? *International Journal of Epidemiology* 34 (2): 306–8.

Mitchell, R., Dorling, D. and Shaw, M. (2000) *Inequalities in Life and Death: What If Britain Were More Equal?* Bristol: Polity Press.

Mitton, L. and Aspinall, P. (2010) Black African in Britain: A diversity of integration experiences. In Stillwell, J. and van Ham, M. (Eds.) *Ethnicity and Integration: Understanding Population Trends and Processes, Volume 3: Ethnicity and Integration.* Dordrecht: Springer, 179–202.

Moore, R. (2015) Britain's housing crisis is a human disaster. Here are 10 ways to solve it. *The Observer.* http://www.theguardian.com/society/2015/mar/14/britain-housing-crisis-10-ways-solve-rowan-moore-general-election (last accessed 23 December 2015).

Morelli, C. and Seaman, P. (2007) Devolution and inequality: A failure to create a community of equals? *Transactions of the Institute of British Geographers* 32 (4): 523–38.

Morris, R. and Carstairs, V. (1991) Which deprivation? A comparison of selected deprivation indices. *Journal of Public Health Medicine* 13 (4): 318–26.

Mullan, P. (2002) *The Imaginary Time Bomb: Why an Ageing Population Is Not a Social Problem.* London: I. B. Tauris & Co. Ltd.

Muriel, A. and Oldfield, Z. (2010) Financial circumstances and consumption. In Banks, J., Nazroo, J. and Steptoe, A. (Eds.) *Financial Circumstances, Health and Well-Being of the Older Population in England. The 2008 English Longitudinal Study of Ageing.* London: The Institute for Fiscal Studies.

Murphy, M. (1989) Housing the people: From shortage to surplus? In Joshi, H. (Ed.) *The Changing Population of Britain.* Oxford: Blackwell, 90–109.

Murphy, M. (2011) Long-term effects of the demographic transition on family and kinship networks in Britain. *Population and Development Review* 37 (1): 55–80.

Nathan, M. (2011) *The Long Term Impacts of Migration in British Cities: Diversity, Wages, Employment and Prices.* Migration Studies Unit Working

Paper 2010/09, London School of Economics. http://www.lse.ac.uk/government/research/resgroups/MSU/documents/workingPapers/WP_2010_09.pdf.

Nathan, M. and Urwin, C. (2005) *City People: City Centre Living in the UK*. London: Centre for Cities.

National Centre for Social Research, Johnson, A., Fenton, K. et al. (2005) *National Survey of Sexual Attitudes and Lifestyles II, 2000–2001*. [data collection]. UK Data Service. SN: 5223.

NATSAL (National Survey of Sexual Attitudes and Lifestyles) (2013) Sexual attitudes and lifestyles in Britain: Highlights from Natsal-3. London. NATSAL. Available from http://www.natsal.ac.uk/media/2102/natsal-infographic.pdf.

NAW (2000) *A Strategic Framework for Promoting Sexual Health in Wales*. Cardiff: National Assembly for Wales.

Nazroo, J., Zaninotto, P. and Gjonca, E. (2008) Mortality and healthy life expectancy. In Banks, J., Breeze, E., Lessof, C. and Nazroo, J. (Eds.) *Living in the 21st Century: Older People in England. The 2006 English Longitudinal Study of Ageing*. London: The Institute for Fiscal Studies.

Neal, S. (2002) Rural landscapes, representations and racism: Examining multicultural citizenship and policy-making in the English countryside. *Ethnic and Racial Studies* 25 (3): 442–61.

NHS (2015, 24/09/2014) *HPV vaccine*. http://www.nhs.uk/Conditions/vaccinations/Pages/hpv-human-papillomavirus-vaccine.aspx.

NHSQIS (2008) *Standards—Sexual Health Services*. NHS Quality Improvement Scotland.

Noble, M., Barnes, H., Wright, G., and Roberts, B. (2010) Small area indices of multiple deprivation in South Africa. *Social Indicators Research* 95 (2): 281–97.

Noble, M., Penhale, B., Smith, G., Wright, G., Dibben, C., Owen, T. and Lloyd, M. (2000) *Measuring Multiple Deprivation at the Small-Area Level: the Indices of Deprivation 2000*. DETR: London.

Noble, M., Wright, G., Smith, G. and Dibben, C. (2006) Measuring multiple deprivation at the small-area level. *Environment and Planning A* 38: 168–85.

Norman, P. (2010a) Identifying change over time in small area socio-economic deprivation. *Applied Spatial Analysis and Policy* 3 (2–3): 107–38.

Norman, P. (2010b) Demographic and deprivation change in the UK, 1991–2001. In Stillwell, J., Norman, P., Thomas, C. and Surridge, P. (Eds.) *Understanding Population Trends and Processes Volume 2: Spatial and Social Disparities*. Dordrecht: Springer, 17–35.

Norman, P. (2013) Whither / wither the census? *Radical Statistics* 106: 13–17.

Norman, P. and Boyle, P. (2014) Are health inequalities between differently deprived areas evident at different ages? A longitudinal study of census records in England and Wales, 1991–2001. *Health and Place* 26: 88–93.

Norman, P., Boyle, P., Exeter, D., Feng, Z. and Popham, F. (2011) Rising premature mortality in the UK's persistently deprived areas: Only a Scottish phenomenon? *Social Science and Medicine* 73: 1575–84.

Norman, P., Boyle, P. and Rees, P. (2005) Selective migration, health and deprivation: A longitudinal analysis. *Social Science and Medicine* 60 (12): 2755–71.

Norman, P., Charles-Edwards, E. and Wilson, T. (2016) Relationships between population change, deprivation change and health change at small area level: Australia 2001–2011. In Wilson, T., Charles-Edwards, E. and Bell, M. (Eds.) *Demography for Planning and Policy: Australian Case Studies*. Dordrecht: Springer, 197–214.

Norman, P., Purdam, K., Tajar, A. and Simpson, L. (2007) Representation and local democracy: Geographical variations in elector to councillor ratios. *Political Geography* 26: 57–77.

Norman, P., Rees, P. and Boyle, P. (2003) Achieving data compatibility over space and time: Creating consistent geographical zones. *International Journal of Population Geography* 9: 365–86.

Norman, P. and Riva, M. (2012) Population health across space and time: The geographical harmonisation of the ONS Longitudinal Study for England and Wales. *Population, Space and Place* 18: 483–502.

Norman, P., Simpson, L. and Sabater, A. (2008) 'Estimating with Confidence' and hindsight: New UK small area population estimates for 1991. *Population, Space and Place* 14 (5): 449–72.

Ofsted (2013) Not yet good enough: Personal, social, health and economic education in schools. London: Ofsted.

Olshanky, J. (2005) *Projecting the Future of U.S. Health and Longevity*. Health Affairs. doi:10.1377/hlthaff.w5.r86.

ONS (2007) General Household Survey: Time Series Dataset, 1972–2004. [data collection]. UK Data Service. SN: 5664, http://dx.doi.org/10.5255/UKDA-SN-5664-1.

ONS (2009) Parents' birthplace. In *Birth Statistics*, Series FM1 No. 37, Chapter 9, Table 9.5. http://www.statistics.gov.uk/statbase/Product.asp?vlnk=14408.

ONS (2010a) Social Trends 40. Retrieved from http://www.ons.gov.uk/ons/rel/social-trends-rd/social-trends/social-trends-40/index.html.

ONS (2010b) *Comparing across Countries' Indices of Deprivation: Guidance Paper*. Office for National Statistics. [Accessed December 2015]. Available from http://www.neighbourhood.statistics.gov.uk/dissemination/Info.do?page=analysisandguidance/analysisarticles/indices-of-deprivation.htm.

ONS (2011a) Divorces in England and Wales 2011. Retrieved from http://www.ons.gov.uk/ons/rel/vsob1/divorces-in-england-and-wales/2011/stb-divorces-2011.html.

ONS (2011b) Mothers in the Labour Market, 2011. Retrieved from http://www.ons.gov.uk/ons/rel/lmac/mothers-in-the-labour-market/2011/mothers-in-the-labour-market---2011.html.

ONS (2011c) Beyond the 2011 Census Project. Office for National Statistics. [Accessed September 2015]. Available from: http://www.ons.gov.uk/ons/about-ons/what-we-do/programmes---projects/beyond-2011/index.html.

ONS (2012a) *Ethnicity and National Identity in England and Wales 2011*. http://www.ons.gov.uk/ons/dcp171776_290558.pdf.

ONS (2012b) Inequality in disability-free life expectancy by area deprivation: England 2002–05 and 2006–09. Statistical Bulletin. Available at: http://www.ons.gov.uk/ons/dcp171778_265133.pdf.

ONS (2012c) *2011 Census: Population Estimates for the United Kingdom*. Statistical Bulletin. London: Office for National Statistics.

ONS (2012d) *Quality and Methodology Information for Long-term International Migration Estimates.* Titchfield: Office for National Statistics. http://www.ons. gov.uk/ons/guide-method/method-quality/quality/quality-information/population/ quality-and-methodology-information-for-long-term-international-migration-estimates--ltim-.pdf.

ONS (2012e) *Polish People in the UK—Half a Million Polish Residents.* Titchfield: Office for National Statistics. http://www.ons.gov.uk/ons/dcp171780_229910. pdf.

ONS (2012f) Cohort Fertility: 2012. Retrieved from http://www.ons.gov.uk/ons/rel/ fertility-analysis/cohort-fertility--england-and-wales/2012/cohort-fertility-2012. html.

ONS (2012g) Families and Households, 2001 to 2011. Retrieved from http://www. ons.gov.uk/ons/dcp171778_251357.pdf.

ONS (2013a) *2011 Census Analysis: Unpaid Care in England and Wales, 2011 and Comparison with 2001.* Statistical Bulletin. London: Office for National Statistics.

ONS (2013b) *Births in England and Wales, 2013.* Statistical Bulletin. London: Office for National Statistics.

ONS (2013c) Full report—Women in the Labour Market. Retrieved from http:// www.ons.gov.uk/ons/dcp171776_328352.pdf.

ONS (2013d) Cancer Statistics Registrations, England (Series MB1) No. 42. London: Office for National Statistics.

ONS (2014a) *What Does the 2011 Census Tell Us about Inter-Ethnic Relationships?* London: Office for National Statistics.

ONS (2014b) *Disability-Free Life Expectancy by Upper Tier Local Authority England 2009–2011 and Comparison with 2006–08.* Statistical Bulletin. London: Office for National Statistics.

ONS (2014c) *Semaphore Research Update.* Titchfield: Office for National Statistics. http://www.ons.gov.uk/ons/guide-method/method-quality/specific/population-and-migration/population-statistics-research-unit--psru-/semaphore-research-update. doc.

ONS (2014d) National Population Projections, 2012-based Reference Volume: Series PP2, Chapter 3: Fertility. Retrieved from http://www.ons.gov.uk/ons/rel/npp/ national-population-projections/2012-based-reference-volume--series-pp2/index. html.

ONS (2014e) Intergenerational transmission of disadvantage in the UK and EU. Retrieved from http://www.ons.gov.uk/ons/dcp171766_378097.pdf.

ONS (2014f) *2011 Census Glossary of Terms.* http://www.ons.gov.uk/ons/guide-method/census/2011/census-data/2011-census-user-guide/glossary/index.html (last accessed 23 December 2015).

ONS (2014g) *Living Alone in England and Wales.* http://www.ons.gov.uk/ons/rel/ census/2011-census-analysis/do-the-demographic-and-socio-economic-characteristics-of-those-living-alone-in-england-and-wales-differ-from-the-general-population-/sty-living-alone-in-the-uk.html (last accessed 23 December 2015).

ONS (2014h) *Marriages in England and Wales, 2012.* http://www.ons.gov.uk/ons/ rel/vsob1/marriages-in-england-and-wales--provisional-/2012/stb-marriages-in-england-and-wales--provisional---2011.html.

ONS (2014i) *The Census and Future Provision of Population Statistics in England and Wales: Recommendation from the National Statistician and Chief Executive of the UK Statistics Authority.* [Accessed December 2015]. Available from http://www.ons.gov.uk/ons/about-ons/what-we-do/programmes---projects/beyond-2011/index.html.

ONS (2015a) *Annual Mid-Year Population Estimates, 2014.* Statistical Bulletin. London: Office for National Statistics.

ONS (2015b) *Migration Statistics Quarterly Report, November 2015.* Statistical Bulletin. http://www.ons.gov.uk/ons/rel/migration1/migration-statistics-quarterly-report/november-2015/index.html.

ONS (2015c) *Births in England and Wales by Parents' Country of Birth, 2014.* Statistical Bulletin. http://www.ons.gov.uk/ons/rel/vsob1/parents--country-of-birth--england-and-wales/2014/stb-pcb-2014.html.

ONS (2015d) *Overview of the UK Population Articles.* Statistical Bulletin. http://www.ons.gov.uk/ons/rel/pop-estimate/overview-of-the-uk-population/index.html.

ONS (2015e) *The 2014-Based Life Tables 1951–2064, UK Principal Projection.* London: Office for National Statistics.

ONS (2015f) *Estimates of the Very Old (including Centenarians), England and Wales, and United Kingdom.* Statistical Bulletin. http://www.ons.gov.uk/ons/rel/mortality-ageing/estimates-of-the-very-old--including-centenarians-/2002-2014--england-and-wales-and-the-uk/index.html.

ONS (2015g) *Population by Country of Birth and Nationality Report, August 2015.* http://www.ons.gov.uk/ons/dcp171776_414724.pdf.

ONS (2015h) *Census Analysis: Ethnicity and Religion of the Non-UK Born Population in England and Wales.* London: Office for National Statistics.

ONS (2015i) *Families and Households, 2015.* Statistical Bulletin. London: Office for National Statistics.

ONS (2015j) *Births by Parents' Characteristics in England and Wales, 2014.* London: Office for National Statistics.

ONS (2015k) *National Population Projections, 2014-Based.* Statistical Bulletin. London: Office for National Statistics.

ONS (2015l) *Life Expectancy at Birth and at Age 65 by Local Areas in England and Wales, 2012 to 2014.* Statistical Bulletin. London: Office for National Statistics.

ONS (2015m) *Trend in Life Expectancy at Birth and at Age 65 by Socioeconomic Position Based on the National Statistics Socio-Economic Classification, England and Wales, 1982–1986 to 2007–2011.* Statistical Bulletin. London: Office for National Statistics.

ONS (2015n) *Healthy Life Expectancy at Birth for Upper Tier Local Authorities: England 2011 to 2013.* Statistical Bulletin. London: Office for National Statistics.

ONS (2015o) *Divorces in England and Wales 2013.* Statistical Bulletin. London: Office for National Statistics.

ONS (2015p) Census 2011. Table DC1109EW 'Household composition by age by sex'. Retrieved from http://www.ons.gov.uk/ons/guide-method/census/2011/index.html.

ONS (2015q) Trends in births and deaths over the last century. http://visual.ons.gov.uk/birthsanddeaths/.

ONS (2015r) Families and Households, 2014. Retrieved from http://www.ons.gov. uk/ons/rel/family-demography/families-and-households/2014/families-and-house- holds-in-the-uk--2014.html.

ONS (2015s) Conceptions in England and Wales, 2013. Statistical Bulletin, Office for National Statistics.

ONS (2016) Long-term International Migration Estimates by Direction, Age (5 year age groups), Sex and UK Area (England and Wales regions), 1991 to 2014. User Requested Data, 17 February 2016. Titchfield: Office for National Statistics.

Osborne, C. and McLanahan, S. (2007) Partnership instability and child well-being. *Journal of Marriage and Family* 69: 1065–83.

Osborne. G. (2014) We need a northern powerhouse. Chancellor's speech at Museum of Science and Industry, Manchester, 23 June 2014. https://www.gov.uk/ government/speeches/chancellor-we-need-a-northern-powerhouse.

Parekh, B. (2008) *A New Politics of Identity*. Basingstoke: Palgrave Macmillan.

Park, A., Bryceson, C., Clery, E., Curtice, J. and Phillips, M. (2013) *British Social Attitudes: the 30th Report*. London: National Centre for Social Research.

Parkes, A., Wight, D., Henderson, M., Stephenson, J. and Strange, V. (2009) Contraceptive method at first sexual intercourse and subsequent pregnancy risk: Findings from a secondary analysis of 16-year-old girls from the RIPPLE and SHARE studies. *Journal of Adolescent Health* 44 (1): 55–63.

Parrado E. A. (2011) How high is Hispanic/Mexican fertility in the United States? Immigration and tempo considerations. *Demography* 48 (3): 1059–80.

Parrado, E. A. and Morgan, S. P. (2008) Intergenerational fertility among Hispanic women: New evidence of immigrant assimilation. *Demography* 45 (3): 651–71.

Peach, C. (2005) Social integration and social mobility: Spatial segregation and intermarriage of the Caribbean population in Britain. In Loury, G. C., Modood, T. and Teles, S. M. (Eds.) *Ethnicity, Social Mobility and Public Policy*, 178–203.

Peach, C. (2006) South Asian migration and settlement in Great Britain, 1951–2001. *Contemporary South Asia* 15 (2): 133–46.

Peach, C. (2009) Slippery segregation: Discovering or manufacturing ghettos? *Journal of Ethnic and Migration Studies* 35 (9): 1381–95.

Pensions Commission (2004) *Pensions: Challenges and Choices*. First Report of the Pensions Commission. London: The Stationery Office.

Pensions Commission (2006) *A New Pension Settlement for the Twenty-First Century*. Second Report of the Pensions Commission. London: The Stationery Office.

PHA (2014) Sexually Transmitted Infection surveillance in Northern Ireland 2014. An analysis of data for the calendar year 2013. Belfast: Public Health Agency.

PHE (2014a) GRASP 2013 Report. The Gonococcal Resistance to Antimicrobials Surveillance Programme (England and Wales). Collindale: Public Health England.

PHE (2014b) HIV in the United Kingdom: 2014 Report. London, Public Health England.

PHE (2014c) United Kingdom National HIV surveillance data tables. No. 1: 2014. London: HIV and Sexually Transmitted Infections Department, Public Health England.

PHE (2015a) Human Papillomavirus (HPV) vaccine coverage in England, 2008/9 to 2013/14: A review of the full six years of the three-dose schedule. London: Public Health England.

PHE (2015b) Infection report: Sexually transmitted infections and chlamydia screening in England, 2014. Health Protection Report. London: Public Health England.

PHE (2015c) Sexually transmitted infections and chlamydia screening in England, 2014. London: Public Health England.

PHE (2015d) Table 1: STI diagnoses and rates in England by gender, 2005–2014. London: HIV and Sexually Transmitted Infections Department, Public Health England.

PHE (2015e) Table 2: STI diagnoses and rates by gender, sexual risk and age group, 2010 to 2014. London: HIV and Sexually Transmitted Infections Department, Public Health England.

Phillips, D. (2015) Claiming spaces: British Muslim negotiations of urban citizenship in an era of new migration. *Transactions of the Institute of British Geographers* 40 (1): 62–74.

Phillips, D., Athwal, B., Robinson, D. and Harrison, M. (2014) Towards inter-cultural engagement: Building shared visions of neighbourhood and community in an era of new migration. *Journal of Ethnic and Migration Studies* 40 (1): 42–59.

Phillips, D., Davis, C. and Ratcliffe, P. (2007) British Asian narratives of urban space. *Transactions of the Institute of British Geographers* 32 (2): 217–34.

PHW (2013) HIV and STI trends in Wales: Surveillance Report, December 2013. Cardiff: Public Health Wales Communicable Disease Surveillance Centre.

Pickard, L. (2015) A growing care gap? The supply of unpaid care for older people by their adult children in England to 2032. *Ageing and Society* 35 (1): 96–123.

Pickett, K. and Pearl, M. (2001) Multilevel analyses of neighbourhood socioeconomic context and health outcomes: A critical review. *Journal of Epidemiology and Community Health* 55 (2): 111–22.

Pike, A., MacKinnon, D., Coombes, M. et al. (2016) *Uneven Growth: Tackling City Decline*. York: Joseph Rowntree Foundation.

Planning Advisory Service (2014) *Objectively Assessed Needs and Housing Targets*. London: Local Government Association.

Pollard, N., Latorre, M. and Sriskandarajah, D. (2008) *Floodgates or Turnstiles? Post EU Enlargement Migration Flows to (and from) the UK*. London: Institute for Public Policy Research.

Pornet, C., Delpierre, C., Dejardin, O. et al. (2012) Construction of an adaptable European transnational ecological deprivation index: The French version. *Journal of Epidemiology and Community Health* 66 (11): 982–89.

Portes, T. and Zhou, M. (1993) The new second-generation: Segmented assimilation and its variants. *Annals of the American Academy of Political and Social Sciences* 530: 74–96.

Pound, P., Langford, R. and Campbell, R. (2015) Qualitative synthesis of young people's views of sex and relationship education. *The Lancet* 386, Suppl. 2: S65.

Price, S., Barrett, G., Smith, C. and Paterson, C. (1997) Use of contraception in women who present for termination of pregnancy in inner London. *Public Health* 111 (6): 377–82.

Rae, A. (2013) English urban policy and the return to the city: A decade of growth, 2001–2011. *Cities* 32: 94–101.

Ratcliffe, P. (2009) Re-evaluating the links between 'race' and residence. *Housing Studies* 24 (4): 433–50.

Raymer, J., Wiśniowski, A., Forster, J. J., Smith, P. W. F. and Bijak, J. (2013) Integrated modeling of European migration. *Journal of the American Statistical Association* 108 (503): 801–19.

Rees, P. (2008) What happens when international migrants settle? Projections of ethnic groups in United Kingdom regions. In Raymer, J. and Willekens, F. (Eds.) *International Migration in Europe: Data, Models and Assessment.* London: Wiley, 329–58.

Rees, P. and Butt, F. (2004) Ethnic change and diversity in England, 1981–2001. *Area* 36 (2): 174–86.

Rees, P., Wohland, P. and Norman, P. (2009) The estimation of mortality for ethnic groups at local scale within the United Kingdom. *Social Science and Medicine* 69: 1592–1607.

Rees, P., Wohland, P. and Norman, P. (2013) The demographic drivers of future ethnic group populations for UK local areas, 2001–2051. *Geographical Journal* 179: 44–60.

Rees, P., Wohland, P., Norman, P. and Boden, P. (2012) Ethnic population projections for the UK, 2001–2051. *Journal of Population Research* 29: 45–89.

Reher, D. S. (2007) Towards long-term population decline: A discussion of relevant issues. *European Journal of Population* 23 (2): 189–207.

Rendall. M., Couvet, C., Lappegard, T., Robert-Bobée, I., Ronsen, M. and Smallwood, S. (2005) First births by age and education in Britain, France and Norway. *Population Trends* 121: 27–34.

Rijs, K. J., Cozijnsen, R. and Deeg, D. J. H. (2012) The effect of retirement and age at retirement on self-perceived health after three years of follow-up in Dutch 55–64-year-olds. *Ageing and Society* 32: 281–306.

Rindfuss, R. R., Morgan, S. R. and Offutt, K. (1996) Education and the changing age pattern of American fertility, 1963–89. *Demography* 33 (3): 277–90.

Robards, J., Berrington, A. and Hinde, A. (2012) Estimating the fertility of recent migrants to England and Wales (1991–2001)—Is there an elevated level of fertility after migration? Presentation at European Population Conference 2012, Stockholm, 13–16 June 2012.

Robards, J., Vlachantoni, A., Evandrou, M. and Falkingham, J. (2015) What became of the carers in 2001? Informal caring in England and Wales: Stability and transition between 2001 and 2011. *Advances in Life Course Research* 24: 21–33.

Robinson, D. (2010) The neighbourhood effects of new immigration. *Environment and Planning A* 42 (10): 2451–66.

Robinson, D., Reeve, K. and Casey, R. (2007) *The Housing Pathways of New Immigrants.* York: Joseph Rowntree Foundation.

Robinson, G. M. (1998) *Methods and Techniques in Human Geography.* Chichester: John Wiley.

Rogers, A. (1990) Requiem for the net migrant. *Geographical Analysis* 22 (4): 283–300.

Rogers Report (1999) *Towards an Urban Renaissance.* Final Report of the Urban Task Force. London: Department of the Environment, Transport and the Regions.

Rolston, B., Schubotz, D. and Simpson, A. (2004) The first time: Young people and sex in Northern Ireland. *Journal of Youth Studies* 7 (2): 191–207.

Rothon, C. (2005) *An Assessment of the Oppositional Culture Explanation for Ethnic Differences in Educational Attainment in Britain.* Sociology Working Paper, Department of Sociology, University of Oxford.

Rowlands, S. (2007a) Contraception and abortion. *Journal of the Royal Society of Medicine* 100 (10): 465–68.

Rowlands, S. (2007b) More than one abortion. *Journal of Family Planning and Reproductive Health Care* 33 (3): 155–58.

Rowlands, S. and Hannaford, P. (2003) The incidence of sterilisation in the UK. *BJOG: An International Journal of Obstetrics and Gynaecology* 110 (9): 819–24.

Rowlingson, K. and McKay, S. (2005) Lone motherhood and socio-economic disadvantage: Insights from quantitative and qualitative evidence. *Sociological Review* 53: 30–49.

Rowthorn, R. (2015) *The Costs and Benefits of Large-Scale Immigration. Exploring the Economic and Demographic Consequences for the UK.* London: Civitas.

Royal Institute of British Architects (2015) *Space Standards for Homes.* http://www.building.co.uk/Journals/2015/12/01/s/k/t/Homewise-Report.pdf.

Rugg, J., Rhodes, D. and Wilcox, S. (2011) *Unfair Shares: A Report on the Impact of Extending the Shared Accommodation Rate of Housing Benefit.* York: Centre for Housing.

Rumbaut, R. G. (2007) Turning points in the transition to adulthood: Determinants of educational attainment, incarceration, and early childbearing among children of immigrants. *Ethnic and Racial Studies* 28 (6): 1041–86.

Rydin, Y. (1993) *The British Planning System: An Introduction.* Basingstoke: Macmillan.

Sabater, A. and Simpson, L. (2009) Enhancing the population census: A time series for sub-national areas with age, sex and ethnic group dimensions in England and Wales, 1991–2001. *Journal of Ethnic and Migration Studies* 35 (9): 1461–77.

Sacks, R. J., Copas, A. J., Wilkinson, D. M. and Robinson, A. J. (2014) Uptake of the HPV vaccination programme in England: A cross-sectional survey of young women attending sexual health services. *Sexually Transmitted Infections* 90 (4): 315–21.

Salt, J. (2009–2014) *International Migration and the UK.* Annual Reports of the UK SOPEMI Correspondent to the OECD. London: Migration Research Unit, University College London.

Salt, J., Dobson, J., Koser, K. and McLaughlan, G. (2001) *International Migration and the United Kingdom: Recent Patterns and Trends.* RDS Occasional Paper 75. London: Home Office.

Salt, J. and Millar, J. (2006) Foreign labour in the United Kingdom: Current patterns and trends. *Labour Market Trends*, special feature, ONS, October 2006: 335–55.

Saxena, S., Copas, A. J., Mercer, C. et al. (2006) Ethnic variations in sexual activity and contraceptive use: National cross-sectional survey. *Contraception* 74 (3): 224–33.

Sayer, L. C., Bianchi, S. M. and Robinson, J. P. (2004) Are parents investing less in children? Trends in mothers' and fathers' time with children. *American Journal of Sociology* 110 (1): 1–43.

Schubotz, D., Simpson, A. and Rolston, B. (2002) *Towards Better Sexual Health: A Survey of Sexual Attitudes and Lifestyles of Young People in Northern Ireland.* Belfast: The Family Planning Association.

Schünmann, C. and Glasier, A. (2006) Measuring pregnancy intention and its relationship with contraceptive use among women undergoing therapeutic abortion. *Contraception* 73 (5): 520–24.

Scott, K. and Stanfors, M. (2011) Second generation mothers: Do the children of immigrants adjust their fertility to host country norms? In Salzmann, T., Edmonston, B. and Raymer, J. (Eds.) *Demographic Aspects of Migration.* Wiesbaden: VS Verlag.

Scottish Executive (2005) *Respect and Responsibility: Strategy and Action Plan for Improving Sexual Health.* Edinburgh: Scottish Executive.

Scottish Government (2014) *Housing Statistics for Scotland 2014: Key Trends Summary.* Edinburgh: The Scottish Government.

Scottish Government (2015) *A Stronger Scotland.* Edinburgh: The Scottish Government.

Senior, M. (1991) Deprivation payments to GPS: Not what the doctor ordered. *Environment and Planning C* 9: 79–94.

Senior, M. L. (2002) Deprivation indicators. In Rees, P., Martin, D. and Williamson, P. (Eds.) *The Census Data System.* Chichester: John Wiley, 123–37.

Senior, M., Williams, H. and Higgs, G. (2000) Urban-rural mortality differentials: Controlling for material deprivation. *Social Science & Medicine* 51: 289–305.

Shaw, M., Davey-Smith, G. and Dorling, D. (2005) Health inequalities and New Labour: How the promises compare with real progress. *British Medical Journal* 330: 1016–21.

Shaw, M., Dorling, D., Gordon, D. and Davey-Smith, G. (1999) *The Widening Gap: Health Inequalities and Policy in Britain.* Bristol: Policy Press.

Shelter (2015) *Building the Homes We Need.* http://www.shelter.org.uk/__data/assets/pdf_file/0019/802270/Building_the_homes_we_need_-_a_programme_for_the_2015_government.pdf (last accessed 23 December 2015).

Shuttleworth, I., Barr, P. J. and Gould, M. (2013) Does internal migration in Northern Ireland increase religious and social segregation? Perspectives from the Northern Ireland Longitudinal Study (NILS) 2001–2007. *Population Space and Place* 19: 72–86.

Shuttleworth, I. G. and Lloyd, C. D. (2009) Are Northern Ireland's communities dividing? Evidence from geographically consistent Census of Population data, 1971–2001. *Environment and Planning A* 41 (1): 213–29.

Simons, L., McCallum, J., Friedlander, Y. and Simons, J. (2000) Healthy ageing is associated with reduced and delayed disability. *Age and Ageing* 29: 143–48.

Simpson, L. (1996) Resource allocation by measures of relative social need in geographical areas: The relevance of the signed chi-square, the percentage, and the raw count. *Environment and Planning A* 28: 537–54.

Simpson, L. (2007) Ghettos of the mind: The empirical behaviour of indices of segregation and diversity. *Journal of the Royal Statistical Society Series A* 170 (2): 405–24.

Simpson, L. (2013) *What Makes Ethnic Group Populations Grow? Age Structures and Immigration*. Dynamics of Diversity: Evidence from the 2011 Census Briefing Series.

Simpson, L. and Finney, N. (2009) Spatial patterns of internal migration: Evidence for ethnic groups in Britain. *Population, Space and Place* 15: 37–56.

Simpson, L. and Jivraj, S. (2015) Why has ethnic diversity grown? In Jivraj, S. and Simpson, L. (Eds.) *Ethnic Identity and Inequalities in Britain: The Dynamics of Diversity*. Bristol: Policy Press, 33–47.

Simpson, L. and McDonald, N. (2015) Making sense of the new English household projections. *Town and Country Planning* 84: 175–82.

Simpson, L., Warren, J. and Jivraj, S. (2015) Do people change their ethnicity over time? In Jivraj, S. and Simpson, L. (Eds.) *Ethnic Identity and Inequalities in Britain: The Dynamics of Diversity*. Bristol: Policy Press, 79–92.

Sinclair, D., Moore, K. and Franklin, B. (2014) *Linking State Pension Age to Longevity—Tackling the Fairness Challenge*. ILC-UK Discussion Paper, February.

Smith, A. and Simpson, L. (2015) In what ways is Scotland's ethnic diversity distinctive? In Jivraj, S. and Simpson, L. (Eds.) *Ethnic Identity and Inequalities in Britain: The Dynamics of Diversity*. Bristol: Policy Press, 93–106.

Smith, C. (2014) What does the 2011 Census tell us about concealed families living in multi-family households in England and Wales? http://www.ons.gov.uk/ons/rel/census/2011-census-analysis/what-does-the-2011-census-tell-us-about-concealed-families-living-in-multi-family-households-in-england-and-wales/sty-what-does-the-2011-census-tell-us-about-concealed-families.html (last accessed 23 December 2015).

Smith, D. P., Finney, H., Halfacree, K. and Walford, N. (Eds.) (2015) *Internal Migration: Geographical Perspectives and Processes*. Farnham: Ashgate.

Sobotka, T. (2008) The rising importance of migrants for childbearing in Europe. *Demographic Research* 19 (9): 225–48.

Sobotka, T. and Lutz, W. (2009) Misleading policy messages from the period TFR: Should we stop using it? *European Demographic Research Papers*.

Somerville, W. (2007) *Immigration under New Labour*. Bristol: Policy Press.

Song, E. Y., Pruitt, B. E., McNamara, J. and Colwell, B. (2000) A meta-analysis examining effects of school sexuality education programs on adolescents' sexual knowledge, 1960–1997. *Journal of School Health* 70 (10): 413–16.

Sonnenberg, P., Clifton, B., Beddows, S. et al. (2013) Prevalence, risk factors, and uptake of interventions for sexually transmitted infections in Britain: Findings from the National Surveys of Sexual Attitudes and Lifestyles (NATSAL). *The Lancet* 382 (9907): 1795–1806.

Stafford, M., McMunn, A. and De Vogli, R. (2011) Neighbourhood social environment and depressive symptoms in mid-life and beyond. *Ageing and Society* 31 (6): 893–910.

Statistics New Zealand (2011) *Population Statistics Domain Plan 2011 Draft Report*. Wellington: Statistics New Zealand.

Stephenson, J. M. (2004) Pupil-led sex education in England (RIPPLE study): Cluster-randomised intervention trial. *The Lancet* 364 (9431): 338–47.

Steptoe, A., Shankar, A., Demakakos, P. and Wardle, J. (2013) Social isolation, loneliness and all-cause mortality in older men and women. *Proceedings of the National Academy of Sciences of the United States of America* 110 (15): 5797–5801.

Stillwell, J. and McNulty, S. (2012) Immigration and internal migration of ethnic groups in London. In Finney, N. and Catney, G. (Eds.) *Minority Internal Migration in Europe*. Farnham: Ashgate, 39–64.

Stillwell, J., Rees, P. and Boden, P. (1992) Internal migration trends: An overview. In Stillwell, J., Rees, P. and Boden, P. (Eds.) *Migration Processes and Patterns Volume 2: Population Distribution in the United Kingdom*. London: Belhaven Press, 28–55.

Stone, J., Berrington, A. and Falkingham, J. (2011) The changing determinants of UK young adults' living arrangements. *Demographic Research* 25 (20): 629–66.

Stone, J., Berrington, A. and Falkingham, J. (2014) Gender, turning points and boomerangs: Returning home in young adulthood in Great Britain. *Demography* 51 (1): 257–76.

Sweeney, M. M. (2010) Remarriage and stepfamilies: Strategic sites for family scholarship in the 21st century. *Journal of Marriage and Family* 72 (3): 667–84.

Thane, P. (1989) Old age: Burden or benefit? In Joshi, H. (Ed.) *The Changing Population of Britain*. Oxford: Blackwell, 56–71.

Thomas, E., Serwicka, I. and Swinney, P. (2015) *Urban Demographics: Where People Live and Work*. London: Centre for Cities.

Timaeus, I. (1986) Families and households of the elderly population: Prospects for those approaching old age. *Ageing and Society* 6: 271–93.

Toulemon, L. (2004) Fertility among immigrant women: New data, new approach. *Population and Societies* 400: 1–4.

Townsend, P. (1987) Deprivation. *Journal of Social Policy* 16: 125–46.

Tripp, J. and Viner, R. (2005) ABC of adolescence: Sexual health, contraception, and teenage pregnancy. *British Medical Journal* 330 (7491): 590–93.

Tromans, N., Natamba, E. and Jefferies, J. (2009) Have women born outside the UK driven the rise in UK births since 2001? *Population Trends* 136: 28–42.

Tromans, N., Natamba, E., Jefferies, J. and Norman, P. (2008) Have national trends in fertility between 1986 and 2006 occurred evenly across England and Wales? *Population Trends* 133: 7–19.

Tunstall, R. (2015) *The Coalition's Record on Housing: Policy, Spending and Outcomes 2010–2015*. London: Centre for Analysis of Social Exclusion, LSE.

UK Abortion Act (1967) Elizabeth II 1967 Ch 23 Abortion Act. An Act to amend and clarify the law relating to termination of pregnancy by registered medical practitioners, 27 October 1967. London: HMSO.

UK Statistics Authority (2013) *The Robustness of the International Passenger Survey*. Monitoring Review 4/13. London: UK Statistics Authority.

UNHCR (2010) *Convention and Protocol Relating to the Status of Refugees*. Geneva: United Nations High Commissioner for Refugees. http://www.unhcr.org/3b66c2aa10.html.

Universities UK (2014a) *International Students in Higher Education: The UK and Its Competition*. Higher Education in Focus Series. London: Universities UK. http://www.

universitiesuk.ac.uk/highereducation/Documents/2014/InternationalStudents-InHigherEducation.pdf.

Universities UK (2014b) *The Impact of Universities on the UK Economy*. Higher Education in Focus Series. London: Universities UK. http://www.universitiesuk. ac.uk/highereducation/Documents/2014/TheImpactOfUniversitiesOnTheUk Economy.pdf.

van der Wielen, N., and Bijak, J. (2015) Welfare participation: A comparison between immigrants and natives in the United Kingdom. *Migration Letters* 12 (2): 67–78.

van Ham, M. and Feijten, P. M. (2008) Who wants to leave the neighbourhood? The effect of being different from the neighbourhood population on wishes to move. *Environment and Planning A* 40 (5): 1151–70.

Vanhoutte, B. (2014) The multidimensional structure of subjective well-being in later life. *Population Ageing* 7 (1): 1–20.

van Solinge, H. (2007) Health change in retirement: A longitudinal study among older workers in the Netherlands. *Research on Aging* 29: 225–56.

Verran, A., Evans, S., Lin, D. J. and Griffiths, F. (2015) The experiences and perceptions of family planning of female Chinese asylum seekers living in the UK. *Journal of Family Planning and Reproductive Health Care* 41 (2): 122–27.

Vertovec, S. (2007) The emergence of super-diversity in Britain. *Ethnic and Racial Studies* 30 (6): 1024–54.

Vidal, S. and Windzio, M. (2012) Internal mobility of immigrants and ethnic minorities in Germany. In Finney, N. and Catney, G. (Eds.) *Minority Internal Migration in Europe*. Farnham: Ashgate, 151–74.

Vivancos, R., Abubakar, I., Phillips-Howard, P. and Hunter, P. R. (2012) School-based sex education is associated with reduced risky sexual behaviour and sexually transmitted infections in young adults. *Public Health* 127 (1): 53–57.

Vlachantoni, A. (2010) The demographic characteristics and economic activity patterns of carers over 50: Evidence from the English Longitudinal Study of Ageing. *Population Trends* 141: 51–73.

Vlachantoni, A., Shaw, R., Willis, R., Evandrou, M., Falkingham, J. and Luff, R. (2011) Measuring unmet need for social care amongst older people. *Population Trends* 145: 56–72.

WAG (2010) *Sexual Health and Wellbeing Action Plan for Wales, 2010–2015*. Cardiff: Welsh Assembly Government.

Waller, L., Berrington, A. and Raymer, J. (2014) New insights into the fertility patterns of recent Polish migrants in the United Kingdom. *Journal of Population Research* 31: 131–50.

Wang, C. and Swerdloff, R. S. (2010) Hormonal approaches to male contraception. *Current Opinion in Urology* 20 (6): 520–24.

Ward, S. (1994) *Planning and Urban Change*. London: Paul Chapman.

Wellings, K., Brima, N., Sadler, K. et al. (2015) Stopping and switching contraceptive methods: Findings from Contessa, a prospective longitudinal study of women of reproductive age in England. *Contraception* 91 (1): 57–66.

Wellings, K. and Johnson, A. M. (2013) Framing sexual health research: Adopting a broader perspective. *The Lancet* 382 (9907): 1759–62.

Wellings, K., Jones, K. G., Mercer, C. H. et al. (2013) The prevalence of unplanned pregnancy and associated factors in Britain: Findings from the third National Survey of Sexual Attitudes and Lifestyles (NATSAL-3). *The Lancet* 382 (9907): 1807–16.

Wellings, K., Nanchahal, K., Macdowall, W. et al. (2001) Sexual behaviour in Britain: Early heterosexual experience. *The Lancet* 358 (9296): 1843–50.

Wellings, K., Zhihong, Z., Krentel, A., Barrett, G. and Glasier, A. (2007) Attitudes towards long-acting reversible methods of contraception in general practice in the UK. *Contraception* 76 (3): 208–14.

Welsh Government (2011) *Household Projections across the United Kingdom, Technical Report.* Cardiff: Welsh Government.

Westerlund, H., Kivimaki, M., Singh-Manoux, A., Melchior, M., Ferrie, J., Pentti, J., Jokela, J., Leineweber, C., Goldberg, M., Zins, M. and Vahtera, J. (2009). Self-rated health before and after retirement in France (GAZEL): A cohort study. *The Lancet* 374. P1889–96.

Weston, H. J. (2003) Public honour, private shame and HIV: Issues affecting sexual health service delivery in London's South Asian communities. *Health and Place* 9 (2): 109–17.

Whitehead, C. M. E. (2011) Migration and its impact on housing costs. In Marsden, D. (Ed.) *Employment in the Lean Years: Policy and Prospects for the Next Decade.* Oxford: Oxford University Press, 38–56.

Whitehead, C. and Williams, P. (2011) Causes and consequences? Exploring the shape and direction of the housing system in the UK post the financial crisis. *Housing Studies* 26: 1157–69.

WHO (2010) *Developing Sexual Health Programmes. A Framework for Action.* Geneva: World Health Organization, Department of Reproductive Health and Research.

Whynes, D. K. (2008) Deprivation and self-reported health: Are there 'Scottish effects' in England and Wales? *Journal of Public Health* 31 (1): 147–53.

Wilcox, S., Perry, J. and Williams, P. (2015) *UK Housing Review 2015: Briefing Paper.* London: The Chartered Institute of Housing. http://www.cih.org/resources/PDF/Policy%20free%20download%20pdfs/UKHR%20Briefing%202015.pdf.

Willekens, F. (1994) Monitoring international migration flows in Europe. *European Journal of Population* 10 (1): 1–42.

Wilson, T. and Rees, P. (2005) Recent developments in population projection methodology: A review. *Population, Space and Place* 11: 337–60.

Wiśniowski, A. (in press) Combining Labour Force Survey data to estimate migration flows: The case of migration from Poland to the United Kingdom. Forthcoming in: *Journal of the Royal Statistical Society, Series A.*

Wohland, P., Rees, P., Nazroo, J. and Jagger, C. (2015) Inequalities in healthy life expectancy between ethnic groups in England and Wales in 2001. *Ethnicity and Health* 20 (4): 341–53.

Wong, D. W. S. (2014) Using a spatial pattern statistic to evaluate spatial segregation. In Lloyd, C. D., Shuttleworth, I. G. and Wong, D. W. (Eds.) *Social-Spatial Segregation: Concepts, Processes and Outcomes.* Bristol: Policy Press, 45–64.

Woodward, A. and Kawachi, I. J. (2000) Why reduce health inequalities? *Journal of Epidemiology and Community Health* 54 (12): 923–29.

Yacyshyn, A. M. and Swanson, D. A. (2011) *The Costs of Conducting a National Census: Rationale for Re-designing Current Census Methodology in Canada and the United States.* [Accessed January 2016]. Available from http://cssd.ucr.edu/Papers/PDFs/Yacyshyn_Swanson_JOS_Aug26_2011.pdf.

Yin, Z., Brown, A., Hughes, G. et al. (2014) *HIV in the United Kingdom 2014 Report: Data to End 2013.* London: Public Health England.

YouGov (2013) *YouGov/University of Lancaster Survey Results.* London. YouGov. Available from http://cdn.yougov.com/cumulus_uploads/document/a0c0uf8c2g/YouGov-Survey-University-of-Lancaster-Results-130130.pdf.

Yu, J. (2010) Sex education beyond school: Implications for practice and research. *Sexuality, Society and Learning* 10 (2): 187–99.

Zetter, R., Griffiths, D. and Sigona, N. (2005) Social capital or social exclusion? The impact of asylum-seeker dispersal on UK refugee community organizations. *Community Development Journal* 40 (2): 169–81.

Zumpe, J., Dormon, O. and Jefferies, J. (2012) *Childbearing among UK-Born and Non-UK-Born Women Living in the UK.* London: Office for National Statistics.

Index

List of Contributors

Ann Berrington is Professor of Demography and Social Statistics at the University of Southampton, where she co-leads the Fertility and Family Research Group within the ESRC Centre for Population Change. Her research interests are concerned with the drivers of family and household change and their association with inequalities across the life course.

Jakub Bijak is Associate Professor in Demography at the University of Southampton, a recipient of the Allianz European Demographer Award (2015) and the Jerzy Z Holzer Medal (2007). As a statistical demographer, he works on demographic uncertainty, modelling and forecasting of migration and population processes, and demography of conflict and violence.

Gemma Catney is Lecturer in Human Geography at the University of Liverpool. Her research is concerned primarily with ethnic diversity, segregation and neighbourhood identity, internal migration, and the significance of geography in understanding the causes and consequences of ethnic inequalities.

Tony Champion is Emeritus Professor of Population Geography at Newcastle University and has a long-standing interest in spatial patterns of population and migration. He was president of the British Society for Population Studies in 2013 to 2015.

Ernestina Coast is Associate Professor of Population Studies at the London School of Economics and Political Science. She has a research agenda focussed on demography and sexual and reproductive health. She was a Council Member of the British Society for Population Studies in 2005–2007.

George Disney is Research Fellow at the University of Otago and Research Associate at the University of Southampton, where he completed his PhD on model-based estimates of UK immigration. He is currently working on the New Zealand Census Mortality/Cancer Trends study investigating socio-economic and ethnic inequalities in health.

Sylvie Dubuc is Senior Research Fellow at the Department of Social Policy and Intervention at Oxford University. Following her PhD from the Sorbonne and postdoctoral work in India, she lectured at Kings College London until 2006. Her main research interests are in social and gender inequalities, migration, family, fertility, reproductive health and policy.

Maria Evandrou is Professor of Gerontology at the University of Southampton, Director of the Centre for Research on Ageing and Co-Director of the ESRC Centre for Population Change. Her research uses a dynamic life course perspective and covers areas such as inequalities in later life, informal careers and the retirement prospects of future generations of elders.

Jane Falkingham is Professor of Demography and International Social Policy at the University of Southampton and director of the ESRC Centre for Population Change, whose remit is to 'improve our understanding of the drivers and consequences of populations change'. She is the current (2015–2017) BSPS president.

Nissa Finney is Reader in Human Geography at the University of St. Andrews, member of the ESRC Centre on Dynamics of Ethnicity (CoDE) and member of the ESRC Centre for Population Change. Her research is about residential patterns, their drivers and consequences and as framed by questions of inequality.

Emily Freeman is Assistant Professorial Research Fellow at the London School of Economics and Political Science. Her research is concerned with influences on and experiences of demographic change and sexual and reproductive health. She sat on the Council of the British Society for Population Studies in 2008–2010.

Ursula Henz is Associate Professor in Social Research Methods at the Sociology Department of the London School of Economics. Her research is mainly concerned with social stratification and family dynamics. Currently, she is involved in studies on work-life balance, assortative mating and fatherhood.

Sarah Lubman is a postgraduate research student in social statistics and demography at the University of Southampton. Her research assesses the policy of dispersal of asylum seekers that was introduced through the 1999

Immigration and Asylum Act, in the context of deprivation. Her research interests also include migration and the demography of conflict.

Alan Marshall is Lecturer in Human Geography at the University of St. Andrews. His research is concerned with understanding how individual characteristics and contextual factors (from national to neighbourhood) interact to influence health across the life course and particularly in later life.

James Nazroo is Professor of Sociology at the University of Manchester. He leads the Frailty and Resilience in Later Life project and the Centre on the Dynamics of Ethnicity. His research interests are concerned with inequality, social justice and underlying processes of stratification focussing on gender, ethnicity, ageing, and the intersections between these.

Paul Norman is Lecturer in Human Geography at the School of Geography, University of Leeds, where he is director of Taught Postgraduate Studies and programme manager of the MSc GIS. His research interests include how health inequalities vary by level of deprivation for individuals and at area level.

Ludi Simpson is Honorary Professor of Population Studies at the University of Manchester and served as Research Officer in West Yorkshire councils and President of the British Society for Population Studies from 2011 to 2013. He has worked on improved sub-national population statistics for planning services in the UK and Latin America.

Athina Vlachantoni is Associate Professor in Gerontology at the Centre for Research on Ageing and the ESRC Centre for Population Change at the University of Southampton. Her research interests cover areas such as informal care provision and receipt, long-term care, ethnic differentials across the life course, pension protection and health inequalities.

Arkadiusz Wiśniowski is Lecturer in Social Statistics at the University of Manchester. His research interest is in developing statistical methods for modelling, forecasting and quantifying uncertainty in population processes with a special focus on migration and combining various sources of data.